Teaching Piano in Groups

Teaching Piano in Groups

Christopher Fisher

OXFORD
UNIVERSITY PRESS
2010

OXFORD
UNIVERSITY PRESS

Oxford University Press, Inc., publishes works that further
Oxford University's objective of excellence
in research, scholarship, and education.

Oxford New York
Auckland Cape Town Dar es Salaam Hong Kong Karachi
Kuala Lumpur Madrid Melbourne Mexico City Nairobi
New Delhi Shanghai Taipei Toronto

With offices in
Argentina Austria Brazil Chile Czech Republic France Greece
Guatemala Hungary Italy Japan Poland Portugal Singapore
South Korea Switzerland Thailand Turkey Ukraine Vietnam

Published by Oxford University Press, Inc.
198 Madison Avenue, New York, New York 10016

www.oup.com

Oxford is a registered trademark of Oxford University Press

Visit the companion Web site at www.oup.com/us/teachingpianoingroups

Library of Congress Cataloging-in-Publication Data
Fisher, Christopher, 1977–
Teaching piano in groups / Christopher Fisher.
p. cm.
Includes bibliographical references (p.) and index.
ISBN 978-0-19-533703-7; 978-0-19-533704-4 (pb)
1. Piano—Instruction and study. 2. Piano—Methods—
Group instruction. I. Title.
MT220.F47 2010
786.2071—dc22 2009015583

Printed in the United States of America
on acid-free paper

Preface and Acknowledgments

"Two are better than one, because they have a good return for their labor" (Ecclesiastes 4:9). Indeed, the potency and effectiveness of group effort have been highly regarded from the beginning of time. Furthermore, the weight of this maxim carries over into the realm of educational endeavor.

As Malcolm Muggeridge once said, "All new news is old news happening to new people." Thus, what follows is nothing new, but rather an attempt to reengage the reader in a discussion of what has been observed for centuries: the powers of group learning. It is my intent to frame this discussion in a way that is fresh and in a manner that clearly and convincingly illuminates this core tenet.

Although it was initially my desire to create a comprehensive narrative on all aspects of group piano teaching, I now acknowledge the futility of such an attempt. To be sure, an honest discussion of this topic transcends that which can be reduced to a single volume. It is my sincere desire that the following pages stimulate a renewed interest in and a thoughtful dialogue regarding group piano teaching. I hope that these chapters will challenge the novice group piano teacher to fully explore the group instructional medium, while inspiring renewed enthusiasm and creativity for the veteran teacher.

I wish to extend my most sincere thanks and gratitude to the teachers and mentors who have directly influenced my interest in and passion for group piano teaching: to Dr. Richard Bobo, who first introduced me to the group piano teaching environment; to Dr. Sylvia Coats, who opened my eyes to the transformative power of group piano teaching, and who inspired and challenged me to higher levels of thinking and creativity; and to Dr. Barbara Fast, who guided me in the refinement of my teaching. Each of you has had a profound impact on my life and my career, and I shall forever be indebted.

I am deeply grateful to Dr. Michael Parkinson, Director, and my extraordinary colleagues in the Ohio University School of Music for their support and encouragement. I am especially thankful to Dean Chuck McWeeney and the College of Fine Arts Creative Research Award, which enabled me to complete this project. A special thanks is owed to Angela Leising for her able research assistance.

Further, I wish to thank the exemplary group piano teachers who graciously agreed to provide their thoughts and perspectives on the subject of group piano teaching: Sylvia Coats, Ted Cooper, Brenda Dillon, Barbara Fast, and Martha Hilley.

I am particularly thankful to the remarkable students who have inspired me in the writing of this book, and who daily teach me and enrich my work.

Finally I wish to thank my amazing wife, Katie, who has been an endless source of encouragement and guidance. Your patience and faithful support are cherished.

Contents

Teaching Piano in Groups

Chapter 1

Group Piano Teaching: An Introduction

The History of Group Piano Teaching

Piano teachers have long recognized the potential of teaching in groups. The application of group piano teaching first appeared in Dublin, Ireland, around 1815 when the German musician Johann Bernhard Logier began instructing piano solely in classes. He argued that the setting was ideal for the introduction of musical theoretical concepts and their subsequent application at the keyboard. Thus, group piano and keyboard harmony classes were born. Piano teachers from America as well as from many European countries attended Logier's classes and returned home to introduce group teaching to their respective countries. The first appearance of such piano classes in America can be traced to girls' schools in the South around 1860. It is also important to note that famous European pianists of the nineteenth century, such as Franz Liszt, Frederic Chopin, and Clara Schumann, taught their pupils in groups in what is typically considered a master class setting. Clearly, European traditions influenced music education in early America.[1]

At the end of the nineteenth century, Calvin Cady, a leading music educator and proponent of group piano in the United States, strongly advocated class piano as a viable means of instruction. In 1889, the U.S. Office of Education officially endorsed and promoted class piano instruction as a desirable teaching procedure.[2] By the turn of the century, the United States had become the world leader in the production of pianos. As a result, the piano found its way into thousands of American homes. Because of this, many elementary schools in the United States saw the establishment of class piano programs, in part due to the high cost of private instruction. The inclusion of piano in the broad curriculum was an effort by the educational system to enhance cultural and artistic awareness.

Pioneers of these early years of class piano teaching included classroom music educators such as Thaddeus Giddings, Hazel Kinscella, Otto Miessner, Helen Curtis, Charles and Gail Haake, Polly Gibbs, Ada Richter, Raymond Burrows, Ella Mason Ahearn, and Fay Templeton Frisch, to name a few. As a result of their efforts, numerous method books and texts emerged, designed explicitly for the purpose of teaching piano as a core component of public, general music education. Examples of early class piano texts include the *Young Student's Piano Course* (1918) by Earhart and Boyd, *Public School Class Method for Piano* (1919) by Giddings and Gilman, and *Steps for the Young Pianist* (1919) by Hazel Kinscella. Central to these methods were the foundational principles of musical notation and repertoire. The text by Giddings and Gilman served additionally as a teacher's manual in that it included chapters on pedagogy as well as classroom organization and management.

The inclusion of piano classes as part of the general public school education showed slow but steady growth from 1920 through 1930. By the end of 1929, a survey by the National Bureau for the Advancement of Education indicated that piano classes were being offered in 873 towns or cities across the United States.[3] Keyboard specialists from the Music Supervisors National Conference produced a manual titled *Guide for Conducting Piano Classes in the Public Schools,* which became an important early training tutorial for group piano teachers. As piano classes gained popularity, the need for specific teacher-training courses for this instructional format became a necessity. These "normal courses" in piano, as they were called, were being offered as early as 1920, when T. P. Giddings offered the course "Children's Classes in Piano" at the Chautauqua Institute. Hazel Kinscella offered two teacher-training certificate programs at the University of Nebraska School of Music in 1920 and 1921. Otto Miessner, author of *The Melody Way* piano method, initiated a vigorous teacher-training campaign from 1924 through 1930 in which he led seminars from New York to California.[4]

In 1925, Columbia University Teachers College launched a program that taught the essential principles of teaching piano classes for children. By the beginning of the next decade, more than 150 colleges and universities followed suit by offering coursework in class piano pedagogy.[5] Public school piano classes continued to thrive until around 1930, when factors such as financial depression, the diversion of the Second World War, and deficiencies in teacher training and interest contributed to a significant decline.[6]

At the same time, Raymond Burrows offered a successful piano class for adult beginners at Columbia University Teachers College. Because of its success, adult courses were incorporated into the college's regular course offerings. Burrows became a leader in the field of group piano instruction for adults, breaking new ground in the development of college piano classes and coursework to train the class piano instructor. Burrows advocated the inclusion of piano classes in all public schools across the United States.[7]

In 1952, Burrows reported in the *Handbook for Teaching Piano Classes* that 256 colleges and universities across the United States offered group piano classes, and 157 offered pedagogy courses in group teaching. The proliferation of group piano programs in colleges and universities during the late 1950s and early 1960s sought to educate the beginning piano student, which often included the music education major, non–music major, and adult hobby students.[8] Such programs were designed according to the philosophy that all music students, regardless of area of emphasis, should receive piano training as a part of their comprehensive music training. Therefore, these course sequences were intended to educate students with fundamental, functional keyboard skills such as sight-reading, harmonization, transposition, and score reading.

The advent of the electronic piano laboratory had a profound impact on the future and direction of group piano teaching. First installed and implemented at Ball State University in 1956, the electronic piano laboratory quickly became the ideal equipment scenario for college group piano programs due to the smaller instrument size, the capacity for both individual and class work, and its relative lower cost as compared with an acoustic piano laboratory.[9] As a result of these technological advancements, in addition to standards mandated by the National Associations of Schools of Music that encourage all graduates to acquire keyboard proficiency, group piano teaching at the college and university levels increased dramatically.

As developments in group piano teaching were being realized in the college classroom, new advancements were taking place concurrently in the private studio. Robert Pace, a student of Burrows and later faculty member at Teachers College, began advocating the use of one partner lesson and one larger group lesson per week for the average-age beginning piano student. Building upon this format, Pace developed a comprehensive group piano method titled *Piano for Classroom Music* (1956), which stressed music fundamentals, playing in all keys (multiple-key approach), harmony, ear training, sight-reading, and improvisation, among other functional skills. Pace further developed the idea of comprehensive musicianship—a sequentially organized and spiral curriculum that transfers broad music fundamentals to highly related concepts and principles—in *Music for Piano* (1961) and *Skills and Drills* (1961).

Other influential piano pedagogues have made strong cases for group instruction in the private studio or preparatory program curricula. James Bastien, in his book *How to Teach Piano Successfully* (1977), contends that young children function especially well in group environments and stand to gain a great deal from this format during their early training.[10] James Lyke, a student of Robert Pace at Teachers College, advocated teaching children in small groups of four students, twice weekly: one lesson for repertoire and technique, and one lesson for musicianship training.[11] Richard Chronister, cofounder of the National Conference on Piano Pedagogy, promoted teaching piano only in groups, with no private lessons.[12] Guy Duckworth, who established the D.M.A. degree in group environments at the University of Colorado, Boulder, endorsed the philosophy of group lessons, with no private instruction, for advanced students.[13]

Frances Clark, founder of the New School for Music Study in Princeton, New Jersey, and coauthor of the *Frances Clark Library for Piano Students,* advocated a combination of both a group and private lessons for beginning piano students. According to her approach, new concepts and literature are to be introduced in the group, while the private lesson is devoted to review of group lesson concepts as well as polishing technique. Louise Bianchi, creator of one of the country's earliest preparatory piano programs at Southern Methodist University in 1965 and coauthor of *Music Pathways,* developed her program based on the model of two group lessons per week for three months for beginning students. From here, students progressed to a partner lesson together with one group lesson per week. During the second year, students attended a one-hour group lesson and a half hour private lesson weekly.

The middle part of the twentieth century saw significant growth in specific resources for the group piano teacher, which included workshops, publications, and new technologies. As early as 1955, the Music Teachers National Association (MTNA) began including group piano workshops on its national convention program. By 1972, MTNA created a specific track devoted entirely to group piano teaching that was chaired by James Lyke. Since this time, four important piano periodicals—*American Music Teacher, Piano Quarterly, Keyboard Companion,* and *Clavier*—have committed many of their pages to articles that emphasize group piano instruction, addressing the topic on a variety of levels.

Around this time, the National Piano Foundation was created and provided group teaching seminars throughout the country. Robert Pace from Columbia University Teachers College spearheaded these workshops and served as the foundation's educational director until 1977. After his retirement, Martha Hilley and

Marguerite Miller continued providing these workshops advertised as World of Piano seminars.

The 1970s launched an era in which group piano teaching emerged as a fully recognized and significant entity of the field of piano pedagogy. This trend was sustained throughout the 1980s, which saw the creation of the first National Group Piano Symposium. Also during this time, university programs such as that at the University of Oklahoma, directed by E. L. Lancaster, and at the University of Texas–Austin, directed by Martha Hilley, established important group piano teacher-training programs.[14]

Recent years have seen a proliferation of new resources for the group piano teacher. One such conference, the National Group Piano and Piano Pedagogy Forum (GP3), first held in 2000, continues to meet biannually. This conference was designed as a platform for college and university group piano teachers to share teaching strategies and related research, along with ideas for shaping the direction of the profession in the future. One day out of the two-day forum is devoted solely to group piano teaching at the collegiate level. Additionally, the MTNA focused discussions on group teaching by devoting the entire 1999 Pedagogy Saturday workshop explicitly to this instructional format. More recently, the MTNA and the National Piano Foundation have created a joint endeavor called the Group Piano Teaching Track, offered during MTNA national conferences. These specialized sessions, which are devoted to group piano teaching at all levels, are a continuation of seminars both organizations have sponsored across the United States in the past.

The resurgence of attention to group piano teaching is illustrated in an increased volume of scholarly research. January 1998 marked the inaugural issue of *Piano Pedagogy Forum*, the first online keyboard journal. Published three times each year, the journal devotes at least one article per issue specifically to the area of group piano teaching and related topics Additionally, *Piano Pedagogy Forum* makes available online proceedings from the National Group Piano and Piano Pedagogy Forum conferences.

The Efficacy of Group Piano Teaching

As group music instruction has gained acceptance throughout the profession, educators have credited the instructional model as a viable and effective format for teaching. In 1982, the International Society of Music Educators met in Bristol, England, and adopted the document "Group Instrumental Instruction" which makes the following assertions:

> Group instrumental teaching can provide a musical environment where good learning may take place beyond what is usually possible in individual instruction; further, a group can provide a social environment in which a student is supported and motivated, even challenged by peers. A group can provide a wider range of experience—discussion, critical listening, the study of historical contexts, structural analysis and collective decision-making; further, a group can be a performing medium for each member in it.[15]

Indeed, when certain requisite conditions are in place, the group environment has the potential to produce learning opportunities that are superior to what could be achieved in an individual, one-on-one format. Group piano instruction provides teachers with opportunities to deliver a comprehensive music curriculum to more students in less time. Those who have adopted this instructional approach are constantly adding to the list of its merits.

The group piano class is a dynamic environment consisting of students who possess unique abilities as well as individual differences. One student may play by ear with exceptional skill whereas another student possesses outstanding sight-reading abilities. By the very nature of the group structure, all students stand to learn something from one another. Therefore, each student can contribute something meaningful to the group.

Students who study piano in groups have greater opportunities for performing experiences, which become a natural part of the educational process. Because performing regularly for peers in a nonthreatening environment is a normal procedure of group piano study, these students often experience less performance anxiety and demonstrate a greater sense of confidence and poise while playing in public. Students in groups also experience performance protocol from the outset, such as bowing and walking onstage.

Because students who study in groups often learn individual repertoire, they are exposed to a wide variety of repertoire through hearing their peers perform. As a result of these performances and the discussions that follow, students may also develop improved critical listening skills. Students are challenged to listen for correct notes, rhythms, tempi, dynamics, phrasing, pedaling, and the myriad of other elements involved in piano playing. After the performance, when students are called upon to articulate a critique or suggestion for improvement, their understanding of the concepts and principles involved is solidified.

When they are not being pressured to perform unfamiliar repertoire, but rather are critically listening to others' performances, students' cognitive load is reduced, freeing them to focus better on the learning task at hand. Here, students can also share common problems they may be encountering in their own repertoire. Furthermore, they are able to make transfers to highly related issues in their own music in regard to questions of style, interpretation, and technical issues, among others.

Thus, groups foster prime conditions for problem solving. Multiple ideas from several students generate many possible ways of exploring a concept and discovering how to apply it. The teacher assumes the role of facilitator rather than lecturer. Consequently, learning is derived from thought-provoking questions posed by the students or facilitator. These questions or problems guide the group's conversations and motivate students to discuss, explore, and analyze the concepts at hand. Therefore, students are not simply told to do something; rather, they are conceptually directed to understanding through group discussion, discovery, experimentation, and implementation. Through both individual initiative and stimulation from their peers, students actively participate in the problem-solving process. By experiencing problem-solving in a social setting, students are exposed to a wider variety of possible solutions and are more likely to take risks by exploring alternate ways of solving musical problems. As a result, small groups foster a form of discovery learning as opposed to receptive learning found in typical lecture-demonstration procedures.

The group setting is a social structure organized according to a common interest: the piano. This dynamic learning environment provides students with the opportunity to develop their keyboard skills among peers who will support and encourage one another along the way. Students develop a sense of camaraderie with their group, which becomes a natural support system. The group has the potential to generate a spirit of enthusiasm and motivation toward the subject matter in a way that the instructor could never achieve alone. It can also be an environment that positively nurtures students' self-confidence. Groups may also present opportunities to motivate students through healthy competition. Group piano students are given constant feedback on how their work measures up to their peers. Thus, the group piano lesson provides students with an array of valuable incentives to learn and develop as pianists.

Additionally, the group environment gives students the opportunity to develop communication and social skills and also aids in the development of leadership initiative. Students assume various roles during specific moments of group work and learn when it is appropriate to lead and when it is more effective to follow. These roles may include that of a critiquer, encourager, listener, leader, and so on. Students also learn how to resolve conflicts and other ways to maintain positive, productive group functioning. Such cooperative skills are certainly important for all students to develop in order to become productive members of society.

The group piano lesson is a prime environment in which to teach functional keyboard skills and fundamentals like harmonization, transposition, improvisation, sight-reading, theory, and ear training. Because of their structure, groups are ideal arrangements for introducing and drilling these skills through games and creative activities, which could not be done in the private lesson. The teacher is able to present and reinforce curricular materials more efficiently in the group as opposed to making the same presentation to each individual student in a private lesson.

The group lesson is an effective place for students to develop a strong rhythmic foundation. The instructor can facilitate a multiplicity of activities in which students can physically express rhythm, such as eurhythmic movement, clapping or chanting rhythmic patterns, playing percussion instruments, or conducting a group ensemble. Along these same lines, the group naturally facilitates the study and performance of piano ensembles, which may include duets, trios, quartets, multiple keyboard ensembles, or accompaniments. As such, students are afforded important opportunities to learn valuable collaborative skills, which emphasize a strong sense of rhythmic pulse and playing ahead regardless of mistakes.

The group environment is a prime location for teaching piano technique. The foundational technical principles involved in playing the piano are applicable for every pianist. Therefore, the instructor can present and encourage students to cooperatively experience these technical principles together. Often important discussion will arise from these experiences where certain technical issues and problems can be addressed. Students can be encouraged to assess not only their own technique (e.g., hand position, posture, finger movement, use of the arm and wrist) but also that of their peers. When students are aware that their peers and instructor are monitoring their technique, they are likely to challenge themselves to develop appropriate and sound technical habits.

Issues of musical interpretation can be effectively taught in a group setting. The instructor must facilitate group discussion regarding each composition studied, leading students to discover the compositional form and structure, as well as historical issues surrounding the piece and how these may affect its interpretation. Students are encouraged to make suggestions regarding all musical details of the work under discussion, such as phrase shape, dynamic shading, pedal technique, and so forth. Students should be encouraged to demonstrate and experience all suggested ideas. When their attention is routinely engaged on issues of expressive playing and musical interpretation, students are more likely to develop a strong sense of meaningful and dramatic musical performance.

Depending on the equipment setup—that is, if a teacher is using a digital piano laboratory—the group lesson can facilitate supervised practice opportunities. This arrangement gives the teacher an opportunity to assess how students spend their individual practice time and offer feedback to encourage greater efficiency.

The aforementioned discussion merely scratches the surface of the potential benefits of group piano instruction. Below is a concise listing of these benefits.

Benefits of Group Piano Instruction

- Students learn from both their peers and their teacher.
- Provides limitless performance opportunities.
- Develops performance confidence and poise.
- Exposes students to a wide variety of repertoire.
- Encourages the development of critical listening skills as students listen to other students perform and then provide comments following the performance.
- Challenges students to develop communication and social skills.
- Aids in the development of leadership initiatives.
- Fosters the development of problem-solving skills.
- Encourages students to make transfers of concepts and principles.
- Provides a dynamic and motivational learning environment.
- Facilitates productive, positive competition.
- Provides a prime environment in which to teach functional musicianship skills such as harmonization, transposition, sight-reading, improvisation, etc.
- Provides a motivational environment in which creative games and exercises may be used to teach and drill concepts.
- Has the potential to sustain student attention through captivating group activities, in turn permitting a longer lesson length.
- Encourages the development of a strong rhythmic sense through group eurhythmic activities.
- Provides a natural environment for the study and performance of piano ensembles (duets, trios, quartets, accompaniments).
- Is a prime location in which to study technique.
- Encourages the development of musical interpretation.
- An efficient and effective means for the presentation of materials for the teacher.
- Facilitates supervised practice opportunities.

The Primary Goals of Group Piano Study

The specific aim of piano study will vary with each student. But regardless of students' personal motivation and goals, group piano teachers embrace and are motivated by several core purposes. First, teachers maintain a passionate belief that all humans can benefit from the life-enriching study of music. The study of piano serves to develop the student holistically, with positive implications in the physical, intellectual, social, emotional, and spiritual realms. Further, it is the intent of most teachers to use music study as a vehicle through which to instill and cultivate character, integrity, and a positive attitude in their students. For others, it is a means to foster and develop talent and human potential.

An abundance of current research supports these beliefs, indicating potential for increased hand-eye coordination and fine motor skills as well as the possibility for increased cognitive development and advancement in abstract and critical reasoning competencies and concentration abilities. Furthermore, the group piano environment enhances students' ability to interact with the world around them.

Teachers aim to develop students who are lifelong, independent learners and appreciators of music in its countless forms. They seek to inspire in their students a sense of musical and intellectual curiosity. Group piano study encourages students to establish high personal standards and to develop qualities of character such as a sense of discipline, perseverance, and a strong work ethic.

Music stimulates the senses and provides students with valuable opportunities for creative, artistic expression. The fundamental precepts of group piano training include the development of technical proficiency, theoretical and historical understanding and application, aesthetic appreciation, critical and sensitive listening skills, stylistic discernment, and confident overall musicianship, which involves repertoire performance, sight-reading, harmonization, transposition, and improvisation.

Qualifications of the Group Piano Teacher

The successful group piano teacher is one who possesses those skills required of the private instructor, as well as many specialized skills that are unique to the group instructional format. Not all teachers naturally possess all of these skills. The successful teacher has a natural gift for leading students to comprehend new concepts and ideas, as well as, and perhaps more significant, a desire to continually learn themselves. The following list is an outline of some of the important competencies of the successful group piano teacher. Such a list may serve as a measurement tool against which one may evaluate oneself, or it may be used to identify areas that can be enhanced or further developed in one's teaching.

- Competent musician/performer
- Possesses solid musicianship skills
- Possesses thorough knowledge of the subject matter

- Able to diagnose problems and construct solutions
- Observant, perceptive
- Able to structure and present the subject in a clear and understandable manner
- Prepared
- Able to manage time
- Flexible
- Imaginative
- Motivational/inspirational
- Sympathetic
- Personable/relational

The successful group piano teacher must be a competent musician and performer. Such skills are necessary in order to effectively model and demonstrate technical and expressive elements to students. Beyond this, excellent performance skills can serve to motivate and inspire students to higher levels of playing. In order to maintain these skills, it is essential for the teacher to continually study new repertoire, and perhaps even further his learning by taking lessons with a colleague or master teacher on a periodic basis.

It is necessary for the group piano teacher to possess solid musicianship skills, being able to sight-read, harmonize, transpose, read a score, and improvise with confidence. After all, it should be the goal of every piano teacher to train comprehensive musicians, not simply students who can play a limited amount of solo literature. What a shame it is to turn out pianists who are unable to play "Happy Birthday" at a family birthday celebration!

Additionally, the group piano teacher should have a thorough knowledge of the teaching literature, as well as an understanding of how to practically level and properly sequence this material. Many excellent resources are available to teachers regarding this issue, including Jane Magrath's *Pianist's Guide to Standard Teaching and Performance Literature.*

A thorough knowledge of music theory and history is also important to the success of the group piano teacher. The group lesson is a prime location for the teaching and application of theoretical and historical concepts. Therefore, prudent instructors know how to effectively facilitate student discovery and experience of these essential elements as part of a complete musical training.

The teacher not only must be a competent performer and a solid musician but also must be able to assess student technical problems and provide solutions to overcome these issues. Therefore, teachers should constantly monitor their own playing, analyzing the mechanical requirements necessary to negotiate certain technical problems. Though strong performance skills are important and necessary, one must note that the successful teacher cannot be evaluated entirely on the grounds of performance ability. For many exceptional concert artists, an understanding of such technical problems and their solutions may be a foreign concept due to the natural technical abilities they posses.

The successful group piano teacher is one who can anticipate potential problems that may arise both during and after the lesson. In this way, the teacher must be perceptive and capable of assessing student issues: social or personal, intellectual (conceptual) or physical (technical). Teachers must be able to diagnose problems and must be capable of constructing and affecting solutions, usually on the spot.

Along these lines, successful group piano teachers must have a sensitive and well-trained sense of hearing. Teachers must be able to recognize individual students who are playing incorrect pitches or rhythms while multiple students are playing simultaneously.

The ability to structure and present subject matter in a clear and understandable manner is a hallmark of exceptional teaching. For that reason, teachers must develop a curriculum that encompasses the foundational principles of music and piano playing, while also appealing to the particular needs of the individual student. Successful pedagogues are those who are constantly considering new methods for imparting the subject matter in a manner that is most effectively understood and applied by the student. These are teachers who themselves are continually learning, who are seeking to grow in their own understanding of the field while developing novel techniques for communicating this knowledge. Furthermore, the teacher must be capable of assisting his students in establishing attainable goals and formulating specific procedures for achieving these goals with maximum efficiency.

The effective group piano teacher is organized and well prepared for each class. Strategic lesson planning is crucial to the success of teaching piano in groups. Therefore, a clear and deliberate plan for the presentation and reinforcement of lesson concepts and principles must be laid out prior to every lesson. Teachers should take time to anticipate student responses or reactions to material, as well as consider possible questions or problems students may encounter. Though the benefits of solid preparation are indisputable, the successful teacher must also be flexible and capable of deviating from the plan in order to imaginatively address certain situations that may spontaneously arise.

Enthusiasm for the subject matter is vital to successful group piano teaching. Students should be able to sense the instructor's passion for his art, and dedication and commitment to the instrument should be the pervasive attitude in his class. Equally important is a genuine concern for his students, as well as a sincere interest in guiding them to achieve their maximum learning potential. For that reason, a personable and relational temperament is a necessary attribute for the effective group piano teacher. Such a teacher is responsive to students' needs and generates a learning environment that is both productive and supportive.

The aforementioned list of qualifications is in no way exhaustive and is therefore merely a jumping-off point. The list below presents additional attributes of the exemplary group piano teacher, many of which are more thoroughly discussed in subsequent chapters.

Additional Principles of Exemplary Group Piano Teaching

An exemplary group piano teacher ...

- Is convinced of the power of group instruction
- Is motivating and encouraging
- Offers genuine praise only
- Assists students in realizing established goals
- Creates an environment that is stimulating as well as empathetic
- Shows students the relevance of that which is being taught
- Asks engaging questions rather than only telling
- Engages students attention
- Encourages metacognition by challenging students to think about their thinking, performing, and practice
- Employs discovery learning
- Transfers learned concepts and skills to highly related concepts and principles
- Establishes sound and healthy technical habits from the outset
- Trains students to be critical listeners
- Teaches students how to successfully practice
- Previews new material; shows students how to be musical detectives
- Trains students to be problem solvers
- Uses an appropriate sense of pacing and sustains interest
- Considers all types of learning styles when designing a lesson/presentation
- Introduces a limited number of new concepts in each lesson, with review of old concepts
- Encourages students to teach others what they learn, verbally restating a concept or principle, thus crystallizing learning
- Involves parents (when teaching children) and encourages parents to assist and guide students
- Teaches with ingenuity, creativity, and a fresh outlook
- Gives concise directions

- Employs humor
- Is enthusiastic about the subject matter and the student
- Is always organized
- Moves about the classroom to observe and assist students
- Establishes and maintains high standards
- Generates a positive atmosphere while giving constructive criticism
- Believes in the subject matter and draws students in to meet it
- Inspires enthusiasm

Chapter 2
Practical and Logistical Issues

Making the Transition to Group Piano Teaching

For the studio teacher who has never taught piano in groups, the prospect can certainly seem daunting. To begin, one should ask the following questions:

1. What is successful in my teaching?
2. What is not so successful in my teaching?
3. How could group teaching enhance my work?

For those teachers who have never experienced the significant power of group teaching, it is imperative that one develop relationships with other group piano teachers in one's area and throughout the country. These teachers are normally very willing to share instructional and logistical strategies as well as other helpful suggestions. It is also worthwhile to observe a variety of group piano teachers and programs in action and to engage these teachers in discussions about the format(s) they use. Fortunately, many workshops and conferences are offered throughout the country that present sessions on the topic of group piano teaching. These include the National Group Piano/Piano Pedagogy Forum, the National Conference of the Music Teachers National Association, and the National Conference on Keyboard Pedagogy. Additionally, many university and college music programs offer pedagogy coursework designed expressly for training students in the many aspects of teaching piano in group environments.

With this said, some of the best learning occurs in the crucible of experimentation. There comes a time when it is simply necessary to jump in and try it. There are many ways to implement a group piano program as part of one's teaching studio. For the first-time group piano teacher, it can be helpful to make the transition by inaugurating a class for average-age beginners. Here, the teacher can focus his energy on the intricacies of facilitating learning in one age-group at a time rather than being forced to deal simultaneously with the many variances found in different age-groups. For those who have special training in early music teaching, a group of preschool students is a good place to begin because these students can usually attend lessons during the day, which will keep the prime after-school teaching hours free for school-age students. Both groups of beginners provide an excellent way to build one's studio enrollment base.

Another desirable introductory format to group teaching is to partner two students of the same age and level into dyads. Each student experiences a fifteen-minute private lesson and a thirty-minute group lesson over the period of one hour of teaching time. The teacher is paid for two forty-five minute lessons but teaches for only an hour. This and other group teaching formats will be discussed in more detail later in this chapter.

The summer is also an excellent time to offer experimental group classes. These months are usually less restrictive in terms of scheduling and can grant the teacher more flexibility in curricular offerings. One might choose to offer a group ensemble camp or a camp designed around special topics such as contemporary music or jazz styles.

Creating a Teaching Philosophy

As a group piano teacher, it is imperative that one wholly endorses the group instructional format and recognizes its many positive attributes. It is important that these convictions are clearly articulated in one's philosophy of education or mission statement. This document should address questions such as the following:

- Why do you do what you do?
- What are the guiding principles of how and what you teach?
- Why do you use groups to teach?
- What is the function of learning the piano?
- What should be the product of piano education?
- What are the roles of the teacher, the student, and the parent?
- How do you create an inspired atmosphere for learning?

A philosophy of education is a fluid and dynamic construct that will change with time and experience. The purpose of the document is to systematically articulate the value, meaning, and significance of that which we do as teachers.

It further serves to codify a teacher's instructional and professional approach so as to enhance his overall effectiveness. One should revisit the document yearly to make revisions that reflect new perspectives. By periodically returning to the document, we stand to be encouraged in our professional pursuits and reaffirmed as to why we do what we do. This philosophy statement should be distributed to and discussed with potential students and their parents during the initial interview along with the studio policy and other important information.

Types of Group Piano Lessons

A wide variety of group piano teaching formats are available to the piano teacher. What follows is a discussion of a few of the most popular. Creative teachers and studio managers are capable of developing group instructional structures that fit the specific needs of both teachers and students. Whichever configuration the instructor selects, one critical precept must prevail: it is the teacher's duty to always teach in a manner that most profoundly impacts each student's learning. The following is an outline of the group instructional formats to be discussed later in the chapter:

Group-Only Instruction

- Dyad or partner lessons
- Overlapping partner/group combination
- Weekly group lessons

Group and Private Instruction Combinations

- Weekly private lessons with monthly group lesson
- Alternating private and group lessons
- Both private and group lessons

Performance Groups

Group-Only Instruction

The application of groups as the sole form of instruction has historically been used as a prime system for the teaching of beginning-level pianists, whether preschool children or adults. Because of its very nature, the group is an excellent setting in which to teach the fundamentals of music and piano playing to beginners. This format eliminates the need to make the same presentation of lesson material multiple times to individual students during a private lesson, negating any unnecessary repetition and redundancy.

Dyad or Partner Lessons

An excellent format for teachers to first experience group teaching, the partner or dyad lesson involves two students who are instructed simultaneously. The students should be close to the same age and level of ability. During the lesson, students learn the same materials and participate in the same activities, though some teachers choose to assign individual supplementary music to foster some feeling of individuality. The dyad structure encourages exchange of student ideas and generates a sense of accountability and healthy competition. Teachers who successfully use this format encourage students to assume the role of teacher by providing comments and feedback for their partners. Such roles help students to develop critical listening skills and to solidify conceptual and skill comprehension. The structure also provides ready-made opportunities for the study and performance of duets and other ensemble materials.

Teachers who employ this format often report increased student motivation and better quality of preparation for the lesson, perhaps in part due to the accountability, cooperation, and peer encouragement that are natural by-products of the structure. Because of this positive social factor, the dyad or partner lesson may serve to lower student attrition, especially during the volatile adolescent years.

Some teachers choose to offer more individualized instruction during partner lessons. While one student is receiving individual attention, the other student may complete theory, ear training, or history activities, perhaps using computer software. Students may also practice or prepare a specific activity at a separate digital piano with headphones so as not to distract the other student. Though it is sometimes necessary, individual work does not genuinely reflect the highest potential of the partner lesson because it eliminates the powerful dynamics of true collaborative work between the two students.

Overlapping Partner/Group Lessons

This format involves two students attending a partner lesson, usually lasting fifteen or thirty minutes, followed by an extended, larger group session involving two more students. The second dyad stays for its partner lesson following the group session. The group meetings allow the teacher to introduce new concepts, review and drill old skills, and provide students with valuable performance opportunities that are not possible in private lessons. Again, for this format to be successful it is critical that students are at a relatively equal level of playing ability and age in order.

Scheduling can be somewhat difficult when attempting to identify compatible times in which students of equal age and ability can attend both partner and group lessons. This structure also requires careful planning and preparation on the part of the instructor. One must have a well-prepared lesson plan with detailed timing and pacing cues. Because of the nature of the schedule, the instructor must utilize every moment wisely in order to stay on time and avoid running over into the subsequent partner lesson.

Weekly Group Lessons

The group lesson is an instructional format that involves three or more students who learn exclusively in groups. This approach boasts many merits. First, students have a social network of peers throughout their piano education. Private piano study and practice can be a lonely enterprise. Group lessons address this issue by providing students with valuable social interaction, including opportunities to encourage and challenge one another to higher levels of playing. Additionally, students stand to learn much from their peers in this dynamic learning environment in which exchange of information and knowledge is central to the group's success. In terms of fiscal issues, the format is more cost-effective, potentially providing students with more instructional time for less money than private lessons.

Group lessons are also quite valuable for the teacher. The instructional medium is very efficient, reducing the number of times the teacher must teach the same lesson material. Furthermore, the format provides the teacher with greater potential to maximize income by teaching more students in less time, freeing up more time to teach additional students.

Group lessons are most effectively taught in an environment in which each student has his own keyboard. Digital piano laboratories provide each student with his own instrument that is outfitted with headphones. Such modern labs are equipped with teacher instructional consoles that allow the instructor to speak and demonstrate to the entire class or to individual students. The system also facilitates group and dyad formations with a click of a button.

Group and Private Instruction Combinations

Many piano teachers choose to employ a combination of group and private lessons in their studios. These teachers suggest that such a design allows them to exploit the advantages of both instructional approaches, giving students opportunities to experience the benefits of each. The application of a combination of instructional mediums requires a well-thought-out and coordinated curriculum. Teachers must develop a sequential course of study and a methodical schedule for its presentation, reinforcement, and evaluation. It is essential that groups consist of students who are at a relatively similar skill level and understanding of essential musical concepts and principles. The group lesson is used to reinforce these important concepts through creative activities and exercises, as well providing a natural environment for the study of ensemble music.

Three Weeks Private/Fourth Week Group Only

Many teachers implement a schedule that includes three weeks of private lessons followed by a fourth week of group lessons only. This format works well for teachers who elect to use the private lesson as the primary means for the delivery of the curriculum but who acknowledge the powerful dynamics inherent in group lessons, and so choose to use the group on a once-monthly basis.

Here, the group lesson is often used to introduce broad, overarching concepts as well as to reinforce these concepts through group activities. The private lesson is used to refine individual technique and to address the specific needs of the student. As is often necessary with group and private lesson combinations, meticulous scheduling is critical. In addition, the instructor must plan wisely in order to keep students progressing evenly in the weeks between group lessons.

Alternating Private and Group Lessons

This arrangement is popular for both students and teachers because of the variety and benefits that result from each teaching format. Here, students receive the benefits of both on a regular basis. As is the case with the use of multiple instructional formats, scheduling can be a great challenge. Both students and parents must be well organized to keep on top of the changing dates and times inherent in the schedule.

Some teachers who use this structure schedule students so that they are teaching some private and some group lessons each week. This approach provides variety for the teacher, but along with it come enormous scheduling obstacles. Regardless, the teacher must be able to create assignments that keep students engaged in practice during the period between private lessons.

Both Private and Group Lessons Weekly

Perhaps most desirable is when students receive both a group and a private lesson each week. One popular arrangement involves a weekly, hour-long group lesson in which new material is introduced and an assignment given. This is followed by a thirty- or forty-five-minute private lesson later in the week in which personalized, individual attention is used to reinforce the assigned concepts. Many programs for first-year piano students employ this procedure.

This structure requires considerable commitment on the part of both students and parents. Students must be very serious about their piano study and must be willing to devote the time necessary to prepare for both a private and a group lesson weekly. Parents must also be willing and able to pay a slightly higher tuition fee, as well as provide transportation to the twice-weekly lessons. In spite of this, such an arrangement can prove especially valuable in reinforcing important concepts as well as the increasing the overall speed of students' development.

Performance Groups

The master class was the first type of group instruction. Master pianists and teachers like Franz Liszt used this method as the primary means for instructing their pupils. A master class involves several student performances followed by constructive feedback by the master teacher. Similar to the master class, the performance group permits all participants, both performers and audience, to contribute insights and suggestions for improvement. The setting also provides students with exposure to a vast amount of repertoire through hearing, analyzing, and providing recommendations on the literature performed by their peers.

Several things must occur for performance groups to be successful. The teacher must foster a supportive environment that is both honest and constructive. Students should always encourage their peers with remarks that are positive and helpful. Overly critical or destructive comments must never be permitted in the performance group. When offering comments, students may use the "sandwich method": begin first with a positive comment, followed by a constructive remark, and concluding with another positive comment.

Importantly, all students must be actively participating at all times. The teacher can facilitate such an environment by asking engaging and relevant questions, which lead students to make important discoveries. These questions can be either objective (e.g., "Did Sally play a staccato in measure 3?") or subjective (e.g., "Was this a colorful performance?"). This is a critical element of successful group teaching.

The performance group is a prime forum for discussion of piano literature and its performance. It is imperative that students are given an opportunity to conduct a preview of the score prior to any given performance, granting them valuable practice in score analysis. Students should be asked to discuss the unique attributes of the score that is under examination, highlighting potential problems, as well as methods one might choose to deal with these problems. Following a thorough preview, teachers might also ask students what they expect to hear from the performance. This encourages students to be able to audiate, or create an aural image based on viewing the score alone.

The instructor may decide to assign each student to listen for one specific element (e.g., correct pitches and rhythms, dynamics, articulation) during each performance. This student is responsible for providing a thorough discussion of his musical element as heard in his peer's performance. Such a procedure lifts the cognitive load, freeing students to listen intently to one particular component. Additionally, it gives students a sense of responsibility and a valued role in the process of evaluation.

For classes that consist of more experienced students, the teacher may choose to select one auditor to play the role of master class teacher. This student must listen intently during the performance and provide helpful suggestions and comments. These experiences can be very valuable, strengthening the student teacher's learning and knowledge by virtue of articulating his constructive commentary.

Grouping Considerations

The structure of groups, including their size and composition, is of paramount importance. Although opinions vary widely, most would agree that more than two or three students constitute a group. In terms of overall group size, four to eight students is usually considered an optimal number.

Ultimately, several factors dictate the size of piano classes. These include the level of student advancement, the purpose and goals of the class, classroom size and configuration, available equipment and technology, length of class time, and the experience level of the instructor. In most situations, the smaller the group the better, except when a teacher wishes to expose students to a wide variety of experiences and opinions.

The following list describes group sizes and their specific benefits:

Larger Groups

- Provide a more thorough resource base (e.g., knowledge, experiences, opinions, repertoire) from which the group can draw
- Best suited for long-term group work rather than smaller, short-term projects

Smaller Groups

- Encourage more interaction among group members
- Promote individual accountability and contributions because students are unable to hide
- Especially appropriate for short-term activities
- Easier to identify any problems student members may be having in working together

Most would agree that the use of relatively homogeneous groups is most effective for piano study. To facilitate having groups with relatively uniform composition, teachers should consider the following criteria:

- Level of advancement and ability
- Age (cognitive and developmental issues by age)
- Personality and disposition
- Common interests
- Background

In group study, it is desirable for students to be able to advance at more or less the same rate. Therefore, the student's cognitive development, physical coordination, and social maturity must be considered, as well as his musical readiness, aptitude, and sensitivity. Student age is also a critical area of consideration. Groups should include students of an approximately equal age, with age gaps never extending to more than two years. Indeed, a few months' difference in age can make a huge difference in a child's maturity and readiness.

Although age must be considered, the student's speed of learning and level of achievement are of primary importance. Even when groups are equal in terms of student leveling, there will always be diversity of student strengths. Each student possesses certain strengths, and these abilities should be distributed equally among group formations so that all students can contribute something meaningful to the group.

It is important to remember that not all students will progress at exactly the same rate as their classmates. For instance, on occasion a six-year-old may progress more rapidly than his seven-year-old peer. In order to maintain efficient and productive groups, students should be evaluated regularly to monitor individual progress as well as their overall contribution to the group. Teachers must be prepared to reassign students to a different group if necessary. In any event, with careful initial student grouping and placement, periodic regroupings will not always be necessary. Regrouping is essential only when groups are consistently unproductive. Teachers should be willing to regroup students to facilitate the highest level of group productivity.

Beyond the aforementioned criteria, it is helpful to consider issues like the student's musical background and other areas of interest, both related and unrelated to music. Teachers must also take into account student personality types and dispositions and how these elements will affect the overall dynamic of the group.

In some situations, including master classes and performance groups, a certain level of heterogeneity can be preferable. The advantages to this configuration are the resulting diversity of personalities, abilities, experiences, interests, perspectives, and reasoning strategies. Perhaps the easiest method for setting up heterogeneous groups is the use of random assignments. This may be accomplished by dividing the number of students by the desired group size or by setting group times and maximum size, and requesting students to select a time that works for their schedule. Alternatively, the instructor may choose to organize groups based on one or perhaps two student characteristics such as learning style or personality type. By using this format, the instructor is able to build groups based on achievement levels, assigning members of both advanced and remedial skill levels to each group.

Teachers must carefully craft lessons and group activities according to the group's size and needs. Curricula should therefore be individualized by group in order to match the members' ages, levels, and progress. Along these lines, group lesson length will vary according to the two important criteria: level and age.

Interview and Placement Examinations

Many group piano teachers agree that a placement examination should be administered at the outset of piano study to assess each student's readiness, aptitude, and current level of advancement. The examination reveals valuable information that will allow the teacher to assign the student to a suitable group, as well as guide him in designing a curriculum that is appropriate to each group's needs. (See chapters 7 and 9 for a more detailed discussion regarding placement examinations.)

Business and Financial Planning

Group piano teaching presents teachers with the opportunity to increase their studio income, at times in a rather dramatic fashion. The group lesson allows one to teach multiple students in a one-hour period, which can equate to an increase in hourly earnings. For students, group piano instruction provides the priceless benefits inherent in the group learning environment, while potentially granting them more instructional time than they would receive in a private lesson.

Teachers who opt to teach entirely in groups have the ability to increase their total studio enrollment by serving a larger student population and, in some cases, the opportunity to increase their overall income. In fact, the group lesson format is a means for teachers to accommodate a large waiting list. The morning, lunchtime, and early afternoon hours are especially suitable for preschool classes, home-educated student groups, or adult student populations. Additionally, teachers stand to serve those communities that have endured cuts in school music programs by providing music instruction to those students who are eager to have such experiences, but for whom no school instruction is available.

A common misconception is that by teaching in groups, one will reduce planning time. In actuality, the reverse is often true. Although group teaching is a more efficient use of instructional time, it demands careful and meticulous planning in advance of each lesson. It is important that parents are educated on this issue.

Teachers who independently own and operate a group piano studio must develop and implement a thoroughly crafted business plan in order for their enterprise to thrive and be profitable. Such a document calls for strategic planning and demands honest assessment of a business's strengths, areas of weakness, and opportunities for growth and development. As part of this initiative, it is wise to research the condition of piano teaching, and specifically group piano instruction, in one's community. This will require the collection and analysis of data, which could significantly impact the success of the business. The business should have a clearly outlined mission statement, which details the specific goals and objectives of the organization. This statement should include the studio's dynamic vision for the future. Also, significant thought should be given to the name of the studio and how this can be used for purposes of marketing.

Further, the business manager must employ prudence in such areas as tax codes, zoning and commercial permits, insurance, and other sound business practices. Should the business structure include hired employees, one must consider payroll, federal, state, and local taxes, and any studio-supported benefits. A variety of resources are available to the teacher in this realm, including those published by the Music Teachers National Association (www.mtna.org). Teachers are encouraged to consult the websites of the U.S. Small Business Administration (www.sba.gov) and the Internal Revenue Service (www.irs.gov), which provide relevant information regarding business deductions and expenses, financing options, tips for business development, and ways to enhance one's services.

There are many variables to be weighed when planning one's potential income. One must first start by asking the following questions:

- What is my desired yearly income?
- How many hours do I wish to work each week?
- How many students will I teach?
- What are my expenses?

The following list presents a basic formula for determining one's business income:[1]

- Desired yearly income.
- Hourly income. This number should be based on a minimum number of students per group.
- Divide desired annual salary by hourly income. The result of this operation equals the number of hours one must teach per year.
- Divide the number of yearly teaching hours by the number of weeks one will teach.
- The resulting number equals the number of hours one must teach weekly.
- Consider whether it is possible to schedule this number of hours each week.
- Subtract estimated yearly expenses, including taxes, from gross income to reach net profit.

Tuition and Fees

When establishing fees, many factors must be considered. First, it is necessary to examine standard lesson fee structures for both group and private instruction in one's community. This information can often be obtained from colleagues who are members of local piano teachers' organizations.

Quality, professional music instruction comes at a price. Students and parents may fail to take their study seriously if the fee is nominal. The fees of a professional music educator should be commensurate with the instructor's level of training and expertise, years of experience, commitment to professional development, range of services provided, and location. Extra fees may be incorporated into the overall fee structure for technology or other unique features of one's curricular offerings.

With this said, it is wise to consider the income level of one's community. Such information can usually be acquired from local government agencies. Rates can be established based on this information and should not exceed the standard of living index for the community in which the instruction occurs.

One must consider not only teaching time but also the time required to prepare for instruction. Clientele must know that each hour of instruction may demand as much as an hour of preparation. Parents and students will often need to be educated on the fact that quality instruction requires thoughtful planning. This involves all other related preparations, including recitals, competitions, music study, and review of new teaching literature, among others.

Additionally, one must consider health insurance, vacation time, retirement, funding for participation in professional development activities such as workshops and conferences, and the overhead expenses involved in operating a studio. These include expenses related to rented teaching space, utilities, equipment, and instructional aids and the host of other budgetary considerations.

There is also a great philosophical debate: Should group study be less expensive than private instruction? If one believes in the group format 100 percent, the tuition charged should be on par with private instruction, and certainly no less. Many would argue that the manifold benefits that are unique to group instruction warrant tuition that exceeds the amount charged for private instruction.

One must also consider whether or not need-based scholarships will be offered and, if so, how these will be funded. Some teachers establish a scholarship account, which is supported by community and business donations. Specific criteria should be defined regarding how these funds may be distributed so as to be clear and fair to all.

Billing and Payment

An instructional calendar should be sketched out prior to launching a new teaching year. The calendar should take into consideration summer instructional offerings, the teacher's vacation period, and one's policy, if any, for makeup lessons. From this calendar, one can determine the number of lessons that will be offered per term, as well as the total number of lessons given per year.

Billing should be scheduled on a yearly or term basis, not by the lesson. These arrangements avoid unnecessary business-related issues prior to or following the weekly class. Families who enroll multiple students may be offered special accommodations in terms of tuition.

Receipts should be distributed immediately after payment has been made. Savvy business managers will have receipts preprepared in a format that can be readily e-mailed to the parent or guardian, bypassing costly postal mailings. Some teachers require a yearly enrollment commitment from all students and extend a small reduction in tuition and fees or waive the registration fee for those students who pay for the entire year in advance.

For teachers with a large waiting list, a nonrefundable deposit can be assessed to secure a seat for the student. Such a policy also helps ensure that students are committed for the duration of the instructional term. Likewise, it is common to assess a late fee, typically ranging from 10 to 15 percent of the total outstanding balance for each month the account is delinquent. It should be communicated that prompt payment is both appreciated and expected. To make paying tuition and fees as uncomplicated as possible, one should identify set procedures such as offering mailing or studio drop-off box options. One must be proactive, with all information related to tuition, fees, and billing clearly articulated in the studio policy in addition to being visibly posted in the studio waiting room. One should then strictly adhere to established billing guidelines in order to communicate the significance of the policy.

Marketing

The best marketing tool is a glowing referral and positive word-of-mouth advertisement. We are business professionals whose product is the success of our students. When establishing a new studio in a city, it is often initially advantageous to engage the community with some form of media advertisement. Print and broadcast media are excellent channels for generating studio interest, although both can be quite expensive. Alternatives include posting flyers and brochures on community bulletin boards such as those found at a public library, shopping mall, or supermarket. At the end of the day, if a community observes exemplary training coming from one's studio as evidenced in student excitement and success, this is worth more than thousands of dollars spent on other advertising media.

Some teachers may elect to offer a demonstration class free of charge during the summer months to attract new students. These offerings present interested parents and students with an opportunity to witness the exciting, quality educational experiences that can result in exceptional group piano lessons.

Participation in one's local music teachers organization is another essential means for marketing. Such organizations can serve as referral networks, with colleagues who are willing and eager to support one another. Public studio recitals and ensemble concerts are another excellent way to showcase the success of one's students. These can be offered in public venues such as libraries or shopping malls as a service to the community. Again, the best advertisement is the success of our students.

Beyond the standard business card, a studio website is becoming a compulsory marketing tool. Here, one can post essential studio information, including tuition and fees, registration forms, studio policies, calendars, newsletters, benefits of group instruction, and studio accomplishments, as well as one's philosophy of teaching and curriculum vita. The marketing potential of a webpage is virtually limitless.

The Learning Environment

When preparing a group piano learning environment, one must bear in mind several important issues. Ultimately, the available studio size and dimensions will dictate the number of students one can enroll in each class. Fortunately, the one-on-one teaching studio can usually be easily modified or retrofitted for group piano teaching. One must also consult local zoning laws, which may determine whether the location and facility are zoned for commercial purposes. These codes may dictate the maximum number of persons permitted in the given space. It is advisable to contact local government officials to acquire this important information to ensure one's business meets local commercial codes.

Along these lines, one must also consider issues like sound overflow, accessibility (with consideration given to the physically handicapped), waiting room space, restrooms, and available parking. The teaching space should be comfortable and organized, as well as free from distractions or clutter so that the teacher and his students can move freely about the room. Further, the room should be well lit, with soft lighting, and should be maintained at a comfortable temperature.

The teaching space should have ample room for storage of materials, games, and equipment, as well as an area for various eurhythmic and other movement activities.

Should one choose to use computer-based learning programs to supplement instructional offerings, it is necessary to determine where the equipment can be most effectively positioned in the studio. Many find arranging computer stations in a separate room to be ideal. It is beneficial to anticipate future facility needs, which may include expansion to accommodate studio growth. One may consider rental space options, including those available from local churches or community buildings.

Selecting Group Piano Materials

Group piano teachers must carefully evaluate and select teaching materials according to their specific instructional purposes. Thoughtful consideration of both old and new materials will provide the teacher with a broad knowledge of the available resources and will allow for the selection of materials that are best suited for the target student population. Teachers must first consider the following criteria to establish the framework for their materials analyses:

- Student population
- Student musical background
- Class size
- Class meeting time (e.g., hour, forty-five minutes)
- Class meeting frequency (e.g., monthly, biweekly, weekly)
- Course length (e.g., fifteen weeks, ten weeks)
- Scope of curriculum

The following list presents specific questions teachers should ask themselves when evaluating methods and materials:

- Is the method attractive and visually appealing?
- Is the page layout well arranged and uncluttered?
- How is the method organized?
- What are the procedures for the introduction of new concepts and principles?
- How are concepts and principles reinforced?
- What is the approach to reading?
- What is the approach to rhythm?
- What is the approach to technique?
- How and to what extent are musicianship skills taught and reinforced (e.g., sight-reading, harmonization, transposition, improvisation, score reading, playing by ear)?
- Of what quality is the solo and ensemble repertoire (e.g., classical, jazz, pop, arrangements)?

- Are the method's structure, sequence, and pacing appropriate for the target student population?
- Are accompaniment resources (e.g., teacher-student duets, MIDI, CD) available?
- Are online resources available to both student and teacher?
- Does the method include a teacher's manual?
- Does the text emphasize one activity or curricular competency over another?
- How easy is the text to use for the student?
- How easy is the text to use for the teacher?
- What are the strengths of this method?
- What are the weaknesses of this method?

Equipment and Technology

Educators must be committed to exploring and exploiting every device possible to enhance and accelerate our students' learning. Thus, one must be dedicated to researching and experimenting with the multitude of new instructional materials and technologies that appear on the market each year.

It is critical to remember that the equipment does not determine the quality of a lesson; it is the people who are involved and their interactions that make the difference. Effective group piano teaching can be achieved with equipment consisting of as little as a single acoustic piano. For this scenario, small groups usually not exceeding four students are optimal. When teaching groups of young children, one or two acoustic instruments can be ideal because there is no apparatus for the children to negotiate.

Although not obligatory, many teachers find the preferred group piano teaching environment to consist of a digital piano laboratory. Here, each student sits at his own instrument, which is linked to a central teacher's controller console. Besides the obvious advantage of instruments that do not require tuning, the modern digital piano lab grants the teacher several instructional options for grouping students while on headphones. Grouping configurations permit the teacher to engage individual students, pairs or small groups, as well as the whole class. Lab controllers allow the teacher to work with groups of students independently of one another, while ensembles or individual students work without being interrupted. The technology greatly facilitates ensemble rehearsal and independent group discussions, although many group teachers agree that the amount of time devoted to on-headset work per class should be limited, allowing students to work collectively off headsets to permit the power of group dynamics to function.

While a digital piano lab is perhaps a more significant financial investment than an acoustic piano, its benefits undoubtedly outweigh the initial cost. The purchase of a lab can certainly be an instructional enhancement, as well as a worthy investment in one's business. While the acquisition of a lab can be costly, it can provide a sizable tax deduction.

Several factors should be kept in mind when considering which technologies to implement in one's instructional arsenal. It is beneficial to begin by defining a specific need. One might consider the following questions:

- How can technology enhance my educational program?
- Which technologies could address this need?
- How will my students' learning benefit from this tool?

It is wise to limit one's focus to one area of teaching at a time. The technological realm is indeed vast, and it is easy to become overwhelmed by the many available possibilities. Lofty dreams must be tempered with reality by concentrating on the specific need that is being addressed.

Should one decide to invest in a digital piano laboratory, it is advisable to examine all options available before making the purchase. To get the best value for the money, one must consider a number of issues. To begin, it is necessary to set down clear parameters from which one will work, including the expressed instructional purposes of the laboratory and the student clientele that will use the equipment. It is also sensible to consider the issue of portability. Will the piano lab be a permanent fixture, or will the teaching space be used for other purposes? If the latter, portable electronic keyboard instruments might be an appropriate option, although most keyboards lack the teacher controller console as an option.

A detailed budget should be generated, with consideration given to how the purchase will fit in the overall studio financial plan. This will determine whether the equipment will be purchased out of pocket, financed, or acquired on a rent-to-own basis. Fortunately, many outstanding technologies are no longer prohibitively expensive, with even the most advanced equipment becoming more and more affordable. One must also decide how the purchase will be funded and how the equipment will be maintained. Many teachers assess a technology fee at the beginning of the teaching year, which is used to procure and maintain the technological components of the studio. For the college or university teacher, it may be possible to make use of student technology fees to fund such upgrades. With time, equipment such as headphones, computer mice, and even big-ticket items such as computers and digital pianos will need to be replaced. Therefore, a long-term financial plan must be constructed and then set in motion.

A thorough investigation should follow, first by searching instrument manufacturer websites to familiarize oneself with the products they offer. Many industry websites can provide unbiased reports on manufacturer products and how their products rate against industry standards. Following this initial research, a trip to several local retailers should be scheduled to play the instruments and experience the variety of available features. As one collects information, it is wise to compare the instruments that are being considered by constructing a list of pros and cons, which should be compared with one's initial guidelines.

When evaluating any type of technology, one should consider the following:

- Who is the target audience (e.g., age, level)?
- Will it engage and sustain student interest?
- What curricular competency or competencies will be served?
- What is the applicability?
- How does the technology fit into the overall instructional mission?
- Will the technology appeal to my student population(s)?
- With regard to software applications, does it offer both depth and breadth in the content? Are the graphics visually appealing? Is the sound of high quality? Does the program offer flexibility?
- Can the technology be readily learned and applied by students?
- Is the technology flexible, and can it be used to fill multiple purposes?
- How does the cost fit into the overall studio financial plan?
- How will it be funded and maintained?
- Does the technology possess proven reliability?
- Should service be necessary, are technicians readily available?
- Will this technology require significant change in how I deliver my curriculum?
- How will I implement the technology into my teaching?
- Are there any alternatives?
- Is special training involved to use the technology? If so, how much time is involved?

After a desirable instrument and lab system has been identified, it is time to begin negotiations with the retailer. The cost of technology is dependent on several variables, including the number of sophisticated, onboard features and the quality of materials used to construct the instrument. Many modern digital pianos come with a variety of orchestral timbres and rhythm machines as a standard feature, with many models boasting built-in sequencers and advanced, interactive instructional applications. Manufacturers and retailers usually offer a range of rental and purchase options to fit the diverse budget needs of their clients. Some offer special multiple-piano purchase discounts as well as discounts for complete lab packages. It is wise to thoroughly discuss all discount and purchase opportunities with the retailer, as well as warranty and service options.

After the equipment has been purchased, one must consider where it will be located in the studio. A logical, appropriate location is one that is free of distractions and promotes concentrated learning. Piano laboratories should be arranged so that the teacher can easily observe all students and their hands. Likewise, students must have a clear view of the teacher and any instructional tools, such as a Visualizer or blackboard. The configuration must also be conducive to movement and other classroom activities (figure 2.1).

It is advantageous to develop a strategic plan for implementation of any technology. The plan should clearly define how the technology will be used and how it will address curricular needs. The policy should also detail the procedures that will be used to introduce the technology to both students and parents. It is wise to alert parents and students in advance of new technology in order to explain the benefits to student learning and how it will be applied in one's teaching. This can be accomplished through a newsletter or an e-mail communication. Some teachers elect to host a demonstration seminar in which the value and purposes of the technology are explained and an introductory exhibition of its features is presented. One's policies regarding the use of the technology must be emphasized, including such issues as washing hands prior to use and protocol

FIGURE 2:1 Sample Piano Laboratory Configuration

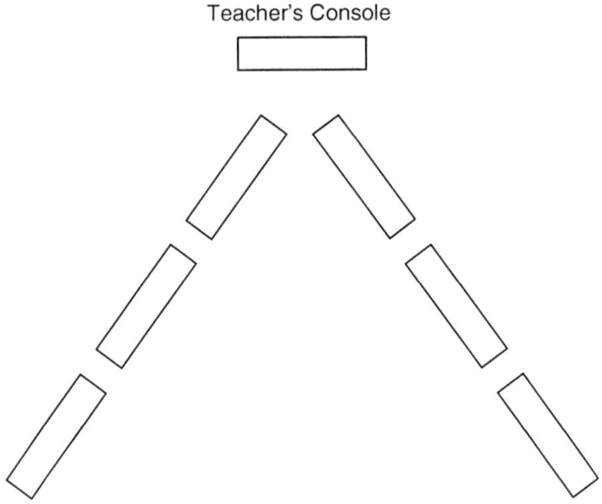

for reporting problems. If an Internet connection is available to students during instruction, it is wise to ask both student and parents to sign a policy contract that outlines acceptable and unacceptable use of the Internet.

In addition to instruments and other technologies, which should always include at least one quality acoustic piano, the group piano classroom may be equipped with tables and chairs at which students can complete theory materials and other games and activities. Chalkboards or marker boards are invaluable instructional tools, with many available for purchase with the staff already adhered. Quality audio equipment such as a compact disc player with digital music interface capability is an important procurement. Compact discs or audio files can be used both during the lesson and at home practice as aural models of current repertoire, as well as for purposes of critical listening and class discussion of performance qualities. They may also be used to play focus music for eurhythmic activities. A projector, document camera, and screen can be used to display PowerPoint slides or other print documents for class discussion. Other instructional aids may include the following:

- Flash cards
- Games and other activities (either purchased or self-created)
- Rhythm instruments
- Supplementary music
- Ensemble materials
- University group piano textbooks
- Software

All equipment should be purchased with consideration of the student clientele by whom it will be used. For instance, a chalkboard should be adjustable to heights at which both very small children and adults can functionally operate. The board should also be long enough for multiple students to use simultaneously. Also, headsets for digital pianos should be adjustable to fit the needs of the student populations who use them.

Chapter 3
Learning Theory: An Introduction

Educators must attempt to understand the underlying principles involved in productive learning as it is occurring in order to enhance one's teaching and, more important, profoundly impact student learning. This chapter will explore important principles related to learning styles, conceptual and discovery learning, and problem solving.

To paraphrase Mel Levine, it is true that to treat all learners the same way is to treat them unequally. Different learners have different learning needs.[1] Quality teaching is situational, meeting students where they are in order to take them where they need to go.

Learning Styles

Each student brings to learning a distinctly personal and unique preference of approach for the acquisition of information and, ultimately, the construction of knowledge. Teaching must therefore address the individual and collective needs of the students involved. Indeed, effective teaching demands thorough consideration of how each student learns best.

Unfortunately, many teachers will hastily declare a student a failure simply because of a perpetual lack of development in a certain skill area. Such a student may be one who is adept at playing by ear but whose reading skills never demonstrate growth. Teachers must avoid classifying such student deficiencies as insurmountable shortcomings, and conversely consider them indicators of a potential disconnect in the reception and processing of information.

The process by which a student acquires, analyzes, stores, and manages information is commonly referred to as the student's learning style. Learning styles usually consist of a dominant and secondary learning modality to which one best responds in any given learning situation. A learning modality is one of three sensory mediums—visual, auditory, and kinesthetic/tactile—through which the learner accumulates information. The following lists explain a few of the various characteristics that are common to each modality:

Visual Learner

- Learns best when information is presented through visual means such as reading and other images
- Carefully observes teaching demonstrations and reads explanations about given concepts
- Appreciates and positively responds to a visually appealing learning environment
- Appreciates well-organized print and visual material

Auditory Learner

- Learns best through listening and responding to both verbal instructions and musical cues
- Appreciates verbal announcement of assignments
- Often verbally repeats or summarizes what he has just learned

Kinesthetic/Tactile Learner

- Learns best by actively doing through bodily movement and manipulation of information and experience
- Is active and may move incessantly

Because each student possesses a dominant learning style, it can then be assumed that all educators have a preferred teaching style through which their own dominant learning modalities are applied. Consequently, a teacher must acknowledge his preferred learning and teaching styles, and then be flexible in his instructional approach in order to effectively reach his students. The wise teacher considers each student's learning preferences and designs instructional situations that target and fulfill these specific learning needs. In the group learning environment, this approach capitalizes on students' individual and collective strengths and utilizes these strengths in the process of developing and shoring up weaknesses. Such considerations result in the most efficient and effective teaching possible, and thus significantly impact the learning outcome(s).

Most research suggests that children experience different dominant modality preferences at various ages during their cognitive development, with the visual modality growing particularly stronger with age. Optimum learning can take place when a student is able to integrate and employ all three modalities.

Many learning style resources are available to teachers for the purpose of assessing student learning preferences, ranging from the use of simple observation to sophisticated testing tools. Whichever method one may choose, it is important that bias of any kind be systematically avoided. Two popular learning style inventories are *Modality Kit* by Swassing and Barbe, published by Zaner-Bloser, and *Learning Styles Inventory*, published by Contact Learning Styles Network (www.learningstyles.net). For those who elect to employ observation as the desired method for determining student learning style preferences, table 3.1 provides musical implications for each modality by category.

It is imperative that the group piano teacher take the time to assess the individual learning preferences within each group. By doing so, the teacher will be equipped with indispensable information regarding the various student learning needs and will thus be able to design lesson plans to address those needs. In this way, the teacher will be able to present lesson concepts and principles in a manner that serves all learning modalities.

Table 3.1 Learning Styles and Musical Implications

VISUAL	Demonstrates exemplary sight-reading skills but has difficulty singing the same melody that is read
	Demonstrates precision and accuracy in reading yet often shows difficulty playing with expression
	Often expresses difficulty with memorization
	Positively affected by the use of flash cards in learning note names and their location on the staff and keyboard
AUDITORY	Plays by ear with ease and skill
	Often struggles with music reading
	May fail to respond to details in the score
	Omits printed pitches, rhythms, or expressive indications
	Plays what he feels sounds most appealing
	Responds to recordings of both himself and other performers
	Responds to counting out loud and verbalization of musical elements (e.g., intervals, melodic movement, harmony).
KINESTHETIC/ TACTILE	Responds best to whole-body and eurhythmic movement activities
	Desires to immediately play or experience what has been verbally discussed
	Responds well to tapping or clapping rhythms
	Constantly moves to the rhythmic pulse of the music
	Wishes to point to place in the score that is being discussed
	Enjoys floor staff activities and other musical games

For example, when teaching rhythms that involve eighth notes, the teacher should do the following:

- Ask students to close their eyes and listen to how eighth notes operate in a rhythmic context by playing a musical example that contains eighth notes (aural).
- Create activities in which students first experience the rhythm through whole body and eventually fine motor movements. This can be accomplished through clapping, tapping, walking, chanting, dancing, and so on (kinesthetic/tactile).
- Visually demonstrate the rhythm in notational form (visual).

Another example might involve the process of announcing a class assignment. The teacher might do the following:

- Write the assignment on the board or display in some visual format (e.g., PowerPoint, overhead, written handout) (visual).
- Explain the assignment verbally, carefully articulating each step. The teacher may also call upon students to read parts of the assignment out loud (aural).
- Demonstrate how the assignment can be completed by giving students the opportunity to model how they will approach learning it (kinesthetic/tactile).

The order in which the learning modalities are presented should be varied so as to give students with each learning style the opportunity to experience their modality first.

Conceptual Learning

To learn conceptually is—as Jerome Bruner would suggest—to serve the future. Conceptual music learning is an instructional approach by which students learn musical concepts and principles and how they can be applied to new situations. Musical concepts are those most basic, fundamental components of music and music making, which include the following:

- Pitch
- Rhythm
- Texture
- Form
- Dynamics
- Articulation
- Tempo
- Timbre

- Style
- Expression
- Phrase

When two or more musical concepts are combined, a musical principle is created. Principles are axioms. They are the big pictures of music: the broad, overarching rules or standards that remain constant. For instance, the combination of the musical concepts of pitch and rhythm will generate a musical principle: melody.

Conceptual learning encourages students to test new concepts and ideas against their repertoire of existing knowledge, understanding, and experience. When faced with new information, students are called upon to question the ways in which the new concepts are similar to or different from existing knowledge. Such analysis yields valuable information that can be integrated into existing cognitive structures. By doing so, students expand and develop the depth and breadth of their knowledge. This information will subsequently inform musical/expressive and intellectual/analytical decisions when one is learning new music.

Given this approach, teaching should avoid imparting concepts or skills in an unrelated fashion but should alternatively seek to communicate how they connect to a broad principle. Students must learn to relate and subsequently apply concepts and principles. The idea of conceptual transfer is a vital component of the conceptual learning approach. To encourage students to transfer knowledge to new situations and in novel contexts, teachers may need to ask leading questions such as, "How is this scale the same as or different from the major scale that we learned last week?" It is also important to note that concepts can be applied from one skill area to the next, mutually promoting one another in a larger context. For instance, a firm grounding in intervallic reading will serve the student well when transposing a melody. Similarly, playing melodies by ear can benefit one's overall confidence when improvising.

Conceptual transfer serves the comprehensive curriculum through the integration of concepts and principles. The goal is for each curricular component, be it concept or skill, to become assimilated into our students' complete working knowledge rather than being an independent entity. Thus, the core intent of this approach is to generate a network of knowledge in which the interrelationships of concepts and principles are clearly understood and readily applied. Indeed, students who learn and transfer knowledge conceptually are able to approach new learning situations with confidence and ease.

To learn within a conceptual framework gives students opportunities for direct application of knowledge. Central to the idea of conceptual learning is the bridging of propositional knowledge with active, working knowledge.

Thus, conceptual learning is more profoundly effective when it is wed with immediate, experiential application. This philosophy underscores the necessity for teachers to create learning experiences that are rich in discovery-based, hands-on activities.

Conceptually based lessons are designed around a central concept and include activities that reinforce understanding of the concept through the transfer of knowledge to related concepts and skills. Such an approach brings focus to instruction by structuring the lesson around a primary theme that pervades the lesson and unifies all activities. The activities used are designed expressly to introduce, drill, and reinforce the central topic. No longer are technique, sight-reading, and harmonization independent lesson units; instead, they are joined by a primary concept. For instance, if the principal lesson concept is the Dorian mode, students may learn how to play the mode, sight-read an example that employs it, harmonize and transpose a melody based on the mode, and improvise using the modal scale.

Teachers must prepare students for the reception of new concepts by orchestrating a variety ways in which students experience the concept. This, of course, should take into consideration the three primary learning modalities. Teachers should lead students to "discover" the fundamental aspects of the concept rather than simply telling them about it. Through the activities, students must be asked to analyze and manipulate concepts so that they comprehend the intricacies involved.

Ultimately, comprehension and mastery of a concept are demonstrated through our students' application of the concept in diverse and unique settings. This may be demonstrated when a student solves a new musical problem by referencing previous conceptual knowledge or by creating music using newly learned musical principles.

In the end, the conceptual approach maximizes learning efficiency by providing students with concrete, practical learning experiences in which information is merged with previous knowledge and readily applied in new learning situations. Indeed, conceptual learning serves the future by developing independent learners and constructors of knowledge.

Discovery Learning

The constructivist branch of epistemological philosophy contends that humans construct and internalize understanding and meaning based on one's present knowledge framework. Built upon the principles of constructivist theory, discovery learning is an instructional approach centered on the idea that learners construct their knowledge from experiencing and manipulating their environment. Thus, the instructional philosophy is an action-based approach to learning founded on the belief that we learn by doing. In this way, discovery learning appeals to all types of learners, merging higher-level thinking and analysis with immediate application and experience.

Discovery learning is also an inquiry-based form of learning in which students consider and wrestle with stimulating questions. The instruction and application of problem-solving skills play a dominant role in this type of learning. Jerome Bruner contends, "Practice in discovering for oneself teaches one to acquire information in a way that makes that information more readily viable in problem solving."[2] In a discovery learning lesson, the teacher guides his students to explore, discuss, analyze, generalize, and compare musical concepts and skills both corporately and individually. Students are conceptually directed to understanding through teacher-facilitated discussion and experimentation, rather than being told what to do and then asked to reproduce what the teacher communicated. As a result, students learn to develop expert question-asking skills where penetrating questions are formulated to which students seek to make informed decisions. Students who participate in discovery learning activities often report a more thorough understanding and greater retention of concepts that they have "discovered" on their own. These students leave the lesson feeling empowered by the fact that they have "discovered" new information, and confident that they can apply this information in new contexts.

To facilitate this type of learning, teachers must create learning situations in which students are trained to search out patterns, investigate relationships, and endeavor to solve problems. Bruner writes, "Emphasis on discovery in learning has precisely the effect on the learner of leading him to be a constructionist, to organize what he is encountering in a manner not only designed to discover regularity and relatedness, but also to avoid the kind of information drift that fails to keep account of the uses to which information might have to be put."[3] Therefore, learning must be accomplished in a practical and logical manner, so that the learner can ably compare new information with that which is already known and tested. Thus, the teacher's job is to generate a learning environment that fosters curious, enterprising, intuitive, and independent learners. The teacher must do his part to pique and sustain student curiosity by presenting the subject matter in a way that is both attractive and relevant. His task is to ask leading questions and to provide helpful hints when necessary, while knowing when to step out of the picture altogether to allow students to explore and experiment on their own.

Discovery learning requires students to take risks. Because of this, teachers must give students permission to do so by inviting them into a world of exploration. Indeed, this type of learning demands a certain degree of courage, as well as a willingness to experiment with and explore uncharted territory. Students must know that trials are likely, but that these challenges will provide valuable information on the road to learning and mastery. Here, the group plays an important role in maintaining, supporting, and encouraging one another despite the surety of failures.

Discovery learning also requires a considerable amount of open-endedness and flexibility from the teacher and at times may demand that the clock be turned to the wall. To be sure, when compared with other approaches, discovery learning may demand more time, but the benefits far outweigh any inconvenience this may cause. Over time, discovery learning has proved to accelerate learning and skill acquisition by ensuring long-term retention and applicability.

Teachers can foster a discovery-based learning environment by designing and orchestrating learning experiences in which students first encounter and operate a concept or skill before a name is assigned and a definition is given. For the piano student this involves experimenting with hearing and producing sounds at the keyboard. This type of music teaching is guided by the principle of "sound before sign," in which students first hear and experience the sound before a symbol is attached to the aural event.

It is helpful to consider an example of a discovery-based learning sequence in which students learn to construct and play major five-finger scales. The teacher begins by modeling and demonstrating a C-major five-finger scale using the right hand alone, with students focusing their attention on the sound. Next, he introduces how to play the pattern entirely by rote, modeling it by using a Visualizer or a keyboard diagram. Students are instructed to place the first finger of their right hand on middle C, with subsequent fingers on D, E, F, and G. The group then plays and experiences the scale.

Working with pairs or small groups, the teacher guides the students to discuss and further explore that which they just experienced at the keyboard. Students are asked to address the following questions:

- How many notes or pitches are played?
- What patterns are found?
- What is the relationship between black and white keys?
- Is there are particular pattern of whole and half steps?
- Does the sequence of notes sound happy or sad?

After several minutes, the teacher facilitates a class discussion regarding student findings. Leading questions such as "What did you discover?" or "How does what you found relate to what you already know?" are used to initiate the discussion. With the guidance of the teacher, the pattern of whole and half steps (start-whole-whole-half-whole) is established as the method for creating a major five-finger scale. Following this confirmation, students return to their pairs or small groups to transfer their new knowledge by transposing this sequence of whole and half steps to other starting pitches.

Note that this procedure began with the teacher limiting the conditions of learning. The objective of the exercise was for the class to discover the pattern of whole and half steps used to form the major five-finger pattern. Notice also that students learned to play the scale first only with the right hand rather than combining hands, which may complicate the matter.

Students are introduced to the scale initially by sound and then are taught by rote using a visual illustration provided by a diagram. Students then play the scale individually, experiencing it both aurally and kinesthetically. It is important to observe that all learning modalities are engaged for this preliminary introduction, beginning first with sound. Also note that the activity did not begin with a complex lecture on how to construct the scale; instead, students discovered the pattern on their own by addressing leading questions posed by the instructor. After students had worked cooperatively to discover the pattern involved, the teacher then led them in a discussion to confirm their findings and then commissioned the students to apply their knowledge to new scales.

Problem Solving

Problem solving is the application of knowledge in a meaningful fashion both within and outside of a given context. Problem solving requires more than simply determining an answer to a given problem. It goes further, demanding that the learner draw upon his knowledge base of previously learned concepts and principles and apply these to the present situation. He must also think creatively, always seeking to find the most effective and appropriate solution to a given problem. John Holt writes, "The test of intelligence [is] not how much we know how to do, but how we behave when we don't know what to do. Similarly, any situation, any activity that puts before us real problems that we have to solve for ourselves, particularly for which there are no answers, sharpens our intelligence."[4]

Thus, central to the development of problem-solving skills is learning to ask oneself the right questions. The purpose of these questions is to lead the problem solver to reference previously learned information and learning experiences that may be useful in solving the problem at hand. As such, effective problem-solving skills are related in part to the learner's ability to process, store, and retrieve information in the first place. Bruner writes, "When you cannot see how to proceed with a problem, try to think of a simpler problem that is similar to it; then use the method for solving the problem as a plan for solving the more complicated problem."[5]

It is true that our job as teachers is to teach ourselves out of a job. With this task comes the challenge of equipping our students with tools to be independent learners and constructors of knowledge. To this end, we must foster an intense curiosity and a bold desire for learning. It is vital that we instill in our students a sense of trust and confidence in their ability to tackle the uncertainties of new and increasingly difficult problems, as well as persistence to keep trying until the problem is solved. In the group learning environment, the struggles of solving problems are divided among the group resources, while subsequently the pleasure of overcoming struggles to making music is multiplied.

One of our primary goals is to teach our students how to become successful problem solvers who think systematically about how to solve musical and technical issues encountered in class and during their practice. When planning the lesson, we as teachers must be cognizant of how the instruction and application of problem-solving techniques can be employed. Problem solving involves four important steps:[6]

- Identification
- Definition
- Experimentation
- Verification

Identification

Identification involves directing our students to an awareness that a problem exists. For younger students, it is often quite necessary for the instructor to help his students identify when a problem is present. Ultimately, we must train our students to independently detect problems so as to increase productivity when they are not under the teacher's supervision.

Definition

Defining the problem is another critical step in successful problem solving. Students must learn to get at the heart of the problem and not be misled by peripheral issues. For instance, some students may define a problem as "When I get to this passage I seem to slow down." Of course, this may be a part of the problem, but it does not address the deeper question of "Why did I slow down at this passage?" Skillful and accurate identification and definition of problems has important implications for success in the following stages.

Experimentation

Here, students endeavor to find the most effective and efficient solution to the given problem. Students are called to reference previous knowledge and consider new solutions in order to identify strategies that may be applied to the present situation. Again, for the younger student it is often necessary to provide suggestions or cues to stimulate personal discovery of viable solutions.

Verification

It is at this stage of problem solving that students apply the strategies they devised to resolve the issue. If the technique works and the problem is corrected, the students have successfully solved their problem and can proceed to uncover new problems. But if the strategy does not solve the issue, one of a few of factors may be at play. First, it may be that the strategy will work but will need a few repetitions in order to correct the problem. Alternately, it may be that the strategy will not work and a new solution must be discovered. Again, accurate assessment of the exact cause of the problem in the first place will significantly influence the success or failure of the problem-solving operation.

Chapter 4

Cooperative Learning Theory and Group Piano Teaching

Group Learning Theory: An Introduction

The study of group dynamics, or how people interact in groups, initially appeared at the outset of the twentieth century in the United States with the work of educator John Dewey. Subsequent study by Gestalt psychologist Kurt Lewin stressed the importance of personal involvement within the dynamic whole of a group as a result of his attempt to generate high productivity within group environments.[1] Herbert Thelen built upon the concepts set forth by both Dewey and Lewin in an educational methodology constructed on the use of small, cooperative groups for the instruction of academic subject areas.[2]

Group dynamics involve the interaction and interpersonal relationships that occur between members of a group and how these influence the group's functioning and productivity. Factors such as emotions, individual differences, and interpersonal influence and conflict all have a significant impact on the efficiency and ultimately the success of any group activity.

Morton Deutsch contends that a group "may be tentatively defined as being composed of a set of members who mutually perceive themselves to be cooperatively or promotively interdependent in some respect(s) and to some degree."[3] Immediately the cooperative interaction among group members emerges as an integral attribute of these dynamic settings.

This cooperative nature manifests itself in the social interaction that transpires among the group's members. Joan Reist describes peer interaction as "the combined or reciprocal actions of two or more individuals that have an effect on each other and work together."[4] Members share common and contrasting goals and experiences, which contribute to the rich variety of knowledge and ideas that are present in a group. Peer interaction is most productive when students freely exchange strategies that will enhance the learning of all involved, while providing support throughout the entire process of learning.

Guy Duckworth suggests that groups typically grow and develop along five dimensions. *Membership* is a stage where individual members assess their involvement in the group and the involvement of others. *Influence* expresses itself as members become comfortable with their specific roles and begin to share in the decisions that must be made. Each member feels he can contribute something to the overall outcome. As membership and influence are attained, *feelings* become important as the members gain confidence that they can express themselves freely. Importantly, *individual differences* emerge as members begin to convey their own unique experiences, skills, and knowledge and come to recognize and value the individual differences that each group member possesses. Finally, and perhaps most important, *productivity* is achieved as the singular ideas of individuals are analyzed, combined with others, and synthesized, generating new ideas that few would have thought of alone.[5] Over time, groups develop an identity of their own, as well as a stable structural framework.

Because of the potentially high levels of productivity groups can generate, they are prime environments for learning. Many psychologists, including Jean Piaget and Lev Vygotsky, contend that one's knowledge and intellectual development are socially constructed through interaction with one's physical and social environments. Piaget argues that "during cooperative efforts participants will engage in discussions in which cognitive conflicts will occur and be resolved, and inadequate reasoning will be exposed and modified."[6] Vygotsky suggests that "groups members exchange information and insights, discover weak points in each other's reasoning strategies, correct one another, and adjust their understanding on the basis of others' understanding."[7]

Groups also provide a habitat for motivation. It is within these groups that relationships are often formed that have the potential to challenge students to achieve their best as part of the built-in system of accountability. These relationships are even powerful enough to change attitudes toward the tasks set before them, providing an incentive to strive for greater success. Furthermore, there is evidence to suggest that even when an individual is rewarded within a cooperative group, all personnel will consequently challenge one another to do their collective best because it is in the group's best interest.

Along these lines, one can contend that a cooperative learning environment may produce a sense of belonging, which can generate high levels of motivation. Many research studies suggest that this type of learning produces significantly higher levels of intrinsic motivation than do other models, at least under some conditions. Robert Slavin stressed that "the critical element was a combination of group rewards and high-level 'elaborated, cognitively involving' peer interactions; simply having one student give another the 'right' answers was not effective."[8] Furthermore, feedback received from peers as well as the instructor serves to motivate and challenge students as long as it is honest and nonjudgmental.[9]

Overview of Cooperative Learning Theory

Cooperative learning is a highly structured instructional methodology that employs small groups of students who work together to maximize their individual and corporate learning. The educational concept of cooperative learning is certainly not new. The instructional approach of small-group learning has existed for centuries, while specific research of cooperative learning theory was more thoroughly developed and researched beginning as early as the 1920s. A surge of activity surrounding the theory was launched in the 1980s, with research continuing today.

Cooperative learning theory and its application were originally designed for use in the public school classroom. Important developers of the instructional approach include David and Roger Johnson (University of Minnesota), Robert Slavin (Johns Hopkins University), and Spencer Kagan (University of California). Building upon the research of educational and social psychologists of the past such as John Dewey, Kurt Lewin, Jean Piaget, and Lev Vygotsky, these pioneers recognized the enormous potential of groups as prime learning environments and consequently built an instructional theory based on this understanding.

At the heart of cooperative learning is the idea that two heads are better than one. Any group of people or students encompasses a rich diversity of ideas, knowledge, and experiences. The members' collective knowledge and ideas are greater than those of any one individual.

What, then, happens during cooperative learning? First, and very important, the group is actively involved in every stage of the learning process. There is no room for idle group members in cooperative efforts. All participants must take an active role in order for the group to succeed. In cooperative learning, the teacher assumes the role of facilitator and no longer serves in the dominant role as the font of information. The teacher is present to guide students in the learning process and help them discover collectively the desired concepts and principles. Throughout the cooperative lesson, students participate in group activities that serve to research, teach, drill, or review concepts and principles. These activities are structured so that the groups must cooperate to achieve a common goal.

Research involving cooperative learning reveals many benefits. Students are actively involved in all parts of the learning process; therefore, learning is participatory, not passive. Students directly and immediately apply information and knowledge from the outset to the very finish. There is no longer a delay in receiving information and the subsequent processing and application of this new material. Participants also have the support and encouragement of their peers. Because students work together cooperatively, pressures are lifted, and students typically experience less anxiety. Due to the nature and structure of cooperative learning activities, students are called upon to use higher-level reasoning strategies and increased critical reasoning competencies. Students are also challenged to view situations from others' perspectives. Additional benefits include the following: the potential for more positive student attitudes, higher achievement levels, increased retention of knowledge, higher levels of self-esteem, and a strengthened ability to articulate ideas through verbal communication.

Five Essential Elements for Cooperative Learning

The simple act of organizing students into groups and instructing them to work together does not necessarily produce results. Cooperative learning must be carefully structured for success. Cooperative learning specialists David and Roger Johnson have identified five essential elements or criteria that must be present for cooperative learning to be successful.[10] The presence of these elements sets apart the cooperative learning activity from other group work. *Positive interdependence* is a mind-set that results in each student's promotion of other students' learning and achievement. Cooperative learning activities are structured so groups must cooperate to achieve a common goal. Therefore, the philosophy "We, not me" prevails. Students are both individually and collectively responsible for learning the assigned material. Positive interdependence can be facilitated using the following: mutual learning goals (e.g., ensuring each member learns the assigned materials), joint rewards (e.g., receiving bonus points for collectively high scores on individual examinations), and divided resources (e.g., each member presents a part of the total information necessary to complete an assignment).

Face-to-face interaction involves communication among group members in order to explain how to solve a given problem, offer a personal insight, present an analysis of a lesson concept, or make connections and transfers from past to present learning. The result is an academic and social network in which students encourage one another to make transfers between previous information and knowledge to the understanding of a new concept or principle. The instructor/facilitator must always attempt to foster a spirit of sharing and encouragement among students and must model this behavior from day one. Ideally, students will become aware of those students who need more assistance or support along the way. The classroom should be arranged in a way that allows teams to easily communicate and work together.

Individual accountability is the element that holds each student responsible for his own contributions to the group and to his individual, personal understanding and growth. This aspect ensures that each student takes personal responsibility for learning. Therefore, cooperative learning is designed so that students are assessed both individually and collectively. This key element prevents "freeloaders," or those students who rely on others to complete the sum of the work. Students realize that it is in their best interest not only to thoroughly learn the material themselves but also to assist team members in mastering the concepts. Accountability can be structured by randomly selecting one student's work to represent the entire group or by having each student explain or teach a concept to his peers.

Social skills are essential for progress in groups. For many students, this is not a natural skill or part of their disposition. Therefore, the teacher must design activities that call for cooperation in order for the exercise to be successful. Teachers must also model positive social behaviors to the class such as offering praise, giving constructive criticism, accepting criticism, checking for understanding, demonstrating efficient use of time, and taking turns. One must demonstrate to his students that leadership, decision making, and communication are most effective when they are participatory. The teacher/facilitator must reinforce and reward positive social skills as they develop. Oftentimes these skills take time to emerge and mature, but eventually they will become a part of the normal group operations.

Group processing, serving as an executive function, occurs when members assess their progress and develop techniques to maintain and enhance their advancement. This is an opportunity for groups to take step back and consider their work in retrospect. It is the metacognitive function of thinking about one's thinking and asking questions such as "What's working?" "What's not?" "How can we do this better?" The instructor may facilitate group processing by asking each group to complete a questionnaire that examines those things the group did well and those things the group could improve upon, as well as highlighting the accomplishments and assistance of each member. The result of effective group processing is the development of a large storehouse of problem-solving strategies as well higher-level reasoning skills.

Preinstructional Planning for Cooperative Learning

Proper planning for the implementation of cooperative learning is critical. The instructor must make many preinstructional decisions that will have a significant impact on the success of the cooperative lesson. First, he must generate a clear list of objectives, both academic objectives and those involving social skills. In terms of academic objectives, the instructor must decide if the lesson will be used to introduce new concepts or instead to review material or make a transfer to related material.

Elizabeth Cohen proposed two types of learning and the subsequent types of interaction that may result from each. *Conceptual learning* is that which introduces and processes abstract, conceptual ideas and usually involves the application of higher-order cognitive skills. Here students contribute and exchange ideas to be thoughtfully considered and analyzed by the group. The result of this type of learning is typically the articulation of reasoning strategies or new discoveries. *Routine learning* occurs when concepts and principles are reviewed through the process of drill, fact recall, or demonstration. During this type of learning, students usually interact through question asking and answering, and by providing helpful and patient explanations of their responses.[11]

It is also important to identify specific social skills that will be emphasized in the lesson. The instructor may accomplish this by monitoring groups over a period of time, noting specific social skill deficiencies. He should continually ask students to identify those social skills that could improve their teamwork and overall efficiency. Perhaps most obvious and important, he must consider those social skills that are imperative for the successful completion of the given assignment or task.

Group Size and Composition

After both academic/musical and social skill objectives have been clearly established, one must carefully consider the formation of each group. Throughout the literature, most researchers agree that the smaller the group the better. In most cases, cooperative learning groups range from two to six members.

There are many elements one must consider when determining the size of a group, all of which may ultimately determine the success of the cooperative activity. It is true that with the addition of each member there are increased resources, including experiences and knowledge. But one must not let this wholly determine the size. Oftentimes the length of time available for the activity may dictate the size of the group. Generally speaking, the shorter the activity time, the smaller the learning group should be. Also the specific materials available to complete the task may have a bearing on the group size.

One must consider both the advantages and the disadvantages of the possible group sizes. Typically, smaller groups are more useful for students who are novices to group work and to cooperative learning in particular. Within these small groups of two to four members, students are challenged to participate more freely and are therefore unable to hide and avoid contributing an equal share of the work. Also, smaller groups require less complex cooperative and social skills in order to optimally function. Furthermore, instructors/facilitators are more readily able to identify problems students may be having in working together and then can suggest solutions to remedy these issues.

Each additional group member contributes to a richer and wider range of knowledge and experiences. Larger groups have the potential to generate more ideas and solutions, which in turn places them at an advantage when dealing with issues that require more complex and higher-level reasoning. With this, though, comes the demand of maturity in terms of social skills so that all students are given equivalent opportunities to share, exchange insights, and contribute to the task at hand.

David and Roger Johnson suggest the use of the acronym TEAM when grouping students: *T* stands for time and involves the length of time available for the activity, as well as the duration of the group; *E* stands for the experience or advancement level of each student member; *A* stands for the age of each individual member of the group; and *M* considers the materials available for the academic task or goal.

For some types of learning, heterogeneous groupings can be a preferred type of group composition. The advantage to this configuration is the resulting diversity of personalities, abilities, experiences, interests, perspectives, and reasoning strategies. Random assignment is the easiest method for creating heterogeneous groups. This may be accomplished by dividing the number of students in the class by the desired group size. Students are then given a number based on the result, and all students with the same number constitute a group. The instructor should also consider issues of race, ethnicity, and gender when formulating groups.

Duration of Groups

How long should groups stay together, and which duration is best for a certain type of learning goal? A key factor for determining group duration is productivity. A group should remain together only as long as it is producing high-quality results and is functioning with positive social interaction. Many long-term groups develop sophisticated mechanisms for constructive teamwork, which enables them to deal with complex tasks and learning goals. These skills are often derived from the powerful connection that is forged among group members who have worked together over an extended period of time.

Teachers must continually monitor group productivity, including both social and academic outcomes, to proactively deal with potential problems. When groups demonstrate unproductive behaviors, it is critical for the teacher to avoid regrouping students too soon. These can often be opportunities for students to learn how to resolve conflicts or problems in their cooperative functioning, as well as a time to reevaluate specific social skills that have been applied in group activity. The development of social skills that help students be constructive members of society is a central purpose of cooperative learning.

David and Roger Johnson have identified three types of cooperative groups. *Informal cooperative learning* groups are temporary groups that last no longer than a class period and are used to focus attention on lesson material, ensure the processing of lesson material, or provide a summary of the given lesson. *Formal cooperative learning* involves students working together from the short to long term to achieve shared learning goals and to complete given tasks and assignments. In the academic classroom, these might include composing a report, conducting a survey or experiment, or reading a chapter and answering questions. Finally, *cooperative base groups* are long-term, heterogeneous groups whose members provide mutual encouragement and support, influencing one another toward consistently higher levels of achievement.[12]

Explanation of the Learning Task

Establishing solid groundwork for the academic task is essential to the success of the cooperative lesson. During the orientation segment of a lesson, the instructor presents a concise introduction featuring the salient features of the cooperative activity, including the basic concepts, objectives, and desired outcomes for the task. An explanation of specific procedures that should be followed to successfully complete the task may be offered. One may find it helpful to distribute activity overview cards to the groups, which list a clear, detailed explanation of the task. This step may be omitted if the instructor desires the students to be creative in their problem-solving efforts. It is important that the instructor convey the expected standard of performance by listing specific criteria for the successful completion of the task, while noting implications for both the individual and the group. He may also choose to remind students of productive cooperative roles during this phase.

It is during this stage that the instructor must foster the central element for the success of cooperative work: positive interdependence. Joint goals should be established so that each individual group member clearly understands that the success of the task hinges upon attainment of the collective goal. Students must know they are responsible for individually learning the material and for ensuring all members of their group have learned the central concepts as well. This can be supplemented with some form of positive reward such as bonus points or special recognition.

A necessary adjunct of positive interdependence is the structuring of individual accountability. In cooperative work, students challenge each individual member of their group to higher levels of learning and comprehension. Such accountability can be promoted by individually evaluating students and by requesting students to teach or summarize a given concept to a peer.

Cooperative Learning Structures

Following is an overview of several of the most popular cooperative learning structures that can be easily adapted for use in group piano teaching.

Groups of Two (Dyads)

Think-Pair-Share

Think Pair Share is designed to develop conceptual knowledge and is particularly useful for short-term activities (e.g., those lasting a few minutes). The structure lends itself well for use by students who are novices to cooperative learning activity and may be effectively employed by learners of all ages. Students first independently think about a topic or question given by the instructor and then are assigned to pairs to discuss their ideas. Students are challenged to reach a consensus and provide justification for their reasoning, afterward sharing their thoughts with the entire class. This structure easily stimulates student participation and involvement.

Groups of Four

Pairs Check

Pairs Check is a prime method for practicing and reviewing lesson concepts. Students work in pairs within groups of four. Within their pairs, students alternate—one solves a problem while the other coaches. After every two problems, the pair checks to see if they have the same answers as the other pair. This structure may be effectively used to encourage student sharing, especially in the initial stages, as well as for developing more creative interaction. Additionally, it has implications for both the acquisition of knowledge and the promotion of a positive social environment. For instance, Pairs Check would be most useful to test students' knowledge of a particular skill or basic lesson concept. By coaching each other, each student may solidify his own understanding of that particular skill or concept.

Groups of Four or More

Round-Robin

Round-Robin is a structure that encourages team building as each student shares in turn with his teammates. By doing so, students express their ideas and opinion through equal participation. The structure is appropriate for reviewing lesson concepts or soliciting ideas and opinions from classmates. The activity is designed so that each member contributes an opinion or answer to a question.

Send a Problem

Send a Problem may be used to review and summarize lesson concepts. Each student from a group poses a question to his team members, who in turn respond with a consensus answer. The same questions are then forwarded to another group to answer. The groups then discuss their collective responses and attempt to achieve a thoroughly reasoned collective response.

Teams-Games-Tournament

In *Teams-Games-Tournament* (TGT), the teacher teaches directly through lecture or discussion. Afterward, teams consisting of four to five members of mixed levels of achievement study or practice together to ensure that all team members know the material. Next, team members divide up to play academic games or compete in tournaments that cover the lesson concepts. Scores are figured and the students are recognized for their achievement, though grades are designated on an individual basis of performance.

Student Teams–Achievement Divisions

In *Student Teams–Achievement Divisions* (STAD), students take a weekly quiz instead of playing games. Recognition is awarded for the combined improvement represented in team members' scores. The amount each student contributes to the collective team score is determined by the degree to which his quiz score exceeds his past quiz average. The highest-scoring teams are recognized by the inclusion of team member names in a newsletter or by some other form of reward.

Group Investigation

Group Investigation is a cooperative learning strategy that combines interaction and communication with the process of academic inquiry. Students form groups according to common interests in a given topic. They internally organize the research, analysis, synthesis, and presentation of their finding. As a collective, students plan a research study to examine a particular problem or issue. When all groups have completed their research, students present their findings to the class, summarizing how their information regarding a subtopic connects to the broader subject.

Fundamental to this philosophy is the idea that students will invest their energies to explore and learn about a topic that is of personal interest. Constructed to address issues of scaffolded learning and problem solving, this approach is usually most effective and useful for large, complex, and open-ended projects. Such projects typically require considerably longer periods of time in which to unfold.

Jigsaw

The *Jigsaw* method involves all groups being assigned the same broad topic, while each member is assigned one unique part of the topic to learn and teach the other members of the group. The groups combine their findings to create a complete understanding of the topic. As such, group personnel cannot gain a comprehensive knowledge of the material unless each member thoroughly completes his given task. The procedure encourages each student to take ownership in his specific area of a larger learning objective, becoming an expert on one portion of the composite topic. The format is perhaps most applicable for the discovery, collection, and synthesis of information to complete a significant long-term learning unit.

Cooperative Learning and Group Piano Teaching

By the very nature of its structure, the teaching of piano in groups lends itself well to the application of cooperative learning theory and techniques. Joseph Goliger, in his study "Implementation of a Program of Cooperative Learning in an Urban Secondary Piano Laboratory" (1995), developed and realized a group piano program curriculum for high school students based on cooperative learning theory.[13] Goliger summarized a list of the potential outcomes of cooperative learning set forth by Johnson, Johnson, and Holubec in 1988:

1. Higher achievement and increased retention
2. Greater use of higher-level reasoning strategies and increased critical reasoning competencies
3. Greater ability to view situations from others' perspectives
4. Higher achievement and greater intrinsic motivation
5. More positive, accepting, and supportive relationships with peers regardless of ethnic, sex, ability, or social class differences or handicapping conditions
6. More positive attitudes toward subject areas, learning, and schools
7. More positive attitudes toward teachers, principals, and other school personnel
8. Higher self-esteem based on basic self-acceptance
9. Greater social support
10. More positive psychological adjustment and health
11. Less disruptive and more on-task behavior
12. Greater collaborative skills and attitudes necessary for working effectively with others

Based largely on Slavin's TGT and Johnson and Johnson's "Learning Together" models, Goliger's study identified many positive results, including "indicators of caring within family groups, the development of a 'we' feeling, the growth of acceptance (in most cases) of positive interdependence, as well as some very refreshing and surprising musical and creative outcomes." Further, Goliger found a "dramatic improvement in grade results" in final exam scores.[14]

Piano teachers have long recognized the merits of studying piano in group environments. Such validating remarks from piano pedagogues confirm a common perception that the format can indeed be a most effective mode of teaching. It is my belief that, supported by these assertions, a specific methodology of group piano teaching could be adapted and developed based on the principles and desirable outcomes set forth by cooperative learning theorists.

Selected Applications of Cooperative Learning Theory to Group Piano Instruction

The following instructional strategies and activities are designed to demonstrate the applicability of cooperative learning theory to selected curricular competencies for piano instruction conducted in group learning environments. This is not a comprehensive listing of applications but an introduction to selected examples. I hope the reader will be inspired to experiment with these activities and invent additional applications of cooperative learning principles to specific group piano teaching scenarios.

Skill competency areas are divided into individual units: technique, sight-reading, harmonization, transposition, improvisation, and solo and ensemble repertoire. Each unit includes a succinct description of the cooperative learning theory structure from which the activity is derived, followed by a thorough explanation of the activity design and detailed procedures for its implementation. A rationale for each exercise is given, with a discussion of the application's educational merits and values.

Technique

Title: Technique Tournament
Piano Competency: Technique (e.g., scales, arpeggios, études)

Cooperative Learning Theory Source

The Technique Tournament is designed largely on the principles of Robert Slavin's structures titled Student Teams–Achievement Divisions and Teams-Games-Tournaments. Drawing upon the major components of both STAD and TGT, the Technique Tournament uses many of these elements—some in modified form—which include the following: class presentations, teams, games/quizzes, individual improvement scores, tournament, and team recognition. Following direct presentation of class material by the instructor, teams of mixed levels of achievement play games or compete in tournaments that deal with the lesson content.

Application Design and Procedure

A complete listing of all technical exercises and studies (e.g., scales, arpeggios, études) to be studied throughout a given period is distributed to students at the outset of the term. Each technical skill or exercise is systematically presented and demonstrated by the instructor during regular class time throughout the quarter. All requirements and specifications are thoroughly discussed at this time. A final Technique Tournament is held at the close of the term, at which point students are required to have mastered each technical element and are asked to demonstrate competency of each skill. Table 4.1 shows a sample of technical skills to be evaluated in a Technique Tournament:

Table 4.1

Round	Technical Skill	Requirements
1	All major scales/arpeggios	Two octaves, hands together
2	All harmonic minor scales/arpeggios	Two octaves, hands together
3	Hanon exercises 1 and 2	Two octaves, hands together

The class should be divided into two heterogeneous teams of mixed ability at the beginning of the quarter. Teams must be carefully assembled by the instructor so that each team represents a cross section of the class in terms of demonstrated proficiency and competency levels, sex, and race/ethnicity. To accomplish this, the instructor can assess each student's strengths and weaknesses or consider student work or grades from previous terms. The size of each team will vary depending on the number of students in each class.

Time should be allotted during each group class for teams to meet and practice. During this time, usually five or ten minutes, the instructor may target a specific technical skill or exercise for the teams to practice or review. For university music major class piano students, teams can be required to meet outside of class to prepare for the tournament. These teams should be asked to schedule a weekly or biweekly meeting in which they practice and assist team members with specific difficulties or concerns they may have regarding the technical materials. Precollege students may also choose to meet together outside class, although this may be a significant challenge due to scheduling and transportation issues.

A Practice Technique Tournament may be held midway through the term. This event is constructed on a smaller scale and is much less formal than the final tournament. The Practice Technique Tournament may contain only a few of the overall technical skill competencies. Additionally, regular (e.g., weekly, monthly) matchups such as round-robin tournaments (comparable to the weekly games and quizzes of TGT and STAD) can be played to give students an opportunity to assess their individual and collective progress. During the round-robin tournament, students are assigned to play a scale by their peers. While a student plays the scale out loud, his peer partner observes and then offers feedback regarding fingering or missed notes. All other students play the scale silently, off headset, with their digital pianos turned off. This gives students the opportunity to review each scale as it is played by the target student, keeping all students involved at all times. This procedure also gives the instructor the opportunity to monitor group and individual progress and to intervene with suggestions for improvement when necessary. Unlike TGT and STAD, the Practice Technique Tournament and weekly matchups do not function as individual point-earning opportunities.

The Final Technique Tournament is conducted near the close of the term. The prescribed technical elements are divided into tournament rounds (e.g., round 1, major scales and arpeggios; round 2, harmonic minor scales and arpeggios; round 3, Hanon exercises; round 4, Czerny exercises). Scales and arpeggios are evaluated on the basis of continuity and the use of correct fingering. Some teachers may establish a specific tempo at which students must play the materials. Études or studies should be assessed with consideration of the specific technical concept involved, in addition to continuity. Advanced classes may be required to render each component with the metronome at a given tempo.

A representative from each team is asked to play a given scale or technical exercise individually. The instructor/judge determines if the technical component was acceptable and awards one team point for a correctly played performance. No points are granted to performances deemed unacceptable. The instructor records points privately rather than announcing them publicly following each performance so as not to embarrass student participants. For university classes or for teachers who provide students with grades, the instructor may also choose to separately grade each performance and assign a letter grade to be recorded as part of a quiz or exam. Therefore, points and grades are separate entities. At the close of the tournament, all points are tallied, and the team with the most points is awarded a prize. In some cases, a play-off round may be necessary. The winning teams may be awarded bonus points to be applied to their overall final exam technique grade. The instructor should be particularly careful to structure these bonus points so as not to radically inflate the student's overall grade.

Rationale and Benefits

The Technique Tournament is a viable means for the instruction and development of piano technique. It is designed to stimulate excitement as well as both individual and group accountability throughout the learning process. Additional positive outcomes related to the Technique Tournament include advancement in technical proficiency, increased levels of confidence at the instrument, and an overall increased motivation to practice technique.

Because teams consist of students from varied levels of playing ability, all members stand to gain something. Students who possess a more advanced technique solidify their understanding as they encourage and assist less-advanced students. The latter benefit as they receive support and tutoring from their more advanced peers.

A variety of ideas and approaches to a given technical problem are exchanged among members. Although at first some students are more reluctant to offer feedback, with time most will willingly offer and accept advice from their peers. As a result, students may find an alternate manner in which to approach a technical issue that they may not have discovered on their own. Students may remind one another of specific fingerings for scales or arpeggios or may provide more abstract technical advice such as appropriate hand position or the proper use of wrist rotation for a given technical issue.

Of course, the instructor should closely monitor in-class group activity, including the exchange of student ideas, noting any unconstructive or socially harmful activity. Intervention by the instructor is at times necessary to control radical or unproductive suggestions and to direct students to alternate approaches to a given technical problem. The instructor should advise students when their comments are not particularly appropriate and give students credit when their suggestions are valuable.

Unsupervised practice among early-level students may reinforce mistakes and bad habits. Therefore, it is important that students explain any suggestions made outside class to the instructor by submitting a brief report that details their ideas. These reports can be as simple as a handwritten note detailing a specific problem the team encountered and a description of the suggestion(s) to solve it. The instructor may additionally wish to follow up on these written reports by asking students to provide a verbal and physical demonstration of their suggestions. An alternative may be to permit only more advanced students to practice outside of class, while earlier levels practice solely in class. This arrangement would allow the instructor to carefully monitor student exchanges.

Positive interdependence is a critical element for the success of the Technique Tournament concept. Team members recognize that in order to achieve bonus points and ultimately, and most important, develop their technical skills, they must assist each other in learning and mastering the required materials. As a result, students begin to challenge each other to higher levels of playing, acknowledging that their individual performance has a direct impact on the collective achievement of the team. Students often develop a strong sense of group spirit and pride. They begin to acknowledge the study of piano technique as an essential element of piano training rather than as a task of drudgery, resulting in a highly motivated personal and cooperate challenge.

Other Applications

The tournament concept may be easily adapted to other group piano curricular competencies such as sight-reading, harmonization, transposition, or score reading. An instructor of group piano might adapt and implement skill tournaments on a rotational schedule, for example, Sight-Reading Tournament in the fall term, Harmonization/Transposition Tournament in the winter term, and Score-Reading Tournament in the spring term.

Sight-Reading

Title: Sight-Reading Drill Pairs with Eye Check
Piano Competency: Sight-Reading

Cooperative Learning Theory Source
Sight-Reading Drill Pairs with Eye Check is an instructional strategy based on Spencer Kagan's Pairs Check, a method for practicing or reviewing concepts or skills by employing teams consisting of two pairs. Within each pair, one student takes a turn at completing a task or solving a problem while the other student coaches. The pair then switches roles. Following the completion of two or more problems, the pair compares their responses with the other team pair. When both pairs agree on the answers, both pairs receive positive reinforcement. If there is disagreement, teams must engage in discussion in order to come to a consensus.

Application Design and Procedure
Students are assigned to dyads (student A and student B) and are given a sight-reading example that has been divided into two halves, one half for each partner. They are asked to examine their portion of the example individually, noting all details such as key and time signatures, melodic/intervallic movement, harmonic progression, accidentals, fingering, and so on. Students must then prepare their score by marking potential problem spots. After this initial analysis, student A explains to Student B potential problems found in his portion of the score and how he plans to negotiate them effectively. Student B then provides additional comments or suggestions that student A may have overlooked. Following this exchange, a tempo is established and the metronome is set. Students should be challenged to select a tempo that facilitates continuity and precision. Student A plays his portion of the exercise while counting. As he plays, student B is given the responsibility of counting how many times student A looks down at his hands (eye check), as well as taking note of specific problems the performer encountered, noting reasons that these occurred.

After the performance, student A provides an evaluation, taking into account his initial explanation of potential problems and the effectiveness of his strategies to play the example well at sight. Student B then offers his assessment of the reading, adding any further insights or suggestions for improvement. Student B also provides a tally of how many times the performer looked at his hands during the reading. Students should be asked to discuss how looking at their hands may have impeded a fluent reading of the example. The roles are then switched and the steps are repeated. After each student has played his portion of the example, the same strategy is used to learn the other student's part. Finally, the partners are asked to play the entire example together using the metronome and counting out loud.

When the pair feels confident with the reading of their example or after an established time period elapses, whichever comes first, the students are joined with another pair that has completed the same example using the same procedure. The pairs exchange insights about the sight-reading example, discussing problematic sections and specific difficulties, as well as methods they used to play these passages successfully. The groups then set the metronome and play the example together, counting as they play. Finally, the entire class plays the example together out loud while counting.

It is important to note that careful selection and leveling of the sight-reading examples is critical for the success of the structure. One should carefully consider the level of each student in the class, attempting to find materials that are appropriate for each pair's reading ability. Students can then be paired up according to their specific sight-reading levels and can be assigned reading exercises that are appropriate for these levels.

Although the initial presentation of the structure can be somewhat time-consuming, it should be noted that efficiency usually improves dramatically during subsequent applications of the activity as students become more accustomed to the procedures involved. Longer and more complex sight-reading examples may require more time to allow students a sufficient period to analyze, discuss, and play.

Rationale and Benefits

In Sight-Reading Drill Pairs with Eye Check, students function in two roles: thinker/player and coach/motivator. Students work together to preview and analyze a score prior to playing. This provides a broader, more thorough perspective than can be obtained by a single student. Collectively, the dyad is able to conduct an exhaustive preview of the example. It is during the preview that students engage in dialogue regarding possible challenges found in the reading example as well as discuss practical methods to contend with these potential pitfalls.

Because students ultimately play the sight-reading example with their partners and with a metronome, they are challenged not only to maintain and internalize a given tempo/pulse but also to read ahead despite any missed notes or other mistakes. This demands that students concentrate on the score and not on their hands. Additionally, students are given immediate feedback on how many times they looked at their hands, as well as an explanation of how this affected the overall continuity in their reading. The structure may be effectively used to encourage student sharing, generating a more creative and highly motivational interaction scenario than individual sight-reading while also promoting a positive social environment

Other Applications

Drill Pairs may be easily adapted and used to reinforce other keyboard skills. The structure can be used to drill various reading scenarios, ranging from the intervallic movement of a simple melody to more complex readings in a variety of clefs. Drill Pairs may also be used to drill technical skills such as scales and arpeggios and can be adapted for use in learning and polishing repertoire.

Harmonization

Title: Harmonization Think-Pair-Share
Piano Competency: Harmonization

Cooperative Learning Theory Source

Harmonization Think-Pair-Share is based on Spencer Kagan's Think-Pair-Share. Students first think individually about a given problem and then formulate an answer. Next, they are paired with a partner to discuss and compare their answers. If their answers differ, they must engage in discussion to create a single team response. Students are required to fully justify their responses. Think-Pair-Share works particularly well for the development of conceptual knowledge. It is most appropriate for short tasks rather than long, open-ended projects.

Application Design and Procedures

Students are assigned a melody to be harmonized and are supplied with a list of potential chords and their inversions to be used (for advanced students, this list may be withheld). To acclimate students to the melody, the class sight-reads it together. Students are then given approximately five minutes to individually select appropriate chords that complement the melody. Students should write possible chord choices above each melodic note. They are initially prohibited from testing their chord choices by playing them and are challenged to select harmonies based solely on an assessment of the melodic notes using their theoretical knowledge.

After the students have completed the harmonization individually or following the five-minute time allowance, they are paired with another student and are asked to compare and rationalize their chord selections. Should any disagreement arise, students are challenged to reach a compromise and also provide an explanation as to why they chose each chord. Once all pairs have settled upon a final version or following the five-minute time allowance, the instructor rotates through the class, requesting a single representative from each pair to share one or two chords from the complete exercise while explaining their justification for each chord. The instructor may also request alternate suggestions from the class. If an appropriate answer does not surface, the instructor may interject with the correct response and explain why it is both appropriate and necessary.

When the class has reached a collective agreement on the exercise, each pair is asked to prepare the example for performance. The instructor should suggest that each pair first play the scale and chord progression of the piece together to acclimate themselves to the key. Responsibilities are then divided between the pairs: one student is asked to play the melody while the other student provides an appropriate accompaniment. Then the roles are reversed and the new parts are rehearsed. Finally, the pairs rehearse playing both the melody and the accompaniment hands together. The instructor then calls upon each group to demonstrate its rendition for the class.

For those students who individually finish harmonizing the example early, the instructor may assign additional tasks such as creating and preparing an original accompaniment pattern or orchestrating the example with various timbres using digital piano resources.

Rationale and Benefits

Harmonization Think-Pair-Share is advantageous in many ways. First, students are given time to think individually about which chords most appropriately complement the melody. This challenges each student to independently formulate an answer and justify his choice, which in turn requires him to be knowledgeable of the concepts and principles involved.

Ultimately, students work together to find the best possible chord choices for the given melody. Working together rather than alone gives students a broader perspective on potential chord choices. After students are paired, any disagreements in terms of chord selection must be thoroughly discussed and resolved. Collectively, the students construct a composite rationale for their chord choices. Students acknowledge that part of their joint responsibility is not only to choose appropriate chords but also to understand why their choices were better than others.

Students learn both parts of the harmonization example (right hand and left hand/melody and accompaniment), first hands independently and then together, after which they perform their rendition for the class. While playing together, both in practice and in performance, students are challenged to maintain a set tempo and continue playing despite any missed notes or rhythms. Also, students may be potentially less nervous when playing the harmonization example with a partner rather than giving an individual performance. Furthermore, Harmonization Think-Pair-Share fosters a strong sense of positive interdependence among student dyads, while building increased confidence in basic principles of keyboard harmonization.

Other Applications

Think-Pair-Share may be applied in the teaching of other keyboard skills, including selecting appropriate fingerings for passages in reading materials or repertoire. The structure may also be used in critical listening exercises, in which students listen to two or more performances of a given work for piano by different artists and then answer questions about what they heard, first individually and then with a partner. Finally, students may discuss their answers with the entire class.

Improvisation/Creative Activities

Title: Styles Improvisation Investigation
Piano Competency: Improvisation

Cooperative Learning Theory Source

Styles Improvisation Investigation is based on the principles of Shlomo and Yael Sharan's Group Investigation, which contends that students will readily and eagerly engage in research and activity that is related to personal interests. For example, students form groups according to common interests in a given topic. Together they formulate a plan to research, analyze, synthesize, and present on their given subject. Each group's final presentation must summarize how their findings relate to the broader topic. Group Investigation works particularly well in the development of problem-solving skills and is especially useful for large, long-term projects that require a significant amount of time to unfold.

Application Design and Procedures

Following an overview lecture-presentation by the instructor on various styles of piano playing such as jazz, blues, rock and pop, folk and country, students are asked to form groups according to a common interest in a given style. The number of students per group will depend on the overall size of the class, with each group consisting of no fewer than three students. No specific criteria are employed in forming groups other than the students' interest in a given style.

Each group is responsible for conducting further research on its selected style of piano playing, while exploring the intricacies of how it is performed. The groups are given the task of creating an ensemble improvisation based on a simple melodic or rhythmic cell that represents their chosen style. Students are encouraged to use their melodic or rhythmic cell as an ostinato accompaniment pattern. Each member of the group must play the accompaniment parts as well as an improvised melody at some point during the performance.

The groups must also present to the class a detailed lecture-presentation on their selected style with the goal of teaching their classmates the salient features of their style of piano playing. As part of the presentation, groups are asked to provide a handout to the class that lists the prominent elements of their chosen style. Students may be encouraged to use audio and video resources during their presentation, and each presentation is to culminate in a performance of their ensemble improvisation.

Because the project demands significant planning, research, and practice from each group of students, it is advisable to grant groups a minimum of two weeks in which to prepare. Depending on the type of group for which the structure is used (e.g., precollege, university music majors), the instructor may require students to prepare their project outside of class or may devote one or several class periods solely to student practice and preparation. For those that meet primarily outside class, the teacher may elect to devote five minutes of each class meeting prior to the presentation so that students can communicate about their next meeting time or other project-related issues. The instructor can also monitor in-class meetings and assist with any questions that may arise.

The following are two examples of how groups may structure their presentations. Group A offers an overview of the history of the blues as well as important pioneers of the style. The group plays recordings by both legendary blues artists and current pop artists whose work is strongly influenced by the blues. Significant time is spent detailing the twelve-bar blues pattern and how it can be manipulated in performance. The presentation concludes with a performance of the group's ensemble improvisation, which is based on the twelve-bar blues pattern. Three parts, including a bass ostinato, chordal/harmonic pattern, and improvised melody, are distributed among the three group members. The pattern is played three times, which permits all members to play each part.

Group B presents its discoveries related to the jazz style. The group begins by discussing the origins of jazz and continues with an explanation of the many varieties of jazz styles (e.g., classic jazz, hot jazz, Chicago style, swing, Kansas City style). Next, the group discusses three common methods of jazz improvisation, which included melodic, harmonic, and motivic. Then the group presents a list of important jazz figures and elements of their style and plays recordings of each. A discussion of common jazz chords and harmonic progressions follows, along with mention of important Web resources related to the topic of jazz piano playing. The group concludes with a performance of its improvisation, which includes four parts: an original bass ostinato, a complementary harmonic progression, an additional rhythmic pattern, and an improvised melody. The ensemble is performed four times to give all four members an opportunity to play each part.

Rationale and Benefits

Styles Improvisation Investigation is an effective means for introducing intermediate-level pianists to various styles of piano playing while giving students an opportunity to explore, in detail, a particular style that is of both personal and collective interest. By collaborating with peers who share their particular interest, students are likely to delve more deeply into all facets of the topic and address areas that otherwise might be passed over. Members of the group come to the project with varying strengths and experiences and are able to contribute something unique to the collective whole.

The project seeks to generate mutual excitement in a given topic within each group. Members of each group are responsible for becoming "resident experts" in their given style of piano playing; theoretically, such a task should create a sense of group pride and camaraderie. Additionally, the requirement for personal and collective creativity in the creation of an original ostinato pattern and improvisation of stylistic melodies is inherent to the project. By virtue of the potentially high level of group motivation and support derived from their teammates, students who participate in Styles Improvisation Investigation often exhibit increased confidence with regard to improvising and are usually more willing to take creative risks. Additionally, students stand to enhance their collaborative music-making skills by participating in a sophisticated ensemble activity.

Here, positive interdependence plays a vital role. Group members must embrace a strong sense of accountability in order for the project to be successful. Groups decide on and assign specific roles for each member (e.g., researcher of the history of jazz, researcher of common chords and harmonies, researcher of pioneers and their music). All parts must therefore be thoroughly investigated and presented in order for the project to be effective as a whole. Additionally, all members are responsible for learning and performing all parts of the ensemble (e.g., bass ostinato, harmonic progression, rhythmic pattern, melody). Students are also given the opportunity to share their learned knowledge, as well as a chance for the entire class to learn from their peers' expertise. When teaching others, students must be knowledgeable of the subject matter and be able to organize and present the material effectively. By doing so, students' individual learning is strengthened.

Other Applications

The Group Investigation structure may be easily adapted and used to teach a variety of keyboard skills and I have modified this structure to create several student projects. One such project, titled "Piano: An Integral Part of My Profession," is an assignment in which first-year university music major group piano students are divided into groups according to their major (e.g., choral music education, instrumental performance, music therapy). Students are asked to interview a professional in their field regarding the application of keyboard skills in that person's daily work, to discover specific ways these skills are used, as well as specific strategies that will enhance the students' preparation.

Another such project targets choral music education majors during the third year of piano study. Students are asked to explore how various piano technical exercises can be modified to create choral warm-ups. Students must compose four choral warm-ups and learn to play them in all keys. The students must produce a computer-generated version of their exercises and provide an annotation that explains what skills they develop for the singer. The group then generates a compilation notebook, which includes each member's warm-ups, and a copy is distributed to all members of the group for their future use. The project culminates in a student-led demonstration of the warm-ups from the keyboard, with the class serving as the rehearsal choir.

Solo and Ensemble Retertoire

Title: Practice Partnerships
Piano Competency: Solo and ensemble repertoire, among other competencies

Cooperative Learning Theory Source

Practice Partnerships is based on a concept known as Cooperative Base Groups, articulated in Johnson and Johnson's Learning Together model. Although not always the case, these groups are typically heterogeneous in membership and often reflect mixed levels of ability and achievement motivation. Cooperative Base Groups meet on a regular basis for extended periods of time, frequently for the duration of the class over the course of a semester or a year. The primary responsibilities of these groups are to provide support, assistance, and encouragement to their partners on various levels, including academic and personal tasks, as well as routine activities related to class issues. The partnerships are responsible for holding each other accountable to learn course materials to the best of their ability.

Application Design and Procedures

While Practice Partnerships was initially designed for use in university music major group piano courses, it can be adapted for and successfully employed in precollege group piano teaching environments. Students form partnerships with another classmate. These partnerships may be self-selected or may be formed with some intervention by the instructor. Students should be advised to secure a partner with whom their schedule is compatible, and with whom they would enjoy working throughout the term. For classes that contain an odd number of students, groups of three will be necessary.

Establishing partnerships of relatively comparable levels of playing ability is an issue that must be given consideration. To this end, students should be paired according to a standard of relative equality in terms of playing ability, and pairs should not include two students of vastly differing abilities. Structuring an arrangement of relative equivalence will likely facilitate balanced interaction among partnerships and contribute to a positive exchange of information and feedback.

The partnerships are to meet over the course of an entire academic term or longer. Students are required to meet outside of class weekly for a minimum of thirty minutes to practice and perform class materials for one another. The weekly meeting is also a time for students to assist one another with difficulties, to solve problems, both technical and theoretical, and to answer questions. The time may also be used to practice assigned duet literature. Other partner assignments may include Technique Tournament preparation and repertoire performance analysis.

Each partnership is required to complete a Practice Partnership Session Report (PPSR) form weekly for each meeting. These forms are to be submitted to the instructor by noon each Friday of the term in order for credit to be given. Forms are to be left in an envelope on the instructor's office door. The form requests a description of what transpired during each practice meeting. Students are also asked to list specific problems that were addressed, methods they used to correct the problems, and whether or not this approach resolved the issues. Students are additionally requested to notate any new discoveries that were made during their meeting. Specific forms are used to provide feedback related to solo and duet repertoire performances, and for critical listening exercises. These forms include various performance aspects that were to be considered as part of the critique (e.g., accuracy, articulation, balance, dynamics, phrasing).

Participation in this program is required of all students. A partnership grade is weighed in the composite course grade through weekly credit, with credit awarded to each student partnership that submitted a PPSR form weekly. The Practice Partnership Grading System is presented in figure 4.1. Joint rewards in the form of bonus points (e.g., ten additional points) may be offered to student partnerships and granted to those teams that demonstrated exceptional improvement.

Students are informed that, if during the course of the term they experience difficulties in their working relationship, they must first attempt to resolve the situation on their own. Should the problem persist, they are instructed to schedule a meeting with the instructor to discuss the situation.

Rationale and Benefits

In response to the common lack of practice and preparation by university group piano students, Practice Partnerships was designed to stimulate excitement and motivation in student practice. Though students are asked to consistently practice individually outside of class, they must also meet weekly with their practice partner. The joint practice session is a low-pressure situation for students. Although students must be prepared when they come to the meeting, the joint practice session is intended to be a place where they can exchange ideas and make new discoveries, as well as a time to provide practice solutions for various keyboard skill-related problems they may be facing.

Requirements	Points
Meet nine (9) weeks and submit nine (9) PPRSR forms	20 points = A
Meet eight (8) weeks and submit eight (8) PPRSR forms	14 points = B
Meet seven (7) weeks and submit seven (7) PPRSR forms	8 points = C
Meet six (6) weeks and submit six (6) PPRSR forms	2 points = D
Meet five (5) weeks or less and submit five (5) PPSR forms or fewer	0 points = F

FIGURE 4.1 Practice Partnership Grading System

Students who participate in Practice Partnerships often acknowledge that practicing with a partner affords them an opportunity to assess and compare their progress with their classmates. These students also communicate the truth that learning is strengthened when one is called upon to teach. Students are given this opportunity weekly during their partner practice when coaching their peers on various course-related topics.

Practice Partnerships have the potential to generate a sense of accountability and positive interdependence. Students are given the task to encourage and assist each other in mastering course materials with the intent of improving their overall keyboard skills. They are also called to challenge each other to higher levels of performance. The instructor may periodically remind students of their responsibility to challenge one another to achieve maximum understanding and proficiency with course concepts and skills. Without such reminders, students can become complacent in their roles of accountability.

Students bring certain strengths and weaknesses to their partnership. For instance, some students may be more proficient at sight-reading whereas others are better at harmonization and transposition. Because of their individual strengths, students stand to learn and grow from the coaching they receive from one another. Students also are aware of the partnership grade that is weighed in their overall course grade, as well as the potential to receive bonus points for partnerships that demonstrate exceptional improvement.

Interdependence is also illustrated by students' preparation and performance of duet repertoire. The Practice Partnerships serve as an automatic duet team in which students can gain valuable collaborative music skills. Artistic decision making is necessary throughout the rehearsal stage of the duets, calling on students to decide on a mutual interpretation.

Instructors must also encourage the development of roles during each practice. Each partnership must devise its own rules and procedures for practice and must establish deadlines to complete specific tasks. Roles may include clarifying and summarizing concepts and new discoveries and completing the PPSR form.

The instructor may also facilitate a cooperative and interdependent spirit, both between partners and among partnerships, by reserving a small lesson segment each week in which students can discuss new discoveries and practice suggestions that were made during their partner practice. This conversation also gives the instructor an opportunity to assess student ideas that were exchanged during unsupervised practice and to address any unproductive or harmful suggestions made by students that might reinforce mistakes or bad habits.

Other Applications

The concept of Cooperative Base Groups may be easily used for activities like the previously mentioned Technique Tournament. Because student partners are scheduled to meet and practice weekly as part of their Practice Partnership responsibilities, the format would eliminate the need to form separate teams for the tournament. Practice Partnerships would be combined to form teams, and the collective teams would meet only periodically. This arrangement would eliminate the challenge of scheduling a time for multiple team members to meet simultaneously on a weekly basis to practice for the tournament.

Chapter 5
Instructional Considerations

Curriculum Development, Implementation, and Evaluation

The development, implementation, and evaluation of a curriculum are vital components of any educational endeavor. As the saying goes, "Unless you know where you want to go, how will you know when you have arrived?" A curriculum is the central aim of instruction. It details the information to be conveyed to the learner. Further, the curriculum is the vehicle through which learning occurs. For the group piano teacher, the curriculum serves as a guide to assist in presenting the fundamentals of music and piano playing in the most organized and sequential fashion, and in a manner that is most appropriate for the students involved. Curricula must be flexible enough to be tailored to each group of students, with consideration given to students' varying and divergent skill levels.

A curriculum is a multidimensional and organic construct. It involves the content of learning—that which is taught—and its interrelationship with other concepts and principles. In addition to the content of learning, a curriculum involves the skills necessary to operate the content. The curricular paradigm should be both progressive and spiral, with basic concepts forming a foundation upon which overarching principles are constructed and grow in complexity with advancement. An understanding of the basic structure of a concept and its subsequent transfer are at the heart of solid curricular design and are therefore inextricably related.

A curriculum considers the goals, both short-term (e.g., weekly and monthly) and long-term (e.g., term or yearly), as well as a detailed plan for achieving these goals. This involves the establishment of objectives and desired outcomes of learning. Goals should explicitly address that which is to be learned, as well as how the learning will be achieved. Key to this process is the establishment of clear curricular competencies and a desired time line for mastery of each standard. It is advisable to launch the construction of a curriculum by beginning first with global, longitudinal benchmarks and then proceeding to fill in the details by term, month, week, and lesson. To be sure, conscientious goal setting can significantly impact the ultimate success or failure of one's teaching, and the implications of this process are certainly far-reaching.

In the case of group piano teaching, one should strive to provide a broad musical education that produces competence in all aspects of piano playing, not technique and repertoire exclusively. Comprehensive musical training seeks to develop not only optimum technique, artistry, and creativity but also the very fundamentals of musicianship, which include sight-reading, ear training, harmonization, transposition, improvisation, ensemble playing, composition, and music theory and history. This type of training produces students who are proficient in all aspects of the language of music and who are capable of understanding, discriminating, singing, writing, and performing music in its various manifestations.

A curriculum also involves the specific experiences in which learning occurs, with consideration given to the materials that will be used, as well as the modes of delivery (e.g., teacher-centered vs. student-centered) and the instructional strategies employed. Teacher-centered presentations involve lectures and demonstrations offered by the instructor in which the teacher carefully controls all aspects of information delivery, whereas student-centered activities grant students freedom to discover and manipulate concepts throughout the process of constructing new knowledge.

When building a curriculum, one should explore all available instructional materials, and determine the method(s) and supplementary materials that will be used to deliver the curriculum. Teachers must not confuse piano methods with an all-encompassing curriculum and thus should avoid using a "page-by-page" approach to teaching. Conversely, the method and instructional resources should serve as tools through which the global curricular standards are presented, reinforced, and integrated into the students' working knowledge. A method must not dictate the structure and progression of a lesson and should not be the central goal of the lesson. Rather, the instructor should manipulate the lesson content in a way that best communicates the curriculum and lesson objectives in the most effective and efficient manner for the students involved. Curricula must always be tailored to the group and its members.

A curriculum also considers the procedures that will be employed to assess student learning. This involves clearly defining curricular benchmarks and the procedures used to evaluate student proficiency and comprehension of each standard.

Curricular objectives must be well defined and justified, and the curriculum as a whole must be regularly evaluated and systematically assessed. One should address the questions, "Why are the curricular objectives important?" and "What is their value?" Following a period of application, one should determine which elements of the curriculum were most successful, which elements were not successful, why they were or were not successful, and how the curriculum could be more effectively delivered or facilitated. Such an assessment can be accomplished most objectively through the use of an unbiased peer review. Ultimately, the findings from this assessment should be used to positively shape the future of the curriculum.

The group piano teacher may refer to several well-developed curriculum and assessment tools when constructing a group piano program curriculum:

- Associated Boards of the Royal Schools of Music (www.abrsm.org)
- Royal Conservatory of Music Examinations (www.rcmexaminations.org)
- National Music Certificate Program (www.nationalmusiccertificate.org)
- American College of Musicians–National Guild of Piano Teachers (http://pianoguild.com/)
- MTNA Assessment Tools (www.mtna.org)

Lesson Planning

Just as an engineer meticulously plans before the construction of a bridge commences, the well-prepared group piano teacher must thoroughly plan for each class he teaches. Detailed, deliberate, and imaginative planning are keys to successful group piano teaching. When planning a lesson, one must give consideration to the following:

- Group size and composition
- Lesson length
- Curricular and lesson objectives
- Preinstructional considerations and procedures

Group Size and Composition

The size and composition of a group will dictate how the lesson will be planned and ultimately carried out. It is important to consider the number of students who will attend the class and the relative equality or disparity of skill level among group members. Consideration should be given to the level of skill competency attained by each student at the given stage of learning. To accomplish this, one might ask the following questions: "What do the students presently know?" "What do I want them to know by the close of the lesson?" "How can I get them to achieve this understanding?" "How can each concept or skill be solidified and expanded through conceptual transfer?"

One must also take into account the age of all involved students, which deals directly with issues related to attention span and physical ability. Unlike their adult counterparts, most children are unable to focus for extended periods. Therefore, length of time devoted to any activity will require some alteration depending on the age of the student population. Similarly, both children and older adults possess physical limitations (e.g., finger strength and dexterity) that are inherent to their specific age groups. Thoughtful consideration of these issues will enable the instructor to establish realistic expectations for their students.

Students bring to learning individual strengths and weaknesses, including unique experiences and bases of knowledge. A group that has been formed using a placement process is likely to yield a more uniform and homogeneous learning environment. With this said, powerful learning can also occur in groups that consist of students who possess varying levels of skill and ability. Whatever the case may be, one must consider that which the students already know, both individually and collectively, including those concepts that have been previously introduced, reviewed, or mastered.

Lesson Length

The scheduled lesson length will have a significant bearing on how the lesson is designed and paced. The size of the group may determine the amount of time spent on each lesson component. Larger groups require more time to allow students to experience and process lesson material, as well as additional time for the instructor to assess and assist student learning. Alternatively, smaller groups may require relatively less time to complete a given task. When conducting small-group activities within the context of a larger group, the shorter the period of time available to conduct the activity usually necessitates a smaller subgroup size. Further, one should be mindful of the overall size of the group in relation to the specific materials available to complete a given task.

Curricular and Lesson Objectives

Viable lesson plans are created in consideration of the broad curricular goals as well as the specific objectives and desired outcomes for each activity and the lesson as a whole. Long-term lesson mapping ensures appropriate sequencing of curricular concepts, while short-term planning works to guarantee the presentation of materials and lesson content in an organized fashion.

It is during this stage of planning that one can assess how the class is progressing toward achieving curricular benchmarks within the established time frame. One must never rush the learning process. Should a class fail to progress according to a set time line, there should be no real cause for alarm. All students and student groups progress at different speeds and therefore require pacing relevant to their specific needs. Some classes will immediately understand a given concept or principle; others will require significantly more drill and reinforcement. It is the responsibility of the instructor to determine if any modifications or interventions can be applied to solidify and perhaps eventually accelerate the learning process.

Preinstructional Considerations and Procedures

When planning for a lesson, one must consider that which will be taught, and how these concepts and skills can be best communicated to the students. Here the instructor will determine the most appropriate mode of presentation (teacher-directed activity or student discovery–based activity) to be used for each of the lesson segments. It is beneficial to try to anticipate possible questions or problems students might have regarding a given concept, as well as helpful responses or solutions to these issues. It may also be advantageous to create a list of questions one might ask to facilitate student interaction and discussion regarding a given topic.

A good lesson plan considers the learning styles of the students involved, ensuring that lesson materials are presented in a way that appeals to aural, visual, and kinesthetic learners. When planning to present or review a concept, one should design activities that address and integrate the reception needs of each modality of learning. One might ask questions such as "How might I best learn about sixteenth notes if I were a aural learner?" or "How would I approach learning about phrase contour if I were a kinesthetic learner?" in order to properly address the students' learning needs.

Most students learn best by doing rather than only being told what to do and how to do it. Consequently, teachers must strive to create concrete, hands-on learning experiences in which students are able to critically analyze and actively manipulate the concepts and principles that are being taught. Such experiences foster the development of critical and intuitive thinking skills and serve to strengthen higher-level reasoning functions.

In the same way, it is important to think about ways one can facilitate active involvement of all students throughout the lesson. For each planned activity, it is wise to structure interdependence among students, which can be accomplished by distributing individual roles among class members. Such a lesson design demands that each student take responsibility for the overall success of the activity, including his or her own mastery of the material. Furthermore, it underscores the importance of each student's direct involvement in the decision-making and problem-solving process.

As a guiding principle, one does well to plan stimulating, captivating activities with which to commence each class in order to engage the students' full attention. Successful introductory activities will establish an exciting tone and will positively impact the overall pace and energy level throughout the class period. These activities should change from class to class so that each lesson begins with a new and inspiring lesson experience.

Likewise, it is imperative that we set our students up for success both during formal instruction in the classroom and during individual practice outside the classroom. Some form of success should be built into each lesson for every student. Successful teaching is inextricably linked to careful planning and a thorough understanding of the students who are being taught. In order to achieve the goal of student success, all learning should commence from an understanding of what students already know and then subsequently develop from this understanding. If, for instance, a portion of the lesson will focus on the teaching of a new technical skill, it is wise to begin with a related technical exercise that students can already play with ease. Such action will produce a level of confidence and establish a positive framework from which to work. Further, it will help to focus the attention of the group and will prepare students to be receptive to the material that is to be taught.

One should avoid teaching without properly preparing students for the reception of new concepts. Hence, there is a need to design lesson experiences that prepare students for this new information. Because of the very nature of music and piano playing, students must first hear that which is being taught, followed by seeing and then doing. Thus, preparatory exercises that emphasize the desired sound are essential. In his teaching, Richard Chronister went further to contend that children should experience new concepts multiple times over the course of several lessons, at least three class periods, before they are assigned to practice the concept independently at home.

During the lesson, it is essential to provide students with ample time to experiment with and manipulate new concepts and skills before moving on to the next concept or skill. It is often tempting to proceed too quickly, without granting students an opportunity for the material to crystallize in their understanding. Therefore, one must be patient, never rushing this critical and vulnerable stage of learning. Moreover, one must create opportunities during the lesson in which students demonstrate their comprehension and proficiency. The instructor is able to glean important information from these experiences, which will help determine whether or not more time is necessary to reinforce the concept or skill, either at that point or in the subsequent lesson.

Teachers should endeavor to build lessons that are rich in concepts and principles that are linked in an interrelated fashion. It is advisable to plan the lesson around one or two broad principles and to design a variety of activities that are all linked to the overarching ideas that are being taught or reinforced. The goal should be to communicate to students, via discovery-based experiences, how these principles transfer from skill to skill or concept to concept.

When constructing a lesson outline, it is necessary to consider ways to ensure that the presentation of new concepts and skills stems from a well-grounded conceptual framework of the material that is to be taught. Thus, the lesson becomes a sophisticated fabric made up of interconnected concepts, which are related to each other and to the broader principles as a whole. To create such a lesson, teachers must demonstrate the gestalt before the minutiae, presenting the big picture, first followed by a discussion of how the details connect to its overarching structure. One must avoid getting bogged down in details before students have first had a chance to experience the global properties of the concept or principle. This approach can be compared to a teacher who begins by showing his class a complex building made of many blocks. After the students have examined the fully assembled structured, they proceed by disassembling the building and then, with the help of the instructor and their classmates, reconstruct it one block at a time.

When presenting a new concept or skill, it is important to limit the conditions of learning by focusing students' attention on one problem at a time. By doing so, the teacher eliminates any unnecessary or even unrelated distractions and frees his students up to fully engage in the issue at hand. Instruction should commence with lesson concepts being reduced to the simplest, most understandable form and should be subsequently built upon in ever-increasing levels of complexity as the student masters each incremental step.

To illustrate this point, consider the process of introducing the chromatic scale. It would be overwhelming to ask a class of students to look at the scale as it appears on the page and immediately play it hands together with correct fingering while naming the notes out loud. A logical progression would be to first lead the class to assess the structure of the scale, which consists entirely of half steps. Next, a discussion of the fingering principles would follow in which students are directed to see that the third finger plays the black keys, while fingers one and two play on successive white keys (i.e., B-C and E-F). Following this, students might play the scale on the keyboard cover or other flat surface, focusing on fingering by saying the finger numbers out loud. Finally, students would play the scale on the keyboard one hand at a time and eventually hands together.

Another important instructional precept is that musical concepts are best understood and remembered when they are experienced directly by the learner in a musical context. For instance, the eighth note and its function in 6/8 meter is best understood if students experience it through movement activities such as clapping, tapping, or walking. A purely verbal explanation of this rhythmic concept would be incomplete without the vital eurhythmic element. Along these lines, it should again be emphasized that musical concepts and principles must always be presented with consideration of all learning modalities—aural, visual, and kinesthetic/tactile.

Lesson material should be framed in new contexts in order to encourage transfer and application of new knowledge and skills. This instructional strategy referred to as decontextualization requires that a concept or skill be taken out of the immediate context in which it was introduced and then transferred for broader applicability in another more abstract context. This can be achieved through the use of various functional skill activities (e.g., harmonization, transposition, ensemble). For instance, students who have learned to construct and play a given chord progression may be asked to apply the learned chords by harmonizing a series of melodies. This procedure strengthens students' understanding of harmonic function and provides an opportunity for students to demonstrate comprehension of the concept or mastery of a skill through application in various practical circumstances.

When planning the lesson, one must consider the most natural and efficient process for introducing, experiencing, reviewing, and synthesizing a concept. The teacher's goal is to achieve a structured plan that progresses in the most logical, sequential, and systematic manner, and one that clearly highlights how concepts and principles are transferred. Because thoughtful sequence in lesson progression is key to generate optimal learning experiences, the activities should flow from one to the next in the most meaningful fashion. In this way, it is also important to plan transitions between activities, in addition to explicit "traffic patterns" related to how students will get from point A to point B, in terms of both attention and physical movement within the classroom. Likewise, equipment needs and any necessary setup or extra preparation should be taken into account. This can be as specific as the need for pencils to complete a written activity or identifying the point at which computers should be turned on and booted up. One can potentially prevent unnecessary disruptions in the flow of the lesson by giving these issues careful thought.

Regarding the issue of timing and pacing, one should have a good idea of how much time will be allotted for each activity. It may be helpful to indicate in the lesson plan, for example, that roughly three minutes will be devoted to triad review exercises, five minutes to scale performances, and so on. Another method is to construct a minute-by-minute notation in the left margin of the lesson plan with the corresponding activities to the right. These will serve merely as time targets to help direct the pace of the lesson and to ensure that the lesson materials are covered. Class activities should be prioritized so that the instructor is aware of those that are most important and those that could be omitted if time is limited.

When planning for each lesson, it is wise to prepare more class activities or exercises than one would usually be able to cover during any given class period. In essence, one should always overplan for each class period. Indeed, it is far better to have planned too many activities than too few. During the planning phase, it is also beneficial to think through possible scenarios one may encounter, with consideration of materials to be covered and the students involved. To this end, and to the greatest extent possible, it is important to try to anticipate potential questions or problems students may have, as well as ways these can be addressed and resolved. Furthermore, teachers must not neglect their own preparation and should therefore practice all of the lesson material.

At this juncture, it is worth noting that sometimes unforeseen issues will arise that will make it necessary to abandon the lesson plan altogether to deal with specific student needs. One should have confidence that this is at times both acceptable and essential. Quality lessons are built on a well-balanced combination of structured activity and creative freedom and flexibility, strategic planning and inspired spontaneity.

Careful planning for variety of activity and experience is a critical element of any lesson plan in order to capture and maintain student interest, excitement, and intrigue. This can be accomplished through frequent changes in student location (e.g., moving from the keyboard to the chalkboard, to floor games, to eurhythmic activities), through the application of a blend of instructional media (e.g., sound and video recordings, PowerPoint, SMARTBoard, Classroom Maestro, Visualizer), by constantly changing student group formations (e.g., grouping students in dyads or small groups, periodic individual work, duet and small ensembles), as well as the continuous use of new games and activities. For children's classes, it is especially important to get students off the bench often, moving from station to station or activity to activity. This will help guarantee that students will stay engaged and focused. With this said, one must be careful not to pace these changes too quickly because of the risk of losing student focus and ability to connect with the activity's purpose.

Technology is notorious for its potential to cause major disruptions in lesson pacing and flow. It is wise to test equipment in advance to be sure it is functioning properly. Moreover, it is advisable to always have an alternate plan should something fail during the class.

It is advantageous to incorporate something new into every lesson. A balanced lesson will involve both the new and the familiar. The level of excitement surrounding learning is in part associated with the instructor's level of creativity. One should be willing to experiment with novel and inspiring approaches for presenting or reinforcing lesson concepts or skills. Following the same lesson structure each week may engender a sense of monotony. Although some things will remain constant, one might explore implementing a new activity or strategy at different points in the class plan each week. This will keep students engaged and "on their toes." One should be sensitive to the students' learning preferences. If the group consists of students who largely benefit from having an established structure, for example, one might avoid excessive week-by-week changes.

Each lesson should conclude with a summary segment in which the teacher recapitulates the ideas and skills that were discussed, how they can be transferred, and specific details of the lesson assignment. The assignment should be clearly displayed, either on a chalkboard or by other visual means. A clear explanation of all facets of the assignment should be planned, as well as how the teacher will review practices strategies and methods that will serve students during individual practice. Assignments need to be given in a way that explains not only "what to do" but also "how to do it." An indispensable tool can be the preparation of assignment cards or handouts, which include clear explanations of the assignment, a helpful summary of lesson concepts, and important practice tips. Kinesthetic learners should be encouraged to write their assignment in an assignment notebook. Such guides can serve to build a bridge between one lesson and the next, eliminating confusion that may develop during this period.

The conclusion of each lesson is also an opportunity for the instructor to ask the key questions: "What did we learn today?" "What concepts are still confusing?" "What and how will you practice this week?" These questions serve to review vital lesson content. They also provide the instructor with important information regarding areas of weakness in student comprehension, giving him an opportunity to record the problems and address the issues during the next lesson.

One must establish procedures that will be used to summarize and assess student understanding of the concepts and skills that were introduced or reviewed throughout the course of the lesson. This can be as informal as the use of a charting system where the teacher checks a box for each student during the lesson when he demonstrates mastery of a given skill, or as formal as individual quizzes and examinations. It might also be beneficial to keep a notebook accessible during the class in which to record notes regarding specific student strengths and weaknesses. This will serve to remind the instructor to find a solution to remedy student problems or issues. These suggestions can then be communicated via e-mail, phone, text message, or, if not immediately pressing, the concerns can be addressed during the subsequent class. Depending on the type of class, one may choose to maintain a daily grade log for every student enrolled. Such a quantifiable system allows the instructor to chart student progress from lesson to lesson and even provides longitudinal perspective over the course of a term or year of study. Figure 5.1 provides a sample conceptually-based group piano lesson plan.

Teaching and Facilitating the Lesson

The act of facilitating learning is one of life's greatest and most rewarding endeavors. With it comes much responsibility on the part of the educator, as well as the student. To be sure, a multiplicity of variables must be in place in order for effective teaching and ultimately successful learning to occur. Indeed, learning is a complex system, involving both formal, planned instructional experiences as well as those that are more informal and impromptu. The act of teaching and learning is a multiple-lane highway linking the teacher with his students. Because of this, teaching and learning demand that both the teacher and his students actively participate in the process by fulfilling their respective roles.

Thus, it is the responsibility of teacher and students to foster a caring and nurturing learning environment in which students' strengths are honored and weaknesses are viewed as opportunities for both personal and corporate growth. The classroom should be a culture of community—a nonthreatening environment in which mutual respect is the common denominator and encouragement is the prevailing the theme.

Group piano teachers must seek to exploit the powers of group dynamics by engaging all students in exciting opportunities to teach and explain their learning process. In this way, we encourage students to be teachers. As Aristotle wrote, "Teaching is the highest form of understanding," and as the Latin proverb so

Group Description

- The group consists of six students, aged eight and nine, who are at an early level of study. The class meets for one hour in a digital piano laboratory.

Lesson Objective

- Review of major five-finger patterns.

Lesson Outline

I. Away From the Piano Warm-Ups

II. Review All Major Five-Finger Patterns
   - Review: Ask students to recall pattern of whole and half steps, while one student writes the pattern on the board. All students write the pattern in their lesson notebooks: start-whole-whole-half-whole.
   - Together students play the D-major five-finger pattern.
   - Round-Robin: Students play major five-finger patterns starting on any pitch.
     - A student teacher assigns a scale to his peer. While the student plays, the student teacher observes. Afterward, he offers specific feedback, and any necessary corrections are made. The performer becomes the student teacher, etc.
     - While student performers are playing, the class may sing the pattern of whole and half steps, finger numbers, or note names. Students may also shape the melodic direction in the air.
     - Nonperformers can play the scale on their keyboard with the volume turned off.

III. Improvisation
   - In a given key, students improvise a melody using the major five-finger pattern. The melody must start and end on tonic. Each student takes a turn improvising along with the teacher's accompaniment.
   - Additional roles may be assigned to those students not currently playing: create a rhythmic accompaniment, call out harmonies used in the teacher's accompaniment, dance or march to the beat in the style of the improvisation, etc.

IV. Harmonization
   - Together, students play the major five-finger pattern of a given melody.
   - Next, students call out the intervallic direction of the melody while playing the melody on the fallboard of their instrument. This may be repeated to include singing finger numbers, note names, or note values.
   - With the teacher modeling, students determine whether a tonic or dominant single note works best for each measure. Students write the harmonic progression that is decided upon in their score. Together students practice playing the harmonic progression, using only single notes.
   - One half of the class plays the melody while the other half plays the harmonic progression. Then the roles are reversed. Slowly, both parts are combined.

FIGURE 5.1 Sample Conceptual Lesson Plan

V. Sight-Reading
- Students conduct a collective preview of a given reading example that employs the five-finger pattern, listing potential problem spots and ways to negotiate each.
- Students sing the melody using solfege.
- On their keyboard covers, students play the melody while singing the intervallic movement.
- Slowly, and while counting out loud, half of the students play the example. The other half observes eye movement and offers constructive feedback following. Then the roles are reversed.
- Together, students transpose the example to a closely related key, while singing the intervallic movement of the melody.
- Students are assigned to compose a four-measure reading example that employs the major five-finger pattern and uses only tonic and dominant single-note harmonies.

VI. Repertoire Preview
- Students conduct a preview of a new repertoire piece, detailing all elements.
- Based on what the score looks like, students explain to the teacher how they anticipate the music will sound. The teacher then plays the piece, giving the students an aural image.
- Students discuss potential problems as well as specific practice strategies that would work well for learning the work. Students write these in their score.
- Students work individually under headphones. The teacher listens in while they practice. Following this and working with the entire group, the teacher addresses challenges students may be having.

VII. Lesson Recapitulation
- "What did we learn today?"
- "What concepts or skills are still confusing?"
- "What and how will you practice this week?"

VIII. Lesson Assignment
- Distribute assignment cards and ask students to write their assignment. Students should write specific tips or strategies discussed for how to practice.
- Place assignment card in lesson binder.

clearly communicates, "By learning you will teach, by teaching you will learn." When students are called upon to teach their classmates, their knowledge is solidified and retention of this knowledge is deepened.

In this type of learning environment, teachers invite students to explore and ponder the realm of possibilities rather than simply transmitting bare, unrelated facts. Successful, transformative teaching produces independent learners who are infinitely curious about the world around them and who continue to explore and develop beyond the classroom. "The most important attitude that can be formed," wrote John Dewey, "is that of the desire to go on learning."

Logistics

When conducting the lesson, it is important to avoid excessive focus on the lesson plan or any instructional technologies that are being used. Concentration should be centered on the students' learning and music making. Solid planning and preparation will grant the teacher the necessary freedom to do so. Therefore, one must know the lesson plan inside and out prior to stepping into the classroom. A well-prepared teacher will have anticipated potential problems and student questions, as well as ways these can be resolved. Initially, the novice teacher may rely more heavily on the lesson plan, but as time progresses and confidence is built, it is important to wean oneself from reliance upon the plan.

While teaching, it is advisable to avoid maintaining a stationary position in the classroom (e.g., comfortably positioned behind the instructor's instrument or console, or standing in one position). Instead, one should be free to walk about the classroom, varying his position often. This provides the teacher with opportunities to engage his students by addressing individual needs while demonstrating to the entire class how a problem can be remedied. Should any students display disruptive behavior, the teacher should move toward that area of the classroom. Often, this simple action will resolve the issue immediately. Students should also be positioned according to mixed levels of ability, with slower learners distributed among quicker learners to facilitate opportunities for students to coach or be coached by their peers.

Communication

One of the primary tasks of any educator is to communicate information in a clear and effective manner. As a result, consideration must be given both to the instructor's speaking voice and to the body language used in conveying information. Effective verbal communication is characterized by varying the speed of delivery, as well as variations in tone, pitch, and inflection. The voice must project to all corners of the learning environment. Thus, the size of the classroom space will dictate the required level of projection. Likewise, a speaking voice that has natural contour and nuance is far more captivating than one that is a monotone.

The use of body language is also a significant aspect of teacher communication. Teachers should be free to move about the room and to use gestures in a manner that best communicates the information being expressed. Engaging teaching may be further characterized by eye contact with students and the use of animated facial expressions.

Dynamic teaching fosters a culture of enthusiasm for the subject matter. Such enthusiasm is contagious if students recognize that it is genuine. Students can easily discern whether or not the teacher is sincerely interested in their comments. The passion for our art can be manifested both verbally and nonverbally. As mentioned previously, when communicating with students, it is important to make eye contact and to convey a sense of genuine interest in what the student is asking or saying. An instructor's lack of authentic attention can undermine the educational endeavor and alienate students.

Teachers should address students by name, which helps students feel as though the teacher is interested in their participation in the learning process and their individual success. This practice also bridges the gap between student and subject matter, conveying to students that both they and the material truly matter.

The goal of any educator is to present information, as well as guide student discussions, in the most logical and sequential order of progression. Moreover, clarity and precision in the use of language for delivery of this information are of paramount importance. As we teach, it is necessary that explanations be given in the most concise yet understandable manner. To achieve this the teacher must put himself in the mind of his students by taking into account questions like "Considering my students' current level of comprehension, how can I explain this concept in a way that would be most easily understood?" Along these lines, the teacher should communicate with his students using age-appropriate language. With this said, many children have advanced vocabularies. Therefore, one should not feel restricted as long as students are comprehending that which is being taught.

Lesson content should be delivered with a maximum level of efficiency. Too often, much of the lesson can be lost to the superfluous—those unnecessary or even unhelpful words that overwhelm our students and generate confusion rather than clarity. Therefore, one must work diligently to communicate only that which is meaningful and serves the explicit objective of the concept or skill that is being taught. To this end, and in advance of the lesson, one should practice explaining a concept using the fewest number of words in the clearest, most logical manner possible.

Real learning requires teachers not only to answer questions but, more important, to ask the right questions in the first place. Therefore, the act of asking purposeful and appropriate questions is critical to engage students in the learning process. Questions can be divided into three categories that call for one of the following:

- Factual response
- Interpretative response
- Personal evaluation and assessment

Questions that require a factual response usually have only one correct answer. An example might be, "What type of dance is this piece, as represented by its title?" If the piece is titled "Minuet," the answer is obviously quite clear. A factual question that may require more explanation may be, "What does the velocity of key descent have to do with dynamics at the piano?"

The other types of questions call for personal insight from the responder and are excellent for generating group discussion. Interpretive response–type questions leave some room for personal interpretation but usually require evidence to support an assertion. For instance, "Why do you think the composer wrote this crescendo before the *subito piano?*" calls for such a response. The answer "So as not to create any excitement" would obviously be off base and unsupported, for dramatic excitement is the very essence of such a series of markings.

Finally, questions that evoke personal evaluations are based purely on one's own opinion and possess no right or wrong answer. Asking, "Do you agree with John's interpretation of the slow movement? And if not, why?" invites the student to make a personal assessment of a performance and to compare his own interpretive ideas with what was heard.

Excessive use of yes- and no-type questions should be categorically avoided because they do not elicit student discussion. Good question asking results in more than the recall of facts. Rather, open-ended questions are preferred because they require application of higher-level critical and abstract thinking skills. These types of questions further solidify student learning and understanding through the process of formulating a response.

Additionally, quality teaching demands that teachers devise and ask questions that require students to demonstrate both declarative and procedural knowledge. Declarative knowledge is related to factual information such as knowing that *forte* means to play loudly, whereas procedural knowledge deals with *how* something is done. An example of procedural knowledge would be the demonstration of how to play a passage *forte* as opposed to piano. Real learning occurs when students can combine and apply declarative and procedural knowledge in a meaningful fashion.

During the lesson, it is usually more productive to ask questions directly of individual students instead of waiting for a response to emerge from the group. We have all experienced those moments when a question is posed to the class at large, and the only response is silence. Usually those students who do volunteer are the ones who are consistently best prepared. When we only call on these students, we leave those who do not understand to fall through the cracks. Question asking and subsequent student responses should be directed by the instructor in a way that gives those who are having difficulty an opportunity for their concerns or problems to be addressed, while giving those with a solid understanding a chance to model for or teach their peers.

Throughout the course of each class period, teachers should attempt to engage each student with at least three or four questions. Such action demands that students remain engaged in order to be prepared to answer the next question that is directed to them. Moreover, if asked in the right manner, these questions will serve the instructor by revealing the condition of his students' understanding. To be consistent with this policy, it may be helpful at first to bring a roster to class to record a mark by the students' names as they are called upon. After every student has answered a question, the teacher can proceed by recycling through the list.

The effective group piano teacher should be committed to finding a balance of direct and indirect communication in the classroom. In her book *Thinking as You Play*, Sylvia Coats presents an adaptation of Ned Flanders's interaction analysis, as well as a thorough discussion of how communication patterns are applied to teaching.[1] Examples of direct communication influences include presenting a lecture, providing specific feedback or criticism, providing an explanation, or giving directions. Indirect communication may include engaging students by asking questions, directing students to expand upon an idea, providing encouragement or genuine praise for positive performance or behavior, or empathizing with students. Although direct communication is at times both necessary and useful, indirect approaches, like asking questions and building upon student ideas, encourage students to think critically and independently. What ensues is a sense of freedom among students to personally engage in decision making, problem solving, and the learning process as a whole. This type of learning environment fosters the development of critical thinking skills and advanced reasoning competencies. Derived from the Latin word *educere*, the word *education* means "to draw out." We stand to learn much from this definition. As the Latin word suggests, we as educators are responsible not for transmitting information to our students but rather for facilitating learning in a way that calls upon students to discover both new knowledge from without and their own abilities from within.

As contended by the Chinese proverb "I hear, and I forget. I see, and I remember. I do, and I understand," an illustration usually communicates an idea more clearly than a thousand words, and by performing that which is being taught, understanding is crystallized. Gilbert Highet supports this assertion by suggesting that people learn more quickly by doing something or seeing something done. Therefore, excessive amounts of lecturing should be replaced with demonstration, and telling should be replaced with modeling. Ultimately, students must be given ample opportunity to manipulate and experience the lesson material in order to synthesize understanding and integrate concepts into their working knowledge. Sophocles wrote, "One must learn by doing the thing; for though you think you know it, you have no certainty until you try."

Teachers must be committed to carefully listening to student questions, with special attention given to the tone of voice and body language. Stephen Covey contends, "Seek first to understand, then to be understood."[2] It is true that much can be gleaned about the state and condition of our students' learning and comprehension through their questions or responses to our questions. Careful listening will allow the instructor to provide thoughtful responses and solutions that penetrate to the heart of the student's needs and concerns. Further, one must also consider not only how a response or solution can answer an individual student's question but also how it can also be applied to the group as a whole.

All too often we as teachers do not give students a sufficient amount of time to respond to our questions. Therefore, we must be committed to waiting for a response, never rushing to provide an answer. Although such a policy can be quite uncomfortable at times, important opportunities for student learning can be dashed by our haste to deliver an answer in order to fill the silence. Bruce Pandolfini, a chess master and highly regarded chess teacher, wrote, "My lessons consist of a lot of silence. I listen to other teachers, and they're always talking.... I let my students think. If I do ask a question and I don't get the right answer, I'll rephrase the question—and wait. I never give the answer. Most of us really don't appreciate the power of silence. Some of the most effective communication—between student and teacher, between master players—takes place during silent periods."[3]

Pacing

Just as an artistic performance of a Chopin nocturne is characterized by imaginative pacing and rhythmic flow, so must our teaching demonstrate these attributes. Pacing, which can be defined as the progression through a planned lesson over a given period of time, involves all activities and the transitions between them. This also includes the frequency and duration of instructional units or episodes and how each fits into the time frame of the lesson.

As teachers, we must endeavor to teach lessons that possess a sense of flow and that are characterized by a logical sequence of experiences as well as an overall sense of purpose. One does well to avoid point-by-point, component-by-component teaching that has no intent or direction. Instead, our teaching should exemplify a rational sense of progression of new concepts and review of old concepts, as well as consideration for how these are related to global principles.

All planned activities should be meaningful and serve a musical purpose. Further, these activities should be varied frequently throughout the lesson to capture and sustain student attention. The wise teacher will carefully plan and balance high-energy group experiences with activities that require more individual, thoughtful focus. Regarding the latter, teachers must strategically incorporate some individual practice time in each lesson to provide students the opportunity to work out individual issues and reflect on the learning that has occurred.

A well-paced lesson balances student activities that are challenging yet attainable. Excessive challenge can generate anxiety, causing students to shut down and resist the task, whereas too little challenge may cause students to lose interest altogether. Such a balance requires the teacher to consider his students' level of comprehension and proficiency while planning the lesson and also during the lesson, as it is occurring. One must be sensitive to these issues and must be able to adjust or modify the level of difficulty for any activity while it is in progress.

When planning lesson exercises, one must give thought to the length of each activity and the time necessary to complete the task. The specific situation may warrant more or less time depending on the students involved and the dynamic of the day. To be sure, one must be conscious of the pace of the lesson to avoid getting bogged down or stalled. Above all, we must be sensitive to our students and the moment. We should be flexible enough to allow the group to help shape the direction and progression of the lesson depending on their immediate needs.

Transitions from one activity to the next must also be carefully planned and orchestrated. Well-designed transitions can sustain student attention and often make or break lesson continuity. Transitions between activities should be smoothly facilitated so they seem natural, and virtually unnoticeable to students. For children, this is critically important because children often have a difficult time shifting from one task to the next. Young students may treat a pause in an activity as an opportunity to create disruption. Therefore, transitions should be seamless, with on-task behavior the expectation.

One of the exciting challenges for the group piano teacher is that of piquing and sustaining student interest throughout the course of a lesson. The dynamic and charismatic educator is able to cultivate a culture of enthusiasm for the subject matter and communicate the relevance of each lesson activity to his students. Students are more likely to engage in learning experiences if they find them both interesting and relevant.

Thoughtful consideration of the age of the student population can have a positive impact on the overall pace of a lesson. With each age-group come variances in the ability to maintain interest and attention, as well as issues related to behavior and attitude. Naturally, most children possess a limited ability to remain engaged during a lengthy learning activity, whereas many adults are capable of sustaining mental engagement for extended periods. Similarly, many adolescents bring to learning particular attitudes and behaviors that are quite different from those of their child and adult counterparts. Consequently, this information will have specific implications for lesson design and procedures.

It is important to be aware of student behavior at all times throughout the lesson. We must be constantly attuned to student needs and be prepared to make provisions to address these needs as necessary. Loss of focus and attention (e.g., students staring off into space) and lack of on-task activity (e.g., restless movement or playing while the teacher is talking) cause classroom disruption. Such indicators may signal that a change of strategy or an alteration of approach to delivery may be necessary at that moment. The resourceful teacher will be flexible and willing to make such adjustments. Teachers may also encourage students to conduct self-assessments of attention and arm them with strategies to help focus attention when it begins to wane. Some teachers suggest changing the class seating arrangement often to keep students focused and provide them with different partners with whom to work on class projects and group activities.

To facilitate the maximum amount of student musical experience, it is important for teachers to talk as little as possible. Excessively long lectures should be avoided. The radio slogan "More music, less talk" certainly applies to our teaching. If a lengthy discussion is absolutely necessary, it is essential to intersperse it with immediate opportunities for students to experience the concepts and skills that are being presented. This allows students to experience the material immediately as opposed to waiting until a lecture has ended. Attention can be lost and comprehension deferred if such opportunities to manipulate essential concepts and skills are delayed.

The flow of a lesson hinges greatly upon the use of successful cueing. Both verbal and nonverbal cues should be used to direct group activity with maximum efficiency. Students need to be taught the instructor's cueing system and vocabulary (e.g., "off headset," "on headset," "line up," "to the board"), which should be used consistently. In a piano laboratory setting, teachers must strive to get students on and off headsets in the most efficient manner because inefficiency in this regard can significantly hinder the forward motion of the lesson.

It is also true that verbal cues can affect musical playing. Cues should be infused with nuance to generate interest, as well as being presented in a manner that demonstrates expressive phrasing. When directing students to play a musical phrase, one can speak and sing the rhythm or pitches with inflection to encourage phrase shape and contour. In the same way, nonverbal cues also affect learning. Nonverbal cues, which include physical gestures or body language, can often be employed to eliminate the need for words and direct student focus toward the sound of the music.

Because it is important to preserve the cooperative unity of the group, it is imperative that we teach to the entire class and avoid teaching an individual lesson for each student. To the detriment of the pace and overall success of the lesson, a group lesson can easily degenerate into a series of six or twelve individual lessons. When this happens, we run the risk of losing the attention of the rest of the class. With few exceptions, this should be avoided, with individual attention being kept to a minimum. Thus, it is critical that we keep all students involved all the time. During group activity, this demands positive interdependence. Learning situations should be planned so that students must do their individual part in order for the activity to be successful. Roles must be assigned, and expectations set in place in order to ensure successful outcomes. In this way, a normal student performance can be transformed simply by giving students individual responsibilities: one plays the piece, one claps the pulse, one counts the rhythm, one sings the text, and so on. These roles can be rotated so that every student has an opportunity to play.

Teachers should strive to teach to the average student, allowing these students to set the pace. Those who quickly grasp the concepts can serve as coaches or peer tutors. In light of this, all students, both slow and quick, should have opportunities to be successful. Wise teachers consider ways to challenge the quickest learners but also ways to help slower learners comprehend and thrive. With this said, one must teach to the prepared students; it is unreasonable to target our teaching to the unprepared student at the expense of those who are prepared. In addition, activities should be structured in a way that accommodates the skills and abilities of all students in the class.

Group Management

It is necessary to establish clearly defined routines, rules, and "traffic patterns" for the group piano learning environment at the very outset of instruction. The teacher should develop a system of expectations, rules of desirable behavior, and acceptable classroom decorum, which should be discussed during the first lesson. One might consider involving students in the process of writing rules of conduct for the class. Because of their involvement in establishing the rules, students may feel a sense of responsibility and an obligation to uphold these policies. Classroom rules and specific consequences for breaking the rules should be clearly posted. Rules such as no talking or playing while the teacher or a peer is talking or playing are critically important. Over time, students will come to appreciate how such policies facilitate smooth and productive learning. Teachers must avoid rewarding unprepared students, but rather reward those who have met expectations for progress and preparation.

A teacher's authority must be established from the outset of instruction. Authority can be expressed through one's tone of voice, as well as through confident body language, including eye contact with individual students. The instructor's natural personality must shine through, though always while demanding an orderly and productive learning environment. It is imperative that the teacher communicate respect as a guiding principle of classroom behavior, clearly and firmly conveying that disrespect in any form will not be tolerated. Students should be considerate of one another's feelings and should seek to understand one another. It is crucial that the instructor model and praise positive behavior through the use of public, verbal affirmation or through the judicious use of rewards.

Discipline must always be consistent and fair. Students are sensitive to this issue and monitor it closely. Justly dealt discipline will engender a sense of student trust. When discipline is necessary, one must select words and actions with prudence. One should also consider how the act of discipline can positively impact the entire group. Problems should be addressed directly, never attacking the student's character or personality but rather redirecting him to the desired path of acceptable behavior and ultimately productivity.

Children, in particular, need direction and leadership. Many children have an innate desire to please authority figures by carefully following directions, and they enjoy the praise that is garnered from obedient behavior. Sometimes students express boredom or act out when they are confused or when they need an additional challenge. Again, it is important that we are sensitive to students' needs, meeting the students where they are and being perceptive of the roots of their behavior on any given day. For instance, the particularly active child might be asked to lead a movement activity, thereby channeling his energy toward a productive outcome.

The lesson should always remain focused on its primary purpose, that of learning about and making music. With this said, at times the teacher may conclude that it is prudent to step out of the picture and allow the unique dynamics of the group to function. Indeed, groups consist of individuals who bring their unique backgrounds and experiences to learning. Therefore, it is important to build on the students' individual differences, carefully working to avoid squelching individual personality and disposition. Sometimes it will be necessary for the group to maintain and support its membership through positive encouragement and other support systems. At other times, the group may need to work through interpersonal problems in order to reestablish group equilibrium. Peer influence can be a powerful tool. The group can be used to discipline misbehavior if it is done wisely and with care. This will begin to happen naturally as students become comfortable enough to exert their influence to solve problems and maintain the group's overall level of productivity. Such activity is a marvelous example of positive group dynamics in action.

Teachers must strive to commence and conclude each class on time. By the same token, we must insist on punctuality and the efficient use of class time from our students. One can communicate an appreciation for promptness and timeliness by arriving early to the class, well prepared and ready to begin. When teachers model such behavior, students come to realize it is not only expected but also beneficial to them and to the quality of their learning experience.

Students should be made aware of the class agenda at the beginning of each class. This "lesson at a glance" can be displayed on the board and briefly explained at the start of the lesson. Students appreciate knowing the order of the lesson, as well as what they will be expected to achieve throughout the course of the class. When armed with this information, students are usually more able to focus on the lesson material, and usually for longer periods of time. Additionally, for those students who arrive early, such an agenda will provide valuable cues to how they can warm up to be best prepared for the lesson.

Concept and Skill Reinforcement

The development of any skill requires thoughtful and deliberate practice and repetition. Certainly, one must avoid meaningless drill at all costs. Thus, repetition must lay claim to students' attention through the application of appropriate challenge based on the degree of the students' present understanding. Learning experiences that are either too easy or too challenging will cause students to disengage from the learning opportunity at hand.

Repetition begets habit. Therefore, any repetition must function as a vehicle for growth and should be done in a way that is both engaging and purposeful. It goes without saying that repetition that is fraught with many mistakes will in turn program those mistakes as part of the habitual response. As such, drill and repetition should be conducted when the student has achieved a certain level of confidence with the concept or skill so as to program it correctly and securely. Teachers must train students to focus their attention on how the correct operation is achieved so as to repeat it in the future and in a performance context. Repetition must be conducted with mindful, thoughtful strategy in order for it to be effective.

It is wise to construct reinforcement plans for individual students who need additional review or drill. Students who have securely mastered the given concept or skill may be assigned additional activities or variations on the assignment at hand. For instance, it students are harmonizing a melody with blocked chords, these students may be asked to practice a more creative accompaniment style such as a two-handed accompaniment.

Furthermore, verbalization, combining a verbal cue with a physical gesture, deepens learning while integrating the physical and cognitive functions involved in learning to play the piano. This may involve saying note names or finger numbers, singing solfege, chanting rhythm, or calling out intervals or chords as students play. Such verbalization also allows the teacher to assess student comprehension.

Teaching Students How to Practice

Lessons should be designed in a way that not only imparts new concepts and skills but also equips students with strategies that will prepare them for and enhance their practice outside the lesson. Exemplary instruction features the integration of concept or skill presentation and reinforcement with a clear demonstration of methods that can be used to most effectively and efficiently prepare the assigned material. Students should leave the lesson feeling empowered and prepared to be successful in their practice at home or in the practice room. Indeed, students must experience some level of success with the material taught during the lesson in order to grant them assurance that they can refine these skills during individual practice.

The teacher must be specific when giving class assignments. Rather than saying, "Complete the sonatina by the next class," it would be more appropriate to also give explicit instructions for how to do so. This involves establishing clearly defined goals and objectives for the week of practice. These can be articulated in the form of an assignment sheet or handout on which the assignment and suggested practice strategies appear. For those who are verbal learners, it is wise to ask students to restate the assignment so they do not forget it. This can be facilitated by randomly asking students to discuss the assignment point by point. Older students can be asked to write their own assignment sheet in language that is relevant and personal. To ensure that all details are included, students can exchange and discuss their assignment sheets. This can be done as a brief one- or two-minute activity.

A discussion of practice techniques should solicit new ideas and suggestions from the group, encouraging and training students to consider innovative ways to maximize their practice time. The instructor can engage students with questions like, "What would you do in this instance?" or "How would you practice this passage?" Student-generated lists of practice strategies encourage students to take ownership in their practice. Moreover, scenario quizzing, such as that which is done by medical students, prepares students to quickly assess problems and subsequently devise procedures to resolve them. For instance, students might be asked, "If I was having trouble with ______, what would you suggest I do to solve the problem?"

The age-old debate over quantity versus quality in the realm of practicing needs to be forever reconciled. Students must know that the quality of practice is far more important than the quantity or time spent practicing. It is not how *long* one practices but rather *how* one practices that matters. Therefore, practicing should be judged not by the clock but by the achievement of clearly defined practice goals. Wise choices in practice strategies equate to less wasted time and more efficient practice.

It is advisable to encourage students to collect questions or problems they encounter during their daily practice and bring them to the following class to be discussed. Students should know that if one person has a question regarding a given topic, it is likely that others will have the same question. For the techno-savvy teacher, an online community discussion board is a great place to exchange practice ideas outside the classroom.

All too often, piano training perpetuates an attitude of perfectionism, leaving no room for mistakes at any stage of learning. On the contrary, healthy, positive teaching encourages students to not be afraid of mistakes but rather to take risks and learn from their mistakes, viewing them as opportunities to learn something new and grow in their skill and understanding. Mistakes are inevitable and have the potential to be of great benefit to any learner. To be sure, mistakes will happen. It is what we learn from these mistakes that matters most.

During their practice, students should learn to regularly pause to address the following questions:

- What did I hear?
- What went well?
- What needs to be improved?
- What may have contributed to the problem?
- How can I correct the problem?

Assessment and Evaluation

Assessment and evaluation deal with the collection and analysis of information related to a learner's performance in order to make an objective judgment regarding his progress and accomplishment. This involves various processes used to document, often in quantifiable terms, the state of a student's knowledge and skills. Robert Duke makes a distinction between assessment and evaluation: "Assessment is the measurement of a learner's performance (e.g., collection of data), while evaluation describes the learner's performance in relation to other learners or according to some continuum of graduated labels."[4] These processes not only attempt to determine what students have learned but also serve to evaluate the instructional program at large and its overall effectiveness.

Assessment is a continual process in which the instructor seeks to measure student comprehension or skill mastery. Assessment must occur throughout all stages of the lesson rather than being delayed until a strategic moment at the so-called end of a learning sequence. Assessment involves careful, keen observation of student understanding and requires an acute awareness of what is happening in the learning environment at all times. On the other hand, evaluation seeks to measure a learner's performance and how that relates to a set of curricular benchmarks. Further, evaluation attempts to understand how the learner is progressing toward achieving the established curricular goals.

As educators, it is one of our primary responsibilities to ensure that what we think we are teaching is indeed what our students are learning. In fact, just because something is being taught does not mean that it is being learned. And just because students appear to be learning does not guarantee they are truly comprehending. Therefore, teaching and learning are not necessarily inextricably related.

Curricular design, instructional preparation and practice, and assessment and evaluation must all be considered concomitantly. They are without a doubt interconnected and must work in concert. As such, assessment and evaluation must be planned with consideration of the curricular goals, as well as the instructional procedures designed to achieve these objectives. Further, a clear understanding of the objectives of the specific learning experience will serve as the standard when assessing whether or not learning has occurred. Questions such as "How can I know that students understand that which has been taught?" and "How will students be asked to demonstrate their comprehension or proficiency?" can serve as valuable assessment guides.

Just because someone can recall a fact, recite information, or play a chord does not mean true learning has occurred. Whether or not a student comprehends a concept or has achieved proficiency in a skill must be evidenced in some tangible manner. As such, authentic learning is demonstrated through active and meaningful application of skill or knowledge. While general observation can be effective in the group learning environment, it is wise to engineer specific, individual opportunities in which students can demonstrate comprehension and mastery.

In the group piano learning environment, sensitive observation of both individual and corporate comprehension will yield important information that can be used immediately to modify or adapt instruction to address students' needs. At times this information may even dictate a major alteration or detour in the original lesson plan. We should be prepared and willing to interrupt the lesson at any point to address confusion. As mentioned previously, deviation from the lesson plan is essential at times. One should never feel constrained to adhere to a class plan but should be willing to make swift adjustments and interventions as needed. Changes and adaptations to the lesson plan should be made according to the immediate needs and interests of the group. For instance, if several students in a class attend a piano concert and return to their next lesson expressing an intense fascination with the music of a particular composer, the instructor should take advantage of this prime learning opportunity to teach his class about the stylistic and compositional traits of the composer and of the period.

Optimal learning happens when students receive and process information and then exercise this knowledge or skill both within the same context and also in novel ways. This may include experiencing the skill in contexts that were not explicitly explained or demonstrated by the instructor. For instance, a student may be able to play a C-major triad but not understand the fundamental procedures for constructing major triads in general. Thus, for the student to demonstrate comprehension of this concept, he should be asked to apply his knowledge by constructing major triads whose tonic is not C while verbally explaining, in his own words, how this procedure is carried out.

With assessment and evaluation comes the responsibility to provide students with frequent feedback concerning their work. The purpose of these comments is to supply students with valuable information regarding the state of their present learning, as well as to influence and motivate students toward a given goal. These evaluative remarks should be delivered in a manner that is meaningful and should be framed in a way that is positive and constructive. Assessment should always reinforce the positive advancements each student makes and should highlight what the student actually did in order to achieve these successes. Our students need to be reassured when they are succeeding and encouraged when they are not. Any negative feedback should be reserved for situations in which it is essential to address unproductive or harmful student behavior. Negative remarks should not be altogether avoided but should be used judiciously to admonish unacceptable behavior or to challenge students to higher levels of productivity.

Indeed, frequent, specific (e.g., where, why, how), and meaningful (e.g., why this is so?) feedback is a critical component of the learning process. For this reason, the group piano teacher must be able to quickly diagnose student problems and prescribe solutions. To do so, the teacher must diligently observe students even while directing the class. This is certainly no easy task. Undeniably, the work of a classroom educator is one of multiple, simultaneous tasks. First, it is crucial that we are attuned to student questions, attitudes, attention, and even body language. Any of these factors may signal a problem or indicate an unanticipated barri to student learning. Further, we should get into a habit of systematically observing each student while directing whole-class activities from the teacher's console or while walking around the room to monitor students during individual practice. Observable signs of comprehension can be demonstrated through students' behaviors and their reactions to planned situations.

Students should be involved in this important process and should be trained not only to identify problems but, more important, to consider many possible solutions to any given problem. It is the job of the instructor to carefully facilitate student discussions in a way that draws attention to common problems or concerns and that leads the class to discover strategies for overcoming these issues. The facilitator must ensure that the comments are presented in a constructive fashion. The suggestions should be specific and relevant, articulating that which needs to be corrected as well as how it can be improved. We do best when we encourage students to offer concrete suggestions for improvement rather than vague, nonspecific assessments.

Students should be trained to develop and implement self-assessment tools. This involves the honing of critical listening skills, which can be a natural byproduct of learning in a group. Students should be trained to complete periodic self-evaluations of the quality of their work and discuss methods or strategies that could potentially serve to better prepare them in the future.

Assessment can be either formal or informal. Formal assessment usually involves planned experiences in which students are assigned a specific grade based on the quality of their work. These situations usually involve some level of comparison relating the student's performance to a set standard. Formal examinations or quizzes must honestly reflect and measure that which is to be learned. Informal assessment can be defined as any other performance experience in which students demonstrate their skills and understanding. These may be as informal as a class performance or answering a question posed by the instructor.

Evaluation of Teaching Effectiveness

Just as student comprehension and proficiency must be evaluated throughout all stages of learning, teachers must also regularly evaluate their teaching. Systematic observation and evaluation is essential for the development of any educator. Objective, honest appraisal of our work as music professionals is essential for, at the very least, maintaining and, ideally, enhancing our professional efficacy and potency. Not only must one seek to describe that which is observed in his teaching, but perhaps more important, one must endeavor to identify and subsequently define those variables that are associated with effective, profound teaching. Indeed, the art of education is ever changing and developing, in part because the world in which we live is also in a state of constant change. There is always room for improvement.

In this regard, two interaction and data analysis software titles are available that enable users to record, observe, and evaluate their teaching. These programs provide users with valuable information, including quantifiable data related to their teaching style and approach. The program eMirror, designed by Birch Browning (Cleveland State University) and Ann Porter (Cincinnati College Conservatory of Music), permits the user to record his teaching and insert comments regarding the observed teaching directly into the video. The software monitors the amount of time devoted to four delivery/interaction methods: on/off headphones, full-group instruction, individual instruction, and small-group instruction. A percentage of each modality is given at the end of the recorded sequence.

The program Scribe, developed by Robert Duke (University of Texas–Austin), allows the user to select and label specific behavior events in both live and recorded videos. The software provides the user with the following valuable data:

- Graphic time lines and chronological records of events
- Interactive time lines representing coded behavior
- Summary tables that describe data recorded over the course of observation intervals

Below is an instructional evaluation protocol consisting of a variety of questions that may be considered as part of one's regular self-evaluation process. The tool may be used as a whole or in part depending on the desired scope of one's evaluation.

Instructional Evaluation Protocol

Professional-Related

- Are you actively involved in a music teacher's organization?
- How many master classes or workshop events have you attended this year?
- Do you subscribe to and read one or more piano-related periodicals?
- How many books related to piano teaching or playing have you read this year?
- Have you read the latest research on instructional methodologies, psychology of learning, doctoral research, etc.?
- Have you actively applied what you gleaned from these readings to your teaching?
- Have you examined new instructional materials on a regular basis? Have you implemented any of these?
- Do you maintain a regular practice routine?
- Have you practiced your students' repertoire recently?
- Have you had a lesson or coaching recently?
- Have you recently given a public performance?
- Are you devoting the necessary, quality preparation time for each class?
- Do you present yourself in a professional manner (e.g., communication, dress)?
- Is your business well managed and thriving? If not, why?
- Do you present a positive, professional image?
- Are your organizational and communication systems effective?
- Do you have a regularly updated website, or are you in regular contact with parents via newsletter or another medium?
- Do you schedule regular parent-teacher meetings to discuss student progress?
- Do you devote careful attention to lesson planning, always considering curricular goals, both short- and long-term?
- Do you regularly experiment with new instructional strategies and materials?

The Instructional Environment

- Is your studio/classroom organized, clean, and tidy? Lighting? Temperature/humidity control?

- Is your studio/classroom attractive, warm, and inviting?
- Are your instruments well tuned and cared for?
- Do you own benches that are the proper height for each instrument?
- Do you have a special footstool or pedal extender for small children?
- Are music and materials properly organized and stored?
- Is the learning environment relaxed and conducive to productive l earning?

Lesson Preparation

- Does the teaching demonstrate solid preparation?
- Is the lesson plan well conceived and constructed?
- Is the lesson plan designed based on a primary concept?
- Is the lesson plan logically sequenced and facilitated?
- Did the teacher establish clear objectives for the class and lesson?
- Are the goals of each activity clear and appropriate?
- Did the lesson include appropriate content?
- Was the lesson content organized and clearly facilitated?
- Are appropriate materials used in the lesson?
- Does the teacher cover multiple skill competencies throughout the course of the class?
- Is technology effectively and efficiently employed?

Pacing and Student Engagement

- Is there a variety of material and activity?
- Is the lesson well paced and facilitated?
- Is there a natural sense of forward progression and sequence?
- Does the instructor linger unnecessarily on one activity to the exclusion of others?
- Does the lesson seem to drag or lose momentum? If so, what might have caused this?
- How much time was spent on each part of the lesson plan (e.g., performing music, drills or review, creative activities)?
- Is the learning environment stimulating and engaging?
- Are students individually and collectively engaged throughout the lesson?
- Are students contributing equally to the class?
- Evaluate the dynamics of the group. Does one student assume a dominant leadership role (e.g., answers all the questions, attempts to demonstrate)? Are there students who are not engaged in the lesson and who do not show interest? How might the instructor respond to these issues?
- What are the students' attitudes toward the subject matter? How might attitude impact learning?

Communication and Delivery

- Does the instructor project his voice clearly and speak in a manner that is understandable?
- Is the speed at which information is delivered or communicated ever too fast-paced?
- Does the instructor vary his location in the room? If so, is this effective?
- Monitor the amount of direct (lecturing, giving directions, criticizing) and indirect (accepting feelings, praising, encouraging, asking questions) teacher influence, as well as student participation during each. Are these properly balanced?
- What percentage of the lesson was devoted to group work versus individual work?
- What percentage of the lesson was devoted to teacher talk in relation to student activity? Could the class be more actively involved?
- Is the teacher teaching to the group or to individual students?
- Are instructions and demonstrations understandable and concise? Are students able to easily follow the teacher's instruction?
- Does the teacher ask thoughtful, relevant, mind-engaging questions? Does the teacher avoid excessive telling and lecture? How do students respond?
- Does the teacher wait for student response or rush to provide an answer?
- Does the instructor call upon individual students by name to answer questions?
- Is the teacher able to effectively respond to and build upon student remarks and reactions?
- Does the instructor appear to be at ease as while facilitating the lesson?
- Is enthusiasm for the subject matter communicated?
- Is feedback appropriate and helpful?
- Does the instructor offer genuine praise for quality work? Is praise ever offered when it is not appropriate or warranted?
- Is encouragement provided to all students?
- Is the instructor sympathetic to the needs of the group as well as individual students?
- Is humor employed?
- Is criticism offered in a constructive manner? Are student strengths and successes highlighted before areas needing improvement are discussed?

Other Teaching-Related Considerations

- Is the teacher sensitive to the specific needs of the individual students and the group as a whole (e.g., learning styles, individual differences)?
- Is there a focus on expressive, musical playing?
- Did the teacher address issues of unhealthy or unproductive technique?
- Did the teacher encourage the application of problem-solving techniques?
- Are discovery-learning principles employed?

- Is the lesson designed and experienced in a conceptual manner?
- Are students sharing in the decision-making process (e.g., areas that require improvement, goal setting, musical decisions, creation of practice strategies)?
- Are appropriate practice strategies discussed and experienced by all students?
- Is the teacher able to quickly and easily adapt or adjust to unpredicted moments or events?
- Does the teacher effectively employ modeling? If so, how many times and at what points during the lesson is modeling or demonstration used?
- Did the instructor maintain discipline and a productive learning environment?
- Is the highest quality of work demanded from each student?
- Were students given ample opportunity to demonstrate comprehension and mastery of concepts and skills?
- Is the teacher able to easily and efficiently assess student problems and subsequently lead students to solve these issues?
- Is the teacher able to effect positive change in the students' playing?

Chapter 6

Instructional Strategies

Creativity and diversity of approach in the delivery of curricula are hallmarks of exceptional group piano teaching. Indeed, imaginative teaching serves to engage and sustain student interest while inspiring curiosity and commitment to the subject matter. Thus, it is essential for group piano teachers to avoid limiting themselves to a handful of overused teaching strategies. Instead, they must be dedicated to exploring and experimenting with inventive means for facilitating learning.

It is an advisable practice to develop and maintain a database or journal of teaching strategies, activities, and games that can be used to teach, drill, or review specific skills or concepts. One should note those that are particularly effective, in addition to how they might be modified for a similar or different purpose in the future. Such a database becomes a priceless resource for the teacher and should be continually revised and expanded.

Teachers may invite intermediate or advanced students to contribute to their class by creating games and activities for the purpose of reviewing specific lesson concepts or skills. Students may be asked to develop a game based on given conceptual parameters and then e-mail a detailed description of how the game is played to the teacher a week in advance. The student, with the assistance of the teacher, can facilitate these games in the subsequent lesson. This approach calls on students to take ownership of their learning by creating entertaining yet practical ways to review important curricular elements. In the process, students are challenged to think as teachers.

The use of small-group learning stations is an excellent way to maintain student engagement in the subject matter while drilling course material through games and other exercises. Here, small groups of two or four rotate through a sequence of activities that review music theoretical and historical concepts or functional keyboard skills. The resulting variety generated by experiencing the games at each station aids in keeping students involved and excited about learning. After all, who doesn't enjoy a good game?

This chapter provides a discussion of the essential competencies found in a comprehensive keyboard musicianship curriculum, as well as a variety of group piano instructional strategies that can be used to teach them. The listing is in no way exhaustive but hopefully will motivate readers to experiment with the techniques and ultimately create their own. The strategies have been designated by level as follows: beginner (B), intermediate (I), and advanced (A). It is important to note that although some activities lend themselves particularly well to the level indicated, most, if not all, can be modified for use with any age-group and level of advancement. The chapter concludes with a description of instructional technologies and how they can be applied to group piano teaching.

Rhythm

Music is organic and visceral. It is alive and is characterized by rhythmic ebb and flow. Because of this truth, rhythm must be a natural part of the student's musical language. Rhythm should never sound pedantic but should be free and dynamic. It must possess elasticity as well as inner momentum and drive. Indeed, rhythm is a fundamental underpinning of all music and one of the most supremely critical musical elements we teach.

It is important that rhythm be experienced aurally and physically before a symbol is assigned or an explanation or definition is given. All too often rhythm is taught as a mathematical construct, which demands the perfect alignment of notes as they fit in a measure of printed music. When rhythm is treated in this manner, as correct as it may be, the result is lifeless and inanimate sound. A conceptual understanding of rhythm is only half of the equation. Rhythm is to be experienced. For this reason, it must first be internalized physically so that it can be expressed musically in a manner that has nuance and vitality.

Eurhythmic movement is an essential part of rhythmic training. The term *eurhythmics* is derived from the Greek word *eurhythmy*, which means "good flow." In essence, eurhythmic movement gets at the heart of the movement of music. Émile Jaques-Dalcroze (1865–1950), the father of the eurhythmic approach to music training, contended that by connecting with one's sense of movement, a natural sense of rhythm can be experienced and applied in music making. Dalcroze writes, "The acuteness of our musical feeling will depend on the acuteness of our bodily sensations."[1] Thus, rhythm, structure, and expression should be taught through movement in some form.

According to the Dalcroze approach, eurhythmic movement should begin with walking the beat, which involves the whole body and requires balance and coordination of the large muscles to avoid falling. Clapping, on the other hand, does not involve whole-body balance and should be delayed until after one has developed large muscle control. Such a sequence will positively impact the development and refinement of the smaller muscle groups involved in clapping and tapping rhythms.

Rhythm should always be related to the pulse, which is the unchanging beat, in contrast to rhythm's ever-changing combinations of note values. Children can first experience pulse by listening to music, either recorded or live, while walking to the beat. The music should include works of various tempi to allow students to experience the full spectrum of musical speed. Students should be directed to walk in the style of the music that is being played (e.g., marching, swaying, skipping). For instance, a student would not march to a slow, melancholy tune. A firm grounding in a sense of steady pulse will undeniably provide a secure point of departure for all other rhythmic training.

From here, students should begin to experience the distinctions between simple and compound meters. As the class walks, the teacher may play chords while accenting either ONE-two (duple) or ONE-two-three (triple). Students should be asked to count aloud with the teacher. Their counting and walking must reflect the emphasis of the downbeat per meter type. They may also use rhythm instruments to accent the strong beat while gently and softly tapping the weaker beat(s).

Later, students can be trained to walk to the beat while clapping and counting the rhythmic patterns found in the music. While sitting, students may also sway to the beat while tapping or clapping and counting the rhythm aloud. Many teachers prefer tapping rhythms because it is more closely related to playing the piano than clapping. More advanced students may be asked to conduct the metric pattern while counting the rhythm out loud.

Audible counting should be a natural part of the group piano experience from the outset. It is necessary to set the standard in which every student counts with no exception. Audible counting of rhythms with inflection should be a natural and, eventually, habitual part of each lesson. When students collectively count out loud, the pressure of this action is lifted from the individual student, making it a group effort instead. Further, anytime a verbal cue can be attached to a physical gesture, learning tends to be reinforced.

The use of words and other rhythmic devices can be of great assistance when teaching rhythm (e.g., "Mississippi Hot Dog" or a syllabic approach such as "ta, ti").

Some teachers choose to allow each group of students to create its own rhythmic devices. Students tend to remember rhythmic systems that are created by the group, and to which they relate.

Rhythm Activities

Rhythm Rhymes: B

- The use of rhymes or lyrics can help the learner to develop a sense of steady beat. Students sing the lyrics of songs found in their methods books.

Student Names: B

- Use student names to represent rhythms. For instance, two quarter notes might equal "Matth-ew," or two eighths and one quarter equal "Jer-e-my."

The Name Game: B

- The class forms a circle. Students individually say their name and clap and/or write the rhythm that results. The group repeats the rhythm. Next, the teacher claps a rhythm of one student's name. The class must identify which name is represented by the rhythm.

Rhythm Safari: B

- The teacher chants: "Goin' on safari, won't you come with me? Hear the animals, name them back to me." The teacher chants and claps, "zebra," and the students respond by chanting and clapping, "zebra." After the animals have been introduced, the teacher repeats, "Goin' on safari, won't you come with me? Hear the animals, name them back to me." This time only the rhythms of the animals' names are clapped. The students must name the animal based solely on the sound of the rhythm.

Body Rhythms: B

- Display various rhythm flash cards on the chalkboard to create a longer, extended rhythm pattern. Students decide how they should be performed (e.g., tap head for quarter notes, clap hands for eighth notes, stomp feet for half notes,). Proceed through the cards in order, while performing the rhythm, always counting out loud. The card order is switched and the process is repeated.
- Variation I: Divide the class into groups by note value (e.g., two students for whole notes, two for half notes, two for quarter notes). Collectively in 4/4 meter, the whole notes stomp on beat 1, half notes tap laps on beats 1 and 3, quarter notes snap on 1, 2, 3, 4, and eighth notes clap on 1&2&3&4&. Then parts are switched.

Strong and Weak Beats: B

- Play a piece with exaggerated strong (primary) and weak (secondary) beats. A tune in 2/4 meter is a good place at which to begin. Students clap or play rhythm instruments on the strong beat and gently tap their lap or play their instrument on the weak beats.
- Variation I: Students bounce a ball on the strong beat.
- Variation II: Students form a circle. On the strong beat, students pass a ball with an emphasized gesture. The object passed can be varied to stimulate and sustain interest, such as using beanbags, tennis balls, balloons, and so on.
- Variation III: While walking, stomp on the strong beat and gently glide or walk on the weak beats.
- Variation IV: Teach students basic conducting patterns, physically demonstrating in the air the strong and weak beats. The easiest meter to conduct is 2/4.
- Variation V: Students create rhythms by combining rhythm cards and adding accent markers to illustrate the primary beats. Student switch seats and clap or tap the rhythms that were composed by their colleagues, always counting out loud.

Rhythm Detective: B

- Give younger students three rhythm cards, two of which are the same. Ask them to determine which rhythm is different and which are the same. For each correct response, they advance to the next rank of detective.
- Variation I: Give all students one rhythm card. The teacher claps one of the rhythms that appear on the cards. The student with that exact rhythm card must raise his hand and identify himself. He then gets a new card.
- Variation II: The teacher places various note value cards around the room. In turn, students shine a flashlight on one of the cards and must explain to the group how many beats that note receives.

Rhythm Card Tic-Tac-Toe: B

- This activity requires laminated rhythm flash cards and a marker to label the cards. The teacher lays cards on the floor or another flat surface and divides the class into teams (*X*s and *O*s). Student representatives from each team who correctly perform the rhythm on the card win the card for the team, indicating their team's possession of the card by turning the card over and marking an *X* or *O* on the back.

Tempo/Rhythm Control: B

- A student or group of students is assigned the role of tempo and rhythm control police for a given exercise or for the day. They are tasked with monitoring the tempo and rhythm, signaling when the tempo is rushing during out-loud playing or a rhythm is incorrect. Tickets may be issued. A soft whistle may also be used.

Echo Clap-Backs/Tap-Backs: B/I

- The teacher claps a rhythmic pattern, and the class responds by clapping and tapping the same rhythm. The patterns can be varied in length, depending on the students' level of rhythmic memory. This activity is an excellent way to introduce students to note values, by putting them in context with notes that are familiar.
- Variation I: I/A: The teacher gives students parameters with which to create and clap a rhythm. For example, students may be asked to clap a rhythm in 6/8 meter, accentuating the big beats. The class must respond by counting and clapping the same rhythm.

Follow-the-Leader: B/I

- Students sit in a circle and clap a steady pulse. The first student says, "Clap back echo after me" or "Rhythm, rhythm that's our game, I'll clap a rhythm, you clap the same." After chanting this introduction, the student claps an original rhythm. The next student in the circle must echo the exact rhythm. If he does it correctly, that student gets to be the leader and follows the same procedure.

Pass the Rhythm: B/I

- This activity is based on the game "Telephone." A student thinks of a rhythmic pattern and taps it on the back of the student next to him. The receiving student then passes the rhythm onto the next student, tapping it on his back. The rhythm is passed around the circle. The final student claps and counts the rhythm out loud. The originator of the rhythm determines its accuracy. This exercise works to develop rhythmic memory and precision.
- Variation I: Each student claps and counts one measure of a written rhythmic example and then passes to the next student in the circle who claps and counts the next measure. The object is to perform the entire rhythm without pause and with perfect continuity and precision.

Rhythm Bee: B/I

- This activity is based on the concept of a spelling bee. Students line up single file. Each student is given a rhythm card and is asked to clap and count the rhythm. Students who incorrectly clap and count their rhythm are out. The last student remaining wins.

Rhythm Math: B/I

- Create rhythm equation worksheets with problems such as the following: One half note plus what equals a whole note? Students complete the worksheets in a timed race.

Rhythm Rock: B/I

- Teacher plays various musical selections while students physically respond to what is played.

Rhythm Ensembles: B/I

- Students compose rhythmic ensembles that include two or more rhythmic parts. They orchestrate the ensemble with percussion instruments or with body percussion (e.g., clapping, snapping, patting knees, stomping, snapping, vocal sounds like "pop"). Each student is assigned a part and is given a few minutes to preview and prepare the rhythm. The class then performs the ensemble. A student may be called upon to conduct the performance. Parts can be rotated and the procedure repeated.

My Note Value: B/I

- The teacher displays a single-line rhythm. He distributes percussion instruments, specifying that each instrument is to play a particular note value (e.g., drums play quarter notes, rhythm sticks play eighth notes). While counting out loud, the students read the example, playing only on their respective note value. Be sure that continuity is maintained throughout.

Rhythm Circle Improvisations: B/I

- Students stand in a circle. A meter is selected. Students in the circle count while clapping or tapping on rhythm instruments a steady beat. A student in the middle of the circle improvises a rhythm using different preestablished note values.

Rhythm Recognition: B/I

- The teacher leads the class in singing tunes that are in various meters. Students are then given a list of the melodies that were sung and are asked to match the title of the tune to the rhythm that is written on the page.
- Variation I: Instead of matching song with rhythm on a worksheet, request that groups write a rhythm on the board for a given tune.

Rhythm Rounds: I

- Students clap a rhythm in canon (as one group reaches measure 2, the second group begins). This exercise challenges students to remain focused on their part.

Dynamic Rhythms: I

- Add dynamics or tempo changes to rhythm cards for variation.

Tempo Indications: I

- Put a series of tempo indication cards in order from slowest to fastest and vice versa.
- Variation I: Students draw a tempo card and must line up in order from slowest to fastest. Students say their respective tempo using the speed of the term.
- Variation II: Students draw a tempo card and must play or sing a passage of any piece currently being learned, using the tempo indicated on the card. The remaining students must guess the tempo.

Rhythm Retrograde: I/A

- The teacher writes a rhythm on the board or displays it using a projected image and asks students to clap the rhythm forward, then backward.

Rhythmic Dictation: I/A

- The instructor plays a rhythm and asks students to write what they heard. Students can prepare their staff with the number of measures, meter, and so forth. Another method is to write multiple circles and then fill in the note values by adding stems.
- Variation I: Rhythm Dictation—Last One Standing: Teacher asks each student to dictate given (e.g., clapped, tapped, or played) rhythms of equal difficulty. If the dictated rhythm is incorrect, the student is out and must sit down. The last one standing wins.

Connect the Rhythms: I/A

- A student develops a short rhythmic pattern and claps it out loud. The next student adds a measure, clapping the entire rhythmic pattern, including the first measure clapped. Each student adds another measure and must remember what has come before. This activity stresses the development of rhythmic memory.

Rhythm Rondo: I/A

- ABACABA, etc.: The teacher establishes an "A" rhythm, which the entire class learns and claps and counts. Each student contributes an improvised rhythmic segment (e.g., "B," "C"). When everyone is finished and in time, the entire class claps the "A" rhythm. The process repeats until all students have had an opportunity to contribute a rhythm to the form.

I Write, You Count: B/I/A

- One student writes a rhythm while his classmates clap or tap and count it.

Find the Beat: B/I/A

- Write or display various rhythms on the board. Students must write in the beat (e.g., in 4/4/ time: 1& 2& 3& 4&).

Rhythm Roles: B/I/A

- Prior to students' repertoire performances, the teacher assigns each student a rhythm role: one student claps a steady pulse, one taps the subdivisions, one person counts out loud, one student points to the notes, and another plays the example. The roles are then switched. Roles help to keep all students engaged in the activity; each student plays a part in the success of the overall activity.

Ear Training

Music is fundamentally an aural art experience. It is a language perceived by the ear. Just as children learn to speak their native language through hearing and imitating native speakers, so they must also listen to and imitate beautifully performed music in order to become literate musicians. Therefore, the natural progression of musical literacy commences with listening, is followed by singing, and is fully realized in music reading and writing. Thus, training of the ear is of paramount importance. Émile Jaques-Dalcroze supports this assertion: "Once the ear is trained to the natural sequences of sounds and chords, the mind no longer experiences the slightest difficulty in…reading and writing."[2]

Indeed, music training must begin with the ear. A solid foundational training of the ear must first precede and later supplement music reading. A specific ear-training curriculum should be developed and implemented as a core component of a comprehensive music curriculum. The group piano lesson is an excellent venue for intensive ear training. The extended length of a typical group piano lesson provides the instructor with more time to develop the ear through various drills and exercises.

Solfege training is an essential element in this equation. Instruction should commence with singing stepwise patterns and then progress to more complicated patterns, which involve skipping and leaping intervals. Complexity should increase with the involvement of rhythmic elements and more challenging intervallic combinations. Concurrently, students need to be asked to replicate melodies at the piano, "picking out" by ear, so to speak, those intervals that are sung. Throughout the process, students must be encouraged to play well-known melodies by ear. Ultimately, reading will have a greater significance when the symbols represented on the page have first been experienced through listening, singing, and playing.

Music encompasses four fundamental elements, all of which are perceived by the ear: pitch, duration, intensity, and quality of sound. In terms of pitch, students must be able to first match pitch, differentiate between high and low pitches, recognize pitch movement and direction, including skips, steps, and repeats, and demonstrate the ability to name intervals, both ascending and descending. Eventually students will develop an aural harmonic vocabulary and will be capable of identifying harmonies, their quality, and relationships to one another.

Students should also be able to perceive a steady pulse both aurally and physically, discern long or short sounds, aurally and cognitively organize the beat into larger groups of two or three, discern a rhythmic pattern stored in short-term memory, and respond by clapping or tapping back the rhythmic sequence. Further, students must be able to differentiate between the gamut of tonal volume—loudness or softness—and the intensity or velocity with which a tone or collection of tones is rendered. Ultimately, student must be able to discern the difference between sophisticated gradations of tonal quality, whether warm and rich, brittle and harsh, or the multiplicity of degrees in between.

Singing, like counting, must be a normal and assumed part of the student's training from the very first meeting. Exercises should be designed to reinforce matching pitch and singing intervals. Imitative singing or "sing-backs" are another excellent tool for developing our students' ears. Here, the instructor plays and sings a sequence of pitches, a few at first and then more as the student becomes increasingly confident and proficient. Students sing what was heard and then play the sequence on the piano. The activity strengthens tonal memory and develops the recognition and application of relationships between intervals.

In the same way, students should be accustomed to singing lyrics associated with method pieces and folk songs and may create lyrics for compositions that have no text. Furthermore, singing through the imitation of beautifully shaped melodies performed by the instructor or peers works to develop student understanding of the natural phrase contour and pacing found in exquisitely performed music.

Music training should begin with a good deal of rote or imitative activity. Students must joyfully experience music making from the outset rather than being bombarded with terminology and symbolism. First and foremost, students must be drawn to the beauty of music and its expressive qualities. This is fostered through the teaching of attractive rote pieces from the very beginning of musical training, which frees students to experience the vast range of sonorities without being faced with the complexities of reading. Rote pieces also allow students to focus on the basic technical skills and touches used to create a diverse assortment of the tonal colors and articulations that the piano is capable of producing.

Ear Training Activities

Pitch Representation: B

- Students stand or sit to reflect high and low sounds or ascending and descending pitches.
- Variation I: Students shape the melodic direction and contour in the air with their hands while singing.
- Variation II: The teacher plays a melody and asks students to draw on paper or on the board the direction and shape of the melody.

Five-Finger Position Playbacks: B/I

- Within a given five-finger position, the teacher names the starting position and pitch and then plays a series of pitches, to be extended in length over time. A good preparatory exercise is to have the class sing the series using solfege prior to playing. One student is selected to play back what was heard, while the other students play on their keyboard with the volume turned down.
- Variation I: Play a major five-finger pattern, but add an incorrect pitch. Ask the students to identify the wrong note and play it both incorrectly and correctly.

The Seeing Ear—Dictation Exercises: I/A

- Students participate in teacher-directed dictation exercises. These may include melodic (based on students' intervallic understanding), rhythmic, as well as harmonic (including chord inversions) dictations. The exercises can be completed by students individually on their own piece of staff paper or collectively at the board. The teacher should count off and may provide the time signature.

Discerning Chords: I/A

- Students form a circle. After playing a scale to establish the key, the teacher plays a chord and calls on a student to name the chord and its quality (e.g., C major, D minor, B diminished) in the given key.
- To focus their listening attention, students may be asked to close their eyes while the teacher plays a chord. Students then hold up the number of fingers to represent the chord name. The latter allows the teacher to see which student comprehends the concept without embarrassing him in front of peers.

Play by Ear: I/A

- The teacher plays a melody. For early-level students, the melody could be a familiar tune. Students are asked to play back the tune within a minute's time. In a piano laboratory setting, students may practice the tune under their headphones. The teacher confirms by playing and/or displaying the melody on the Visualizer.

Play What I Play: I/A

- Based on the game "Telephone," one student plays a short melodic motive and performs for one other student under headphones so that only the two students can hear what is performed. The receiving student may not watch the performer play but may only listen. The auditor must then play back what was heard by ear for the student who is next in line. The performance by the final student in the line must match the motive that was performed by the first student.

Critical Listening Skills

Joseph Lhevinne once said, "Most students hear, but they do not listen. The finest students are those who have learned to listen." Indeed, students must learn to listen critically to their playing and develop the ability to discern the quality of the sound they are producing. There is no substitute for listening to beautifully performed music, both live performances and recordings by outstanding artists. Students should be encouraged to listen to high-quality recordings on a regular basis. Parents can assist here by playing this music in the home or in the car. Teachers can now use the latest MP3 technology to create weekly playlists that can be downloaded in class or from the instructor's website. This is a priceless part of the students' education, exposing them to beautiful tone quality, exquisite phrase shape and contour, and stylistic renderings of the repertoire. The literature should not be limited to the keyboard repertoire; students should be exposed to lyrical singing and opera, concerto and chamber music literature, and great works from the orchestral repertoire.

During each activity, both in class and during their practice, it is essential that students are targeting their attention by listening for some specific musical element. Students need guidance and direction in order to make the activity productive and to avoid inattention. One must keep examples brief to maintain student focus.

Critical Listening Activities

Legato versus Staccato: B

- Students form a circle and hold hands. The teacher plays an example. When the students hear legato, they must continue to hold hands with their neighbor, but when they hear staccato, they must drop their hands to their sides. This can be done with eyes closed, which forces students to listen and not rely on watching what others are doing.

Dynamic Discussion and More: B

- Play a musical example or recordings of music. Ask students to describe the tempo using appropriate Italian terminology, as well as general articulation and dynamic scheme.
- Variation I: For younger students, the teacher plays familiar tunes and asks students to determine if they hear forte or piano, legato or staccato, and so forth.

Let's Take a Vote: B/I

- Students form a circle. The teacher plays a musical example, which clearly demonstrates legato versus staccato, good tone versus bad tone, forte versus piano, and so on. Students must vote according to the quality of sound (e.g., was it legato or staccato?). The teacher tallies the votes and declares which group is correct.

A Blank Slate: I/A

- Students are given a score or score excerpt on which all interpretative markings have been removed. The teacher plays the work either as originally written or with new interpretative decisions, and the students must mark their score in detail to express what they heard. Here, students are transforming what they hear into symbolic notation.

Music Rewrite: I/A

- Each group takes a familiar repertoire piece and rewrites it, adding expressive elements such as accelerandos, ritardandos, staccatos, slurs, and dynamics that are not noted in the score. They must learn the piece with their new markings and perform it. The rest of the class members must identify how the score was modified.

Name That Tune: I/A

- During class, the teacher plays excerpts from a given listening assignment. Students must, in turn, name the title and composer. Older students may be asked to provide additional information such as the style period, genre, and so on.

You Be the Judge: A

- Students are asked to close their eyes and listen critically to two performances of an excerpt from a piece the class has recently studied. One performance contains incorrect dynamics, articulation, and so on, while the other is correct. Students are asked to determine the most appropriate performance.

- Variation I: The teacher plays works that are unfamiliar to the class and asks which performance is more stylistically appropriate.
- Variation II: Students write about and discuss two different performances. Give students specific musical elements on which to focus.

Recording Imitation: A

- Students listen to a recording of a solo instrument other than the piano. Students must attempt to imitate the sound they heard, such as imitating the shape of a lyrically rendered operatic melody or matching the tone quality of a performance of a Bach cello sonata.

Form and Structural Analysis: A

- Students listen to a recorded or live example and must discern the formal structure of the work (e.g., binary, rondo, sonatina/sonata).

Match This.../Copycat: B/I/A

- The teacher plays a phrase or a five-finger pattern with specific dynamics and articulations. One by one, students attempt to describe what they heard, then imitate exactly what was played. This can be as simple as exploring the dynamic continuum by playing a single pitch or two while having students match the dynamic scheme. This is a perfect opportunity to discuss velocity of key descent and how that affects volume. The activity should be done with eyes closed, which forces students to listen critically.

Adjective Assignment: B/I/A

- Students listen to a musical selection while writing adjectives that describe the piece.
- Variation I: Younger students may also represent the music by drawing a picture or writing or telling a story.

Reading

In essence, music reading consists of associating symbols with their sound counterpart, with notes acting as symbols for sounds. Reading music involves the integration and coordination of three components: the ears, the eyes, and the hands, which requires the synchronization of visual, aural, and motor skills. Simultaneously, the cognitive realm negotiates the intellectual operations necessary to successfully organize and process what is read, and then transfers this to the hands to be realized musically. Thus, reading demands significant neuromuscular precision and acuity.

Students should be able to hear a tone or a series of pitches in their mind's ear when looking at its symbol, even before it is sounded on the piano. Some teachers have referred to this skill as the "hearing eye." Edwin Gordon coined the term *audiation*, which takes place when one hears and comprehends music for which the sound is no longer present, or may never have been present in the first place. Gordon makes the following comparison: "Audiation is to music as thought is to language."[3] Thus, reading is more effective and has a deeper meaning if that which is read is a symbolic illustration of melody and rhythm that has been previously experienced both aurally and physically through movement.

It is important for teachers to stress that for the pianist, knowing where a note is located and its relationship with adjacent notes is infinitely more important than knowing the note name. Richard Chronister writes: "In music reading, the letter names of the notes used to form a musical pattern are not at all crucial to the ability to read or understand that pattern—it is the relationship from one note to the next that is crucial. And the student's ability to respond to that relationship easily and readily determines that student's fluency with the language of music, an indispensable aspect of music reading."[4]

Thus, an intervallic reading approach is most viable. Students should learn to read using a combination of both intervallic and multiple-key approaches. At the beginning, landmark notes provide students with points of reference in reading, allowing students to learn other pitches in relation to these landmarks. In a systematic and gradual manner, the staff can be expanded and fully constructed around the given landmarks.

It is imperative that students learn to read intervals rather than individual notes, with the latter being entirely inefficient. Students can be trained to locate starting pitches and then read successive notes in a pattern using intervallic and directional movement. Students must understand that a pianist simply does not have time to name each note when reading a complex score such as a Bach fugue or Ligetti étude. Of course, being able to identify and name notes is a critical, fundamental step in the reading process, but one must move beyond a pure "note-naming" approach to reading in order to become a confident, fluid reader.

Indeed, readers of the English language read not letters but words. The same is true for musicians. We read not notes but groups of notes as found in melody and in harmony. To take this illustration further, we read not merely words but sentences. As musicians we read the accumulation of melody and harmony as found in phrases or longer musical ideas. Thus, attention should be given to reading complete ideas as opposed to individual notes. As such, it is essential for the pianist to be able to discern patterns as found in a musical score, such as scales, chords and their inversions, and arpeggios.

To this end, students should be trained to use a systematic sight-reading preview routine. Here, students examine key and time signature, observe melodic, intervallic direction, including large leaps, conduct a harmonic analysis, identify potential rhythmic challenges, and take note of accidentals, hand position changes, and fingering indications that signal a change in hand position. Young students may use colored pencils to trace the contour or direction of a melodic line, using one color for upward movement, one color for downward movement, and one color for repeated pitches. Prior to playing, teachers may direct their students in speaking or chanting the melodic motion of a piece in rhythm by saying "up, down, down, repeat," and so on.

Students may be given a sight-reading checklist that includes a step-by-step protocol to be considered prior to reading a new example (figure 6.1). It is wise for students to get into the habit of practicing a sight-reading example on their lap or on the keyboard cover while audiating that which they are "practice playing."

Preview Protocol

- ❑ Key signature
- ❑ Clefs (i.e., treble, bass, tenor, alto)
- ❑ Accidentals
- ❑ Time signature
- ❑ Rhythm: tap and circle potential challenges
- ❑ Melodic direction: sing melody (solfege), say intervals
- ❑ Large intervallic leaps
- ❑ Scales
- ❑ Hand position changes
- ❑ Fingering
- ❑ Harmony: common tones
- ❑ Triads and inversions
- ❑ Patterns
- ❑ Play RH on lap (slowly and counting)
- ❑ Play LH on lap (slowly and counting)
- ❑ Play hands together on lap (slowly and counting)

Playing Protocol

- ❑ Select a slow tempo and maintain steady pulse (set metronome, if necessary)
- ❑ Read ahead and anticipate what is coming next in the score
- ❑ Use coordinated, structured, and deliberate eye movement
- ❑ Avoid looking at hands, only for large leaps

FIGURE 6.1 Sight-Reading Checklist

Students need to know that there is no magic wand that can be waved in order to become a competent sight reader. Rather, one must be dedicated to developing this skill through consistent practice. Accordingly, sight-reading demands daily practice of all types of textures, both linear (contrapuntal) and vertical (chordal/harmonic). Students should engage in daily reading, either from a sight-reading method or by reading passages from the piano literature. To facilitate the latter, some teachers maintain a lending library of supplementary reading materials from which students can check out materials for at-home practice.

When sight-reading, students need to be encouraged to play with confidence, avoiding the use of a tentative tone at all costs. Good sight readers wisely select tempos that facilitate not only accuracy but also continuity. The following list describes characteristics of an exemplary sight reader:

- Has a solid sense of keyboard geography and topography
- Has an ability to recognize and discern intervallic relationships between notes, as well as scales and chord patterns
- Has a solid kinesthetic awareness of what triads and inversions feel like
- Employs coordinated and structured eye activity that perceives music in large groups or chunks of notes
- In chordal textures, perceives common pitches that are constant from chord to chord, which frees the reader up to focus on moving voices
- Has an ability to view a measure of music, store it in one's short-term memory, looking ahead to the subsequent measure while playing the previous measure
- Avoids looking at one's hands, only briefly glancing at them during large shifts in position
- Utilizes a consistent system of fingering according to patterns and groups of notes
- Plays with confidence and continues to read ahead despite mistakes
- Has an ability to anticipate that which is forthcoming in the score
- Has an ability to hear (audiate) a score prior to and during reading
- Can play stylistically while reading, observing expressive details such as dynamics and articulation
- Selects a tempo that promotes continuity and precision

Keyboard Geography and Topography

Keyboard Geography: B

- With a rhythmic accompaniment, teacher chants, for example, "Black keys, high keys, two black keys." Students respond in rhythm by playing any group of two black keys.

High and Low Pitches: B

- Ask students to generate a list of things that create high and low sounds. Divide a sheet of paper, using a horizontal line in the middle of the page to represent the middle range. Ask the students to draw the items on their list, with high sounds appearing above the line and low sounds below the line.

Finding Keys by Feel: B

- With their eyes closed, students place hands on the keyboard and feel their way to a given note. For instance, to find D, students will search for a pair of two black keys and go to the white note in between. This activity can be conducted with students lining up at a single instrument, as a partner activity, or as an individual exercise.

Triad Drills: I

- Together with eyes closed, students begin on a C-major root position triad and ascend chromatically through all major triads.
- Variation I: The instructor assigns a starting triad. Students find their position and then close their eyes. The teacher will then say, "Move to a G-major root position triad." Students feel their way to the chord, then check. Eventually, the instructor can include chord inversions and a variety of chord qualities. Students are encouraged to sense and know common tones or anchor notes from chord to chord.

Grand Staff Pitch and Interval Identification

Music Alphabet Forward and Backward: B

- Using musical alphabet flash cards, students must arrange the cards both forward and backward as quickly as possible.

Mnemonic Devices: B

- The teacher asks groups to create their own mnemonic devices to remember the lines and spaces of the staff. Students are more likely to remember the tool if they create it. Beyond this, student-created mnemonic devices are often infinitely more creative than "Every Good Boy Does Fine."

Teacher Chant Drill: B

- Although it can never replace an intervallic approach, drilling note names and their location on the grand staff is an important skill. This can be achieved in a variety of ways. For example, the teacher chants: "Bass clef, third line, name that note." or "Treble clef, fourth space, name that note." In teams, the students must name and play the note described by the chant. The team with the most points wins.

Timed Flash Card Drills: B

- Students are divided into two teams, with each team receiving an equal number of note or pitch flash cards. Students, in turn, must accurately name the pitch on the card and locate and play the pitch on the piano. The first team to accurately complete their stack of cards wins. The teacher should take note of flash cards that give students trouble in order to drill these extensively in a future class.

Floor Staff: B

- The teacher places a beanbag or stuffed animal anywhere on the floor grand staff and asks students in turn to name the note.
- Variation I: Students place the bag on a pitch and call on a classmate to name and play the note. The student must then find that pitch on the piano.

Hide and Go Seek: B

- Students are divided into teams. The teacher hides flash cards around the classroom. Students must find a card, run to the piano, play and say the note name, and place the correctly played card in the team pile. If correct, they get a point and run to find another card. The team with the most points wins. This also can be used to drill triads, rhythms, seventh chords, and so on.

Build a Chord: B/I

- Teachers place a beanbag on any given line or space on the floor grand staff. Students are asked to build a chord on this starting pitch in either root or first or second inversion. They must also name the chord quality.

Visualizer Drills: I

- The instructor plays a series of notes on a Visualizer or other staff device. Students are called upon to name the note that appears. This activity should begin slowly at first, with speed increased as students become more confident. After students name the note, they must play that particular pitch on their keyboard. These activities can be conducted either individually or using a team-based design.

Reading in a Flash: I

- The teacher displays a note on the staff or Visualizer while students' eyes are closed. At the command, by name, a student opens his eyes, and one second later the teacher erases or removes the note from the staff. The student must remember the pitch, name it, and play it on his keyboard.

Timed Worksheet Drills: I

- The teacher distributes a worksheet with various pitches both on the grand staff and off (using ledger lines). When the teacher calls "start," students can begin naming and writing the note names. The first student to complete the exercise wins.
- Variation I: On staff paper, students write various pitches on and off the grand staff. Students exchange papers and identify pitches in the shortest possible time.

Intervallic Reading Exercises

Name That Interval: B

- The teacher places two beanbags anywhere on the floor grand staff. A student is called upon to both name and sing the interval that is created. The student with the most correct answers at the end of a set number of rounds is declared the winner.

Melodic Shape and Contour: B

- Students shape the melodic contour of a tune in the air as it is sung, representing the melody through movement.
- Variation I: Draw the shape of a melody on paper, creating an abstract map or outline of the melodic contour. Play (and sing) the melody next, then transpose the melody to other keys.
- Variation II: Together and out loud, sing the direction of the melody, saying "step, skip, repeat" as the melody dictates.
- Variation III: Divide resources. One student plays the melody while another sings the melody using solfege syllables and another sings the direction (e.g., step, skip, repeat).

Intervallic Visual Representation: B

- Students are given a notated single-line melody or an example from their method or repertoire collection. On the melody, students draw a straight line for stepping intervals, a curved line for skipping intervals, and a squiggly line on pitches that repeat. They can use a different colored pencil for each type of movement.

Melody Transposition: B

- The teacher asks his students to transpose melodies to encourage intervallic reading. As students play, they should sing or say the intervallic movement such as "step up, skip down, repeat."

- Variation I: While solfege singing a melody, students demonstrate the intervallic movement by signaling different body levels. For example, if the melody skips down, students touch their feet. If it skips upward, they touch their head.

Follow the Leader—Interval Style: B/I

- Follow the leader: The teacher says, "Start on F, go down a third, up a second, and down a fifth. What note do I land on?" Students respond by naming and playing the correct pitch. This can be done either at or away from the piano.

Melody Identification Exercises

Melody Detective: B

- Display a melody either on the board (handwritten or projected using PowerPoint) or on a handout. Students must determine the name of the tune simply by audiating or singing the melody.
- Variation I: The teacher plays a musical example while students follow along by reading and listening as it is played. The teacher will make two or three intentional mistakes and ask students to identify the mistakes following the performance.
- Variation II: The teacher plays a musical example while students follow along. The teacher will stop at random moments and ask students, in turn, to identify the exact stopping points.
- Variation III: Students are given a card or series of cards that contains a melody. The teacher plays one of the melodies. The student with the melody must identify himself as the cardholder.
- Variation IV: The teacher gives students a series of melody cards and plays them in a particular sequence. Students must then put the cards in the order that they heard.

Which One Is It?: B

- The teacher or a student leader plays a melody or rhythm. Then two cards are displayed, one of which contains the correct melody or rhythm. Students must identify the card that matches that which was heard.

Sight-Reading Exercises

No Peeking: B/I

- To train students to avoid looking at their hands, while performing partner sight-reading, one student plays while the other student covers the performer's hands with a book or cloth.

Solfege Sight-Reading: B/I/A

- Students sing a melodic line using solfege prior to and while sight-reading a musical example at the piano.

Sight-Reading Chain: B/I/A

- As a group, students sight-read an example, each playing one measure and passing it seamlessly to the next student so as not to break the overall continuity.
- Variation I: One student starts. In the middle of the measure, the teacher calls out the name of a student who will play the next measure. All students read along in preparation in case they should be called.

Partner Sight-Reading: B/I/A

- With a partner, students determine a tempo, set the metronome, and sight-read together. This activity reinforces continuity and the skill of reading ahead despite mistakes. Students may be asked to count aloud as they play. Weaker readers may read only one hand at a time; stronger readers read both hands simultaneously.

Sight-Reading Composition Exchange: B/I/A

- Students compose a brief sight-reading example based on given parameters (e.g., melodic thirds, in a given mode, hymn texture). The compositions are exchanged or drawn from a hat, then sight-read aloud for the class.

Sight-Reading Drill Pairs with Eye Check: I/A

- See chapter 4, "Cooperative Learning Theory and Group Piano Teaching."

Ensemble Sight-Reading: I/A

- Students sight-read duets or other ensemble literature that is at or slightly below the student's current reading level. The exercise challenges each student to continue without pause, maintaining continuity and style.

Flip-Flop: I/A

- The teacher divides the class into two groups. Each group begins by playing either the right hand or left hand. The groups switch hands for each measure.

Contrapuntal Combination: I/A

- The class is divided into two groups. Assign one group to read the right hand and one group to read the left hand of a contrapuntal work. Switch parts.

Finally, combine parts. Listen carefully to the interaction of voices. When using digital instruments, each group may select a different timbre or voice so that each part can be easily distinguished from the other.

Sight-Reading Composition Mix and Match: I/A

- Given set parameters such as note values and melodic range to be used, students compose one measure of a larger composition on card stock. One student is selected to arrange the cards (measures) in any given order. The class must sight-read the resulting composition without pause. Following this step, another student may be asked to reorder the measures of the composition, with the class reading the new arrangement.

Tachistoscoping:[5] I/A

- With a blank sheet of paper or cardboard in hand, a student stands next to the performer/sight-reader and covers first a single note of music after it has been played. Such action prevents the student from looking backward to check for accuracy and rather encourages the student to continue reading ahead.
- Variation I: The teacher or a fellow student covers every beat of music before it is played to force the player to read and instantly memorize the music long enough to play it, while looking ahead to what comes next in the score. Gradually, multiple beats or even complete measures can be covered. The musical example can be practiced multiple times, with the level of difficulty increasing with each repetition.

Quick Memory: I/A

- The teacher gives students a short example (e.g., four bars or so) and one minute to study the example. When the time is up, have students discuss what they saw, recalling such things as the shape of melody, key, accidentals, and so on. Give them thirty more seconds to review the example and then request that they play as much as they can from memory. Gradually the size and level of difficulty of the musical example are increased. Also, the length of preview can be truncated as students become more proficient.

Chorale or Hymn Textures

Important Preparatory Steps for the Following Activities:

- Conduct a harmonic analysis of the chorale or hymn texture sight-reading example.
- Mark common tones from chord to chord.

- Mark instances where one hand must play pitches on a different staff (e.g., right hand must also play a tenor voice)
- Remind oneself to read from the bottom to the top.

Outer Voices: A

- Students play only the outer voices of a four-part texture. When they feel confident with this procedure, they may slowly add the interior voices. This activity serves to direct the eyes to outer voices first, thereby challenging students to perceive complete chords rather than reading individual notes of a chord.

Strategic Eye-Hand Movement: A

- In textures that move in half-note values, give each chord four beats instead of two. This allows the performer to locate the bass pitch on beat 1, the tenor on beat 2, the alto on beat 3, and the soprano on beat 4. The chord may be constructed in a broken fashion or played altogether on beat 4. The procedure organizes eye and hand coordination while reinforcing a steady pulse.

Common Tones: A

- In a four-part texture, students can be directed to play only the common tones from chord to chord. Initially, students may mark common tones with an *X* so that attention is ultimately focused on moving parts. This drill encourages students to quickly observe common tones, freeing them up to focus on the voices that move.
- Variation I: Conversely, students may play only the pitches that change from chord to chord.

Take Two: A

- Similar to Sight-Reading Chain, here one student plays two chords of an example followed by the next student, who plays two chords, and so forth. The purpose is to encourage a seamless transition from chord to chord and measure by measure.

Open Score Reading

Important Preparatory Steps for the Following Activities:

- Mark cross-voices, unison, or octave doublings.
- Mark instances where one hand will play pitches in the opposite clef due to extended hand span or large intervallic distance between two adjacent voices.
- In special situations, due to chords whose range is unplayable, mark the voices to be omitted.

- When playing orchestral or band scores, highlight those parts that are in concert pitch with one color and use another color for other parts that will require transposition.
- When playing orchestral or band scores, mark how parts will be distributed between the two hands.

Divided Resources: A

- As an introductory step to reading an open score, divide the parts among students. This could translate to a single part or two parts, depending on the size of the group. When using digital pianos, each part may be played with a specific timbre or instrument so as to give clarity to the individual parts. This procedure gives students a sound model of the complete score. Gradually all parts can be combined by individual students.

Choral Score Sing-Along: A

- While playing four parts from an open choral score, the performer may be challenged to sing one of the parts. The performer should be asked to play four times, each time singing a different part while playing the rest. Choral music educators are called on to do this sort of activity in rehearsals on a regular basis.

Hymn to Open Score: A

- Students rewrite hymns on four independent staves and practice as an open score.

Choral Score Rehearsal Project: A

- Students select a choral score in three or more parts. College music majors should select a work that is likely to be used in their work as professional music educators. Student prepare each part individually in the appropriate range, and all parts in any combination. During the class presentation, the student will act as a choral conductor/accompanist and will lead the class in a rehearsal of the selected work from the keyboard. The class will serve as the choir. The project culminates in a rehearsal of all parts together from an open score and a final performance with the accompaniment.

Technique

The purpose of technical study at the piano is to arm the pianist with the tools necessary to create captivating music in a healthy and efficient manner. Thus, the primary aim of piano technique is to provide a means with which one can play with maximum ease and fluency. To this end, the instruction of a solid piano technique is grounded in and preserves that which is natural and comfortable for the individual student.

The basic operations of piano playing involve the integration of cognitive as well as gross and fine muscular control. Indeed, the mechanics of piano technique are the result of sophisticated neuromuscular functions that work to produce all necessary actions involved in advanced-level piano playing, including finger dexterity and facility, finger independence, application of arm weight, and the overall efficient use of the entire playing mechanism, to name just a few.

Because of these complexities, technique should be taught, at first, apart from music reading in order to free the student to focus on the specific physical gestures used to produce a desired sound. Both the ear and the physical playing mechanism must work in concert to achieve optimal technical refinement. When teaching technique, it is important that we emphasize that the gesture must match its desired end product: the sound. A beautiful, flowing line should not look stiff and rigid but should be gentle and graceful. Indeed, the gestures that are employed must serve to generate a complementary tonal result.

Because of its very nature, the instruction of technique demands the use of imitation and modeling. Students should first be directed to concentrate on the desired sound and then, by way of demonstration and imitation, the gesture used to produce this sound. Consequently, the teaching of technical exercises through imitation is a preferred method of delivery, thereby allowing the student to devote full attention to the sound and gesture rather than complicating the issue by also involving the element of reading. In the group piano learning environment, students learn technique from modeling after their teacher, as well as by observing and discussing one another's technique.

It is essential that teachers develop a detailed regimen of technical skills and principles for their students, a plan of action for how they will be presented and reinforced, and demonstrable markers of proficiency at each stage of learning. The technical component of the overarching curriculum must be strategically and systematically sequenced so that students build the necessary facility and dexterity to accomplish the tasks set before them in all other areas of the curriculum. The plan should take into consideration the individual students involved and will require a certain amount of flexibility from the teacher to adapt to the needs of each student in any given class.

During the group lesson, it is necessary for the teacher to carefully monitor each student's individual technical development. In a group piano laboratory environment, student-led activities can permit the teacher to walk around the room to address inappropriate technique. For example, a student may be asked to lead the class in playing an exercise by Hanon from the teacher's console, while the instructor moves about the room to assess each student's technical approach.

The group lesson provides a certain advantage over the private lesson in this regard. Here, students are trained to be on the look-out for inappropriate or inefficient technique not only in their own playing but also in that of their classmates. To accomplish this, teachers must first train students to be able to discern good from bad technique by plainly demonstrating the difference between the two. Based on this understanding, students should be encouraged to monitor their own approach while vigilantly inspecting for unnecessary tension or potential bad habits. As students become confident in the desired technical approach, they can be asked to observe their peers playing, responding to questions such as "Did Emily apply wrist rotation in that passage?" or "Did Reid use strong, sturdy fingers at measure 13?" Through observation of the positive technical attributes of their peers, students may be motivated to improve or fine-tune their own approach.

It is advisable for students to focus initially on the production of a rich, warm tone at the mezzo forte or forte volume levels prior to being taught the softer side of the dynamic spectrum. Soft playing is exponentially more difficult to produce and control, especially for the younger student. Once a solid tone and appropriate hand shape are achieved, soft playing can be introduced by asking students to imitate a five-finger pattern, played first fortissimo then pianissimo. This procedure focuses students first on the desired sound, which can then be followed by a demonstration and discussion of how the sound is physically realized.

It is equally advisable to teach a nonlegato touch at the outset of instruction. This can be achieved by teaching exercises that use the forearm on repeated notes of a rhythmic pattern. Too often a legato touch is taught prematurely, before students have developed the refined finger control necessary to produce such a sound.

Technical exercises should first be rendered slowly so that students can concentrate on the proper movements and gestures involved in producing the preferred sound. Speed will follow. To be sure, the basic underpinning of fast playing can be taught first at a slow tempo. To develop velocity and speed, scales and other technical exercises can be taught in small groups of notes and gradually expanded. For scales and arpeggios, hands-separate practice is advised so that concentration can be given not only to correct fingering but also to finger crossings and other principles related to a balanced hand position and the desired resulting speed.

We must be diligent in stressing to our students that the development of technique is a means to an end, with the final desired result being that of producing compelling music. Thus, technique should be practiced not as a digital exercise but as a study in musicality and expressivity.

Posture, Sitting, and Hand Position

Tunnel and Bridge: B

- For groups of beginners and especially young children, the hand position can be related to a tunnel. The position is supported by a tall thumb and fifth finger with a supported archlike bridge. Students can take turns driving a toy car under the tunnel and over the bridge.

Shape the Piano Hand: B

- Another strategy involves one student covering his peer's hand with a towel or piece of paper. The student should learn to shape his best "piano hand" without looking, relying solely on what it feels like. This encourages students to learn how the correct natural position feels without having to examine the hand.

Finger Numbers: B

- With hands positioned on a solid surface, a student leader calls out a number. Students must wiggle or tap that number as quickly as possible.
- Variation I: For added challenge, add right- and left-hand instructions.

Away-from-the-Piano Exercises: B

- "Away from the piano" exercise routines are excellent ways to build awareness of various parts of the playing mechanism, including the fingers, wrists, forearm, elbow, upper arm, shoulders, and back. Beginning students in particular may have difficulty differentiating between each part of the mechanism and often struggle to separate specific joint movements. It may be beneficial to begin every class with such exercises to warm up the body and generate awareness of each part of the playing apparatus.

Posture and Position Police: B/I

- From the outset and throughout the early stages of study, it is necessary for teachers to remind students to examine their posture and hand position, for these are at the heart of a sound technical training. The teacher may assign one student at the beginning of each class to serve as the posture and hand position police.

They are tasked with monitoring their classmates' position and notifying them when they have "broken the laws" of good posture and hand position.

Technical Exercises and Activities

Five-Finger Follow the Leader: B

- A student leader plays a five-finger scale in a given key with a specific dynamic scheme (e.g., soft-loud-soft), and the class must imitate.

Five-Finger Fun: B

- As a group, students play five-finger patterns in chromatically ascending order with a rhythmic accompaniment, be it a prerecorded drumbeat or a student-created accompaniment performed on rhythm instruments. Several published teacher accompaniments are available that provide added interest to scale playing and practice.

Articulation Movement Exercises: B

- When teaching articulation, ask students to physically represent the gesture involved in creating the sound through full body movement.
- Legato: When teaching legato, one might relate the gesture used to play legato to walking in which there is always one foot on the floor. Lead students in a walk around the room, noticing that there is always a momentary overlap when both feet are on the floor.
- Staccato: Have students hop around the room to feel the buoyancy and upward movement involved. Relate this to the physical gesture of lifting when playing staccato.
- Two-note slurs: Ask students to bend at the knees and then raise up. This relates to the downward motion on the first note, and upward motion on the second note of a two-note slur.

Five-Finger Patterns: B/I

- Five-finger patterns and their many variations are excellent exercises for the development of early-level technique. The benefits of these exercises should not be underestimated or quickly passed over. Five-finger exercises can be used to teach the student to develop finger independence, using all fingers of the hand with equal strength. They also serve to teach pattern recognition, combining theoretical principles with practical technical applications. There is a multiplicity of ways these exercises can be varied.
- Variation I: One hand forte, one hand piano. Switch.
- Variation II: One hand staccato, one hand legato. Switch.
- Variation III: One hand eighth notes, one hand quarter notes. Switch.

Pick a Scale, Any Scale: B/I

- Students draw a scale from a hat or cup and then perform the scale for the class. Before playing, the student is asked to name all notes of the given scale, as well as the fingering used per hand. This activity can be used to drill any technical skill such as arpeggios, chords, and even technical exercises or études.

Scale Discovery: B/I

- Scales are best taught using the discovery process. First, teach a single major or minor scale by demonstration only. Ask students to form groups and investigate collectively how the scale is constructed. After the pattern is defined, students apply and transfer the pattern on other starting pitches.

Scale Ensembles: I/A

- Divide students into four groups. If the class consists of only four students, each student will take a singular role. Group/student 1 plays any given scale, two or more octaves, ascending and descending. Group/student 2 harmonizes and accompanies the scale, applying an appropriate chord progression that is either taught by the teacher or composed by the group. Group/student 3 plays an octave bass line from the chord progression, while group/student 4 performs a rhythmic accompaniment using rhythm instruments. The roles are then switched and rotated.

Technique Tournament: I/A

- See chapter 4, "Cooperative Learning Theory and Group Piano Teaching."

Round Robin: I/A

- Students prepare assigned scales, arpeggios, or other technical exercises for this activity. The first student is given a scale to play. In a digital piano laboratory, the student plays the scale, and all other students play along on their keyboard with the volume turned off. This ensures that all students are engaged during the activity and also provides them with the digital practice of fingering the scale. While the student plays, the student who assigned the scale observes and follows the performance with specific feedback and suggestions for improvement. The performer then passes a scale to the next student, and the procedure is repeated.

Scale Jeopardy: I/A

- Modify television game shows, such as Jeopardy, to review or drill scales, arpeggios, or other technical skills. Categories can be created based on a technical skill, with each key or category receiving a set point amount. The team with the most points wins.

Scales in the Round: I/A

- Divide the class into two or more groups. Play first together, then in a round. The result turns monophonic scales into a harmonic rendering, adding interest and texture.

Salsa Scales: I/A

- Practice or perform scales with rhythm accompaniments, which are standard onboard features on most digital pianos. Add a salsa beat or other prerecorded rhythmic accompaniment. Any accompaniment, be it a teacher duet, MIDI, or CD, adds excitement and energy to scale playing.

Chord Progression Call-Out: I/A

- While one small group plays an assigned chord progression in a given key, the other group calls out the name of the chords or Roman numeral indicators. Reverse roles.

Repertoire

The study of the piano repertoire in a group environment is of immeasurable benefit to participating students. The collective preview and analysis of new literature engage students in the process of discovery. Jointly, students uncover the fundamental compositional elements upon which a piece is constructed and discuss strategies to enhance their practice and preparation of the work. Indeed, the manner in which new literature is previewed and introduced has much to do with how it will be ultimately prepared and performed by the student. The group environment lends itself to a variety of captivating and exciting ways in which this can be accomplished.

Group performances of the literature provide students with opportunities to offer and receive feedback and recommendations for improvement, thus serving to develop critical thinking and problem-solving skills. This exchange of ideas demands that students express and articulate their thoughts about music in an intelligent, constructive manner. Every group includes a variety of personalities, each with a unique interpretive opinion of how the music should be performed. The group process calls upon students to think about music not only in a way that will impact their own preparation and performance but also in ways that may inform and shape the interpretive considerations of their peers. For purposes of group reference, it is important that all measures are numbered in the literature to be discussed.

The group experience exposes students to a wide variety of repertoire and musical styles because of the diversity of literature that is studied within a group. Students are given valuable opportunities to hear and examine their peers' repertoire, which may serve to inspire an interest in a particular composer, genre, or musical style, and may even challenge them to higher levels of preparation of their own repertoire. Furthermore, the regular performance of repertoire in the group lesson helps dispel or at least alleviate much of the fear and anxiety often associated with performing for others.

Repertoire Preview: B/I/A

- This is a valuable time in which students should be led to ask questions about the form and style of the work. It is time to assess potential problems and discuss methods to address these problems. The preview should be used to develop students' analytical skills and their ability to formulate appropriate and efficient practice strategies.

Dividing Resources for Preview: I/A

- For extended, more advanced literature, divide the piece into segments, with each student preparing a different segment each week. At the next lesson, each student plays his part in sequence. By doing so, the entire piece is played from start to finish, giving students a complete understanding of how the work sounds as a whole. Here, all students are responsible for solid preparation of their part. If a student is not prepared, the performance of the piece is incomplete. The procedure is rotated among students until the entire work is learned and polished.

Student-Directed Preview: I/A

- The teacher allows students to teach or lead the preview of new literature. Students must thoroughly discuss potential problems and techniques to address the potential problems. This activity gives students a chance to engage their critical thinking skills, as well as an opportunity to demonstrate leadership initiative.

Preperformance Discussion: B/I/A

- Prior to a student performance of a new work, the class should study the score and be prepared to describe in detail what they glean from the music. Questions like "From what you see in the music, what do you expect the character of the piece to be?" and "What specific expressive or technical issues will you listen for?" can be asked to elicit discussion. An examination of the form should

also precede the performance. This exercise encourages the students to audiate, translating visual notation into an aural image.
- Variation I: Allow a student to lead the preperformance discussion.

Performance Auditor Roles: B/I/A

- Prior to students' performances of repertoire, assign specific roles to each auditor to listen explicitly for elements such as dynamics, articulation, phrasing, and so on. Students will feel empowered by their responsibilities, resulting in fully engaged critical listening. After the performance, each auditor is called upon to provide the performer with positive feedback on elements that were successful, as well as constructive criticism on issues that could be improved. Perhaps most important, auditors are commissioned to provide helpful suggestions that could enhance the execution of the specific musical element for which they were responsible.
- Variation I: Provide students with a listening guide. Ask students to write an adjudication sheet for each performer, which conveys the positive elements, those that need improvement, and tips to solve any problems the performer may have experienced during the performance. This activity provides the performer with written feedback that can be referenced during future practice. It also gives auditors the chance to develop critical listening and problem-solving skills.

Postperformance Discussion: I/A

- The postperformance discussion can be a valuable time of learning not only for the performer but also for all students in the class. Here, the teacher should ask leading questions to facilitate the dialogue, such as, "What did you think of the legato touch?" "Was it fluid and smooth?" "Could you hear the transfer of weight and tone from note to note?" The performer should be asked to provide his assessment of the performance as well as thoughts regarding how the performance felt.

Postperformance Reconstruction: I/A

- Without conducting an initial preview and discussion of a work, direct students to listen critically to the performance and imagine what the score must look like. After the performance, students are asked to list all the structural, harmonic, stylistic, and expressive features heard, reconstructing the score through verbal description.

Self-Selected and Prepared Repertoire: B/I/A

- Students should be given the opportunity to select their solo literature from a collection of carefully chosen pieces determined by the instructor. This procedure gives students the chance to identify and prepare works that are of individual interest and that reflect their personal style and taste. Students take complete ownership in literature unlike that which is being studied by their peers. Also, when the group learns a varied repertoire, the entire class gains an opportunity to learn infinitely more literature than that which could be learned individually.

- Variation I: Allow students to select repertoire at the beginning of the term and assign them to prepare it independently. Conduct a self-study repertoire performance class at the close of the term. This is a valuable opportunity for the teacher to assess his students' level of independent learning and self-analysis.

Phrasing

Phrasing lies at the heart of musical expression and interpretation. A phrase is a recognizable musical idea or unit, comparable to a spoken statement or a written sentence. Intelligent, expressive phrasing involves the thoughtful grouping of notes, on both the micro and the macro level.

Ball Toss: B

- To demonstrate the natural rise and fall of a phrase, have students toss a ball, attempting to re-create the archlike pattern.

Imitation Question and Answer: B/I/A

- Modeling and imitation are some of the most effective ways to teach phrasing. To this end, the teacher may play a phrase from a piece that is being studied and request students, in turn, to imitate the sound of the phrase in the exact manner that it was initially played. The teacher should vary the sound each time so that students hear a variety of ways in which the phrase can be performed.

Shaping Sound: B/I/A

- Ask students to demonstrate, through bodily movement, the shape and motion of a phrase. This can be as simple as drawing an arch in the air or more advanced full-body movement.

Rubber Band Pull: I/A

- To help students experience the tension and resolution inherent in a well-contoured phrase, they may be partnered and asked to pull and release one side of a shared heavy-duty rubber band in a controlled manner. By doing so, the students are able to physically experience the tension and subsequent release involved. Following this exercise, students should be asked to transfer this sensation to a musical phrase, imparting the same sense of tension and release to the music.

- Variation I: Music that exhibits phrase tension and resolution or rise and fall is played. Two students stand facing one another. While listening to the music, the students press their hands together as the tension builds and release them as the energy subsides. This exercise is also effective when teaching suspensions and their subsequent resolution.

Improvisation

Improvisation is an integral component of the keyboard musician's equipment. For the young pianist, improvisation can be an effective means for the development of a sense of keyboard topography and geography. Using their newfound knowledge of how the keyboard is organized, beginning students can explore the full range of the keyboard and exploit the capabilities of sound and sonority for each register in what is called free improvisation.

The act of improvising can help strengthen and refine one's understanding of harmony, melody, and rhythm. It can foster the development of the ear and train the mind to recognize and organize music into patterns and coherent ideas. It may also enhance one's ability to rapidly learn and memorize repertoire. As such, improvisation may work to galvanize a kinesthetic awareness of chord shapes and how harmonic progressions operate in given tonalities.

Improvising on a theme from a composition gives students an opportunity to assimilate principles related to the foundational and global structure of the piece prior to embarking on the quest to polish and understand the intricate details of the work as a whole. The creation of music, whether through improvisation or formal composition, provides students with valuable opportunities to demonstrate comprehension of concepts and principles. Further, stylistic improvisation is a highly informative practice that arms students with the skills necessary to negotiate a memory slip during a performance by improvising in the style of the work. To be sure, improvisation is a vehicle for self-expression that provides the pianist with a confident means for the re-creation of sounds at the keyboard that are heard first in the mind's ear.

Improvisation Activities

Soundscapes: B

- Students select a topic (e.g., storm, birds, elephants, speeding locomotive) and attempt to illustrate it through sound. If the student is attempting to illustrate

a bird, the teacher may ask which register of the keyboard could be best used to demonstrate the sounds of a bird. As one student creates music in the upper registers, the others should be directed to raise their hands high above their heads to illustrate the high register of sound. This exercise integrates knowledge of keyboard geography and improvisation. Improvisation activities should be used from the start of students' training. By doing so, it is less likely students will fear improvising. They should be encouraged to experiment with improvisation regularly in their practice, creating their own music using the infinite sonorous possibilities of the keyboard.
- Variation I: The teacher reads a story out loud and gives students an opportunity to provide sound effects, assigning one student to each page.
- Variation II: Ask students to paint or draw a picture and then improvise music to describe their artwork.

Melodic Variation Improvisation: B

- Perhaps the easiest way to introduce students to improvisation is to ask them to play a written melody and then vary the melody by changing the rhythm, melodic direction, mode, or structure. This can be done as a chain exercise in which one student varies a single measure of a larger example. Students play their variation of the original melody in a seamless fashion.

Movement Improvisation: B/I/A

- Assign students to re-create a movement activity such as skipping, hopping, running, or marching through music. An initial discussion of defining characteristics of each and strategies one might use to illustrate it may be helpful for the young student. This is an excellent skill for the general music teacher to possess.

Musical Chairs Improvisation: B

- The class is given basic parameters within which they must improvise. Chairs are lined up à la musical chairs. As the student improviser plays, the other students move around the chairs. When the improviser stops, the others must scramble to find a chair. The person who is left without a chair becomes the next improviser.

Melodic/Rhythm Improvisation: B/I

- Two students work together. Each receives a flash card that displays a one-measure rhythm. The cards are placed on the piano rack, with each student sitting in front of his respective card. Each student practices clapping or tapping his rhythm. When they are ready and from left to right, together the students count and clap the rhythm seamlessly. Next, they select a five-finger pattern and improvise a melody using the rhythm indicated on their card. The students then engage in an improvisation dialogue, using their melodic/rhythmic improvisations.

Call-and-Response Improvisation: B/I

- To reinforce melodic or rhythmic principles that are currently being discussed in class, the teacher may choose to conduct question-and-answer improvisation activities. For instance, if a class has recently learned eighth notes, the teacher could play a rhythmic pattern using set note values (e.g., quarter and eighth notes; the students respond with their own rhythmic answer using the established note values.

Modal Mania: B/I

- Students improvise music using modal scales built on white keys. By using a range of white notes only, students are freed to concentrate on the improvisation rather than being focused on playing "correct" pitches. This is a good way to teach the structure of modes after students have first experienced them through rote introduction and improvisation.
- Variation I: To further simplify the activity, one half of the class can create a harmonic progression using only modal fifths while the other half improvises a melody. Roles can then be reversed.

Simple Improvisation: B/I

- Transfer learned skills by asking students to improvise using recently learned concepts. For instance, give students simple parameters within which to work (e.g., use primary chords, five-finger patterns, end on tonic) to limit conditions at first so that students can focus on the basic concepts prior to spiraling into more complex realms.
- Variation I: Sight-read a simple melody, then assign students to improvise on the given melody using simple parameters such as altering melodic direction, rhythmic durations, and so on.

Styles Improvisation Investigation: I/A

- See chapter 4, "Cooperative Learning Theory and Group Piano Teaching."

Chord Progression Improvisation: I/A

- Using a learned chord progression, students improvise a melody employing only chord tones at first. Later they may add nonchord tones to generate interest. For younger students, one may choose to divide responsibilities, with the group playing the progression while each student takes a turn improvising a melody. This activity is a good way to apply chord progressions in a practical manner.

Repertoire Preview through Improvisation: I/A

- Using the chord progression found in a repertoire piece to be studied, the teacher engages students in the previously mentioned activity titled Chord Progression

Improvisation as a preparatory step prior to teaching the composition. One half of the class can play the chord progression while the other half performs the melodic material. Then the roles are reversed.

Ostinato Improvisation: I/A

- In groups, students create and practice a rhythmic or harmonic ostinato accompaniment. The group then plays its ostinato while the remaining classmates take a turn improvising a melody above the given accompaniment.
- Variation I: Students can generate an improvisation above prerecorded accompaniments or drum tracks, which are often standard onboard features of digital pianos. Drum tracks can also be found as part of sequencing applications such as Garage Band or other titles.

Conversations: I/A

- Ask students to have a keyboard conversation between two or more players without saying a word. Each student takes a turn saying something through sound. The class must guess what the conversation was about.

Stylistic Improvisation: A

- Lead students to improvise in the style of their current repertoire. Discuss the basic stylistic principles that characterize the literature, highlighting cues such as rhythmic, melodic, formal, and dynamic issues. Explore sonority and style by asking students to play their repertoire in a different tonality (e.g., from major to minor), changing rhythm or meter, and exploring different registers of the keyboard. Such an activity solidifies students' knowledge and understanding of given styles of piano playing. It will also provide students with confidence and security during performance of the solo literature.
- Variation I: After students have successfully read a sight-reading example, assign them to improvise in the style of the piece. This calls for immediate assessment and application of the compositional style of the excerpt.
- Variation II: Assign students to create a set of stylistic variations based on any theme such as "Twinkle, Twinkle Little Star." The styles can be based on Baroque, classical, Romantic, or Impressionist and other contemporary compositional style traits. Student may choose to improvise in other popular styles such as rock, jazz, country, or ragtime.

Pattern Piece Improvisation: A

- Create an improvisation using a motive or pattern from a published work such as Satie's *Gymnopedie* or Bartok's *Mikrokosmos*.

Twelve-Bar Blues Improvisation: B/I/A

- The twelve-bar blues progression can be taught shortly after students have learned major and minor five-finger patterns and can be built upon to more advanced stages as the students' facility advances. For a class of beginners, one can first divide responsibilities: one student plays the bass line, one student plays a chordal accompaniment, one student plays a rhythmic accompaniment, and one student improvises a melody. The roles are then rotated. The chords used could be as easy as diminished fifths (e.g., B-flat and E = C7; A and E-flat = F7; B and F = G7), which keeps the hand in a centralized position, requiring only a half-step or whole-step movement.

Musical Emotions: B/I/A

- Write a series of emotions on the board. Give each emotion a number. Students draw a number from a hat, which corresponds to an emotion. Students are given a few minutes to create music that expresses that emotion.

Accompaniment Pattern Improvisation: B/I/A

- Improvise using learned accompaniment structure (e.g., Alberti bass, blocked or broken chords, oom-pah-pah or waltz). Divide the class into two groups. One group will play an established harmonic progression using a set accompaniment pattern such as waltz style; students in the second group take turns improvising a melody above the harmonic structure. Switch roles so that all students have an opportunity to experience both parts.

Additional Improvisation Instructional Tips

- Always encourage students to maintain a sense of pulse.
- Involve other rhythm or percussion instruments.
- Employ various sound, timbres, and drum machine features available on digital pianos.
- Students should be encouraged to improvise in a variety of keys in order to develop a kinesthetic sense of the keyboard. This will also challenge the student to think intervalically.

Composition

Like improvisation, composition is an excellent way for students to demonstrate their level of comprehension of a variety of theoretical and stylistic concepts.

Styles Variations: I/A

- Students select a classical, folk, or popular song and compose a set of variations in contrasting styles. Students may choose to vary melody, harmony, meter, rhythm, or other compositional elements. They are asked to perform their variations for the class.

- Variation I: Using the theme from any of their solo repertoire, students compose a set of variations and perform for the class.
- Variation II: Using a sequencer or drum machine, create additional parts by employing a variety of instruments or sounds.

Sound Settings: I/A

- Assign students to compose a musical setting of a poem, either original or published. Many resources are available from which to choose. Some may elect to set humorous poetry, and others will gravitate toward more weighty works. Students are challenged to illustrate through sound the context of the poetry.
- Variation I: In groups, assign students to create a story using vivid imagery. Collectively, the group is assigned to create a composition to illustrate the story through music.

Composing Accompaniments: A

- Each student selects a tune from a beginning-level band or choral method and composes an accompaniment. The student rehearses the accompaniment with a soloist and performs the work for the class.

Concept/Skill Transfer Compositions: A

- Students compose a work based on a given set of parameters, using skills or concepts recently discussed in class. This is a great opportunity to draw students' attention to the intricate aspects of music composition while applying those concepts learned in their piano studies. Additionally, the activity provides students with priceless transfer of knowledge regarding form and structure (e.g., sonatina form, fugal and simple contrapuntal ideas), antecedent/consequent phrases, harmonic implications, or contemporary compositional techniques. This can be achieved by assigning students to create a sequence using the harmonies found in a recently studied chord progression. Using this sequence as a harmonic foundation, they can create a fitting melody.

Harmonization

Harmonization and transposition are both essential curricular components of the pianist's comprehensive musical training. These important functional skills allow students to play the piano recreationally throughout their life. For some, this may include accompanying community singing activities such as contemporary worship experiences, which often employ a chart-style approach. The ability to harmonize and transpose melodies is not only an important skill for the amateur pianist but also of particular benefit for the professional musician, especially the classroom music educator.

Harmonizing a melody requires the pianist to apply his theoretical knowledge of chords and how they function within the melodic/harmonic context. The manner in which a melody is harmonized should be based first on an understanding of the melodic material and the harmonies that complement the given melody. The final decision of the harmonies to be used is dictated by the ear, the musical style of the given tune, and ultimately the imagination of the pianist.

It is important that students are trained to deal with the variety of harmonization demands encountered by the pianist. This includes lead sheets with pop chord symbols (alphabet chord names), figured bass realization (Roman numerals), and examples that present a melody alone without chord symbols or a list of possible chord choices. Students should become comfortable harmonizing melodies that require the use of not only primary chords but also the entire harmonic spectrum, including secondary chords and secondary dominants and jazz harmonies. For the early-level student in particular, chord inversions should be used to facilitate ease of movement in a closed position. This procedure allows students to learn chord progressions in a practical manner.

Additionally, students should develop a command of a variety of stylistic accompaniment patterns, including but not limited to the following:

- Single notes (e.g., tonic-dominant roots)
- Octaves
- Blocked chords
- Broken chords
- Alberti bass
- Waltz style ("oom-pah-pah")
- March style ("boom-chic-chic-chic" or "boom-chic-boom-chic")
- Boogie-woogie or walking bass
- Two-handed accompaniments in piano style

Students can transfer their knowledge of accompaniment styles by harmonizing folk tunes that employ a given type of accompaniment and then sight-reading written examples at a similar level of difficulty that use the same accompaniment type.

The ability to harmonize familiar tunes by ear is another important skill to be developed by the pianist. Students can learn to "pick out" tunes by ear and apply their harmonic knowledge by selecting chords that most appropriately complement the melody. Teachers should maintain a list or database of familiar tunes that can be harmonized with primary and secondary chords, as well as secondary dominants. A list of melodies and the chords commonly used to harmonize them can be found on the companion Web site.

Harmonization Activities

Harmonization Think Pair Share: I/A

- See chapter 4, "Cooperative Learning Theory and Group Piano Teaching."

All by Ear: A

- In small groups, students pick out a melody by ear such as a folk tune or a popular song and then determine the harmonic progression. Next, they harmonize the melody using a stylistically appropriate accompaniment pattern. Students may be asked to sing along as they play. Finally, students may be asked to transpose their tune to another closely related and singable key. This exercise is particularly relevant to the university music student who is preparing to teach general or elementary music.

Harmonization Dictation: A

- In dyads, students perform for a partner their version of a harmonization example. The student listener must write the harmonic progression used by his partner, identifying the Roman numerals or chord names employed. The student checks his answers, and the roles are reversed. Students determine which harmonization lends itself best to the sound and style of the piece and then practice this version together. Finally, the dyad performs their version for the class.

Lead Sheet/Pop Chord Chart Reading: A

- Using lead sheets such as *The Ultimate Fake Book*, published by Hal Leonard, or contemporary Christian worship charts, student dyads first learn to play the piece as a duet, one student playing chordal accompaniment while the other plays the melody. Then roles are reversed. Finally, students harmonize the tune using a two-handed, piano-style accompaniment. The accompaniment must reflect the style of the piece.
- Variation I: Students may create an ensemble by composing or improvising rhythm and other parts. This may be orchestrated using various digital piano timbral or percussive resources. The parts may be divided among the group.

Transposition

The study of transposition should evolve from an intervallic and multikey approach to reading. To enhance this approach, teachers often employ a "movable do" system of solfege. Transposition must be a part of every lesson from the outset of study, which helps it become a natural part of playing the piano rather than a dreaded task. This can be achieved by transposing reading exercises and by playing technical exercises in a variety of keys during each class. Teachers may also select a key of the week or day and ask students to transpose all class materials (e.g., sight-reading, harmonization, technical exercises) to the given key.

Transposition Activities

The Wheel of Transposition: B/I/A

- The group learns a reading example in a given key. Working in teams, students spin a wheel that displays various keys. The students must transpose the example to the key on which they land. The teacher awards a point to the student's team for a successful transposition, and the team with the most points wins. The level of difficulty of both the reading example and the keys to which they must be transposed will vary by class according to the students' level of advancement.

Transpose by Twos: B/I/A

- Students are divided into dyads and are given a musical example to be transposed. One student must transpose the treble clef while the other transposes the bass clef. The roles are then reversed. Finally, both students must together transpose both parts.

Time Trial Transposition: I/A

- The teacher gives students three minutes to prepare a brief transposition exercise. The example length will vary by student level. Each student must play his exercise for the class while the class scores the performance. Eventually, the prep time should be reduced so that the student is transposing at sight.

Transcription Activities

Group Popular Transcription: A

- Students are assigned to dyads or small groups. The groups select a favorite popular song and bring a recording to class, either on CD or in a digital format. Together students must transcribe the basic chord progression. After the progression has been established, the students are tasked with re-creating a stylistically accurate rendering of the original tune. When the equipment is available, students may utilize digital piano and sequencing technology to add drum tracks or other instrumentation to add authenticity to their performance.

Blind Transcription: A

- Provide students with a CD or digital audio files that include a collection of excerpts from unfamiliar popular tunes. These may be made available via a studio/class website or e-mailed directly to students. Students must play the excerpts in the original key by ear. The goal is to re-create an authentic transcription of the excerpts, using the essential stylistic elements.

Ensemble and Collaborative Piano Playing

The ability to collaborate well with other musicians is a vital skill for the well-rounded pianist. Collaboration with other pianists and musicians opens up a vast array of music-making possibilities to the pianist, including the priceless collection of chamber music repertoire. Ensemble experience in the form of duets, duos, quartets, and other configurations prepares students with the skills for accompanying as well as for chamber music collaboration with other instruments and vocalists.

By virtue of its structure, the group piano learning environment provides teachers and students with priceless ensemble opportunities from the very first lesson. For the student, collaboration is an intrinsic element of one's study and is experienced from the beginning of group piano study. Piano ensembles, whether duets, duos, or larger ensembles, provide students with many valuable skill sets, including the following:

- Promote the development of critical listening, flexibility, balance, and ensemble skills associated with collaborating with other musicians.
- When sight-read, challenge students to continue reading and playing despite mistakes while maintaining a steady pulse.
- Help develop rhythmic acuity and precision, as players are forced to maintain a strict pulse between themselves, as well as negotiate any rubato or expressive/agogic issues with perfect ensemble.
- Encourage the development of communication and social skills.
- Promote the development of decision-making and problem-solving skills, as students are challenged to justify musical decisions with their collaborators.
- Encourage musical analysis and builds general musicianship skills.

Indeed, solo piano playing is a lonely endeavor, with students isolated during hours of individual practice. Collaborative music therefore allows us to share the art of music making with one or more musicians. The social aspect is obviously an attractive one as we are all social creatures to a certain extent.

Beyond this, ensemble and collaborative music making is both fun and motivating. Students become part of a team. The accountability and interdependence associated with peer collaboration challenge students to produce high-quality work, both in preparing their individual parts and in the collective ensemble. In order for the team to be successful, all musicians involved must be thoroughly prepared.

Ensemble recitals are an excellent venue for amateur students to engage in public performance. Because the stage is shared with peers, students do not feel as though they are in the spotlight, thus reducing much of the performance anxiety typically associated with solo performances. Positive ensemble experiences can be a stepping-stone for future solo performance endeavors. Fortunately, for the group piano teacher, a wealth of piano ensemble literature is available to accommodate divergent student abilities and stylistic interests.

Ensemble Activities

Duet, Duo, and Multiple Piano Ensembles: B/I/A

- Students prepare and perform duet, duo, or multiple-piano ensembles. The literature can be performed on a dedicated thematic piano ensemble recital that can feature literature from particular composer or compositional period, a specific style of piano playing such as jazz, blues, or ragtime, or other holiday music, to name just a few.

Scales and Exercises: B/I/A

- Duet teams together play scales or exercises, such as the Hanon studies, striving for a perfectly unified sound.
- Variation I: The secondo player begins a scale and passes it to the primo, attempting to create a seamless transition from one player to the next

Ensemble Precision through Technique: I/A

- Chordal exercises such as chorals are an excellent means for developing synchronization in ensemble playing. Using literature such as *Hymn* op. 280, by Louis Kohler, student duets work to achieve optimal ensemble. The predetermined leader of the team must give clearly defined physical gestures or cues such as a head nod or breath. Using the wrist to conduct these cues is often the most reliable approach. Whatever gesture is selected, it must be consistent and clearly defined. Cues must be rhythmic and clearly indicate the tempo.

Developing Balance and Melodic Projection as an Ensemble: I/A

- Students play a simple two-handed scale together in their respective register, alternating the role of melody and accompaniment. One student plays louder than the other, and then roles are switched.
- Variation I: Students play the same scale, but now play the outer voices forte and the inner voices piano.
- Variation II: Play the same scale, but now project the inner voices.

Improvisation Ensembles: I/A

- Students create ensembles based on a given chord progression. Each student takes a specific role: one improvises a melody, one a countermelody, one a blocked chordal accompaniment, one a broken chordal accompaniment, one a sustained bass, and so on. Utilize rhythm instruments and onboard instrumental timbres featured on digital pianos to generate interest.

Two-Handed Accompaniment: I/A

- Transform a harmonization exercise into an accompanying exercise. Students create and perform a two-handed accompaniment in piano style while the class sings and/or plays the melody on their pianos or other instruments.

Piano Accompaniment Composition Project: A

- Assign a melody or permit students to select a melody of their choosing. Ask students to compose a piano accompaniment for their melody. They may choose to write their accompaniment in any style (e.g., jazz, blues, rock, classical, Romantic). They must then learn and perform their accompaniment with a soloist.
- Variation I: Building on the preceding assignment, ask music major students to compose and perform an original accompaniment for elementary band or choral method materials.

Accompanying a Soloist: A

- Students select and prepare the piano accompaniment of an approved art song or early or intermediate instrumental solo. Students rehearse and perform their selection with a soloist for the class. Prior to the performance, students should discuss rehearsal strategies and cueing techniques employed as well as tuning protocol.

- Variation I: Students practice sight-reading the simplest of accompaniments while their classmate sings or performs the melody on the piano or another instrument.

Rhythm Ensemble Composition and Accompanying Project: A

- Students work together to compose a rhythm ensemble with piano accompaniment. The rhythm parts should be at an early or intermediate level and may be composed of simple rhythmic cells or ostinato patterns. After the instrumental parts have been composed, each pianist is responsible for composing an individual piano accompaniment that complements the rhythmic parts. The accompaniments should be original and should represent a particular style. Students then take turns playing their piano accompaniments while the other students or class at large play the rhythm parts.

Choral Warm-Ups: A

- This activity is geared toward university choral music education students. The students compose original choral warm-ups and prepare the exercises in all keys. The students are asked to play and demonstrate each exercise while leading the class from the keyboard, with the class acting as the choir. Students must generate a notated version of each exercise as well as an annotation that details the pedagogical objective of each. Warm-ups from all students are combined to create a choral warm-up compilation. All members of the group are responsible for learning not only their own warm-up but also those composed by their group members.

Music Theory Activities

Key Signature Drills: I/A

- Students are divided into two teams. By team, students line up at the chalkboard. In turn, students build the order of sharps, then flats. The team to finish first wins.
- Variation I: By team and in turn, the students must quickly write the key signature for a key tonality called out by the teacher (e.g., B major, C minor). The first team to correctly write the key signature gets a point. The team with the most points at the end of the tournament wins.
- Variation II: The class is divided into two teams. By team and in turn, students line up behind the "flash card display persons" each of whom holds an equal number of key signature flash cards. Students must name the key signature that appears on a flash card, then go to the end of the line. The team that correctly identifies its stack of flash cards is declared the winner.

Tempo Terminology: B/I

- Create or purchase flash cards that include Italian tempo indications. Students work together to put them in order from slowest to fastest. To reinforce this exercise, students walk each tempo, beginning with the slowest and progressing to the fastest. The teacher can accompany the exercise with improvised or prerecorded music. The teacher may also call out a tempo at random, and students must follow in tempo.
- Variation I: The teacher performs a work at any tempo. Students must guess which tempo indication matches the tempo of the work being heard.

Dynamic Gradations: B/I/A

- The teacher asks students to put dynamic sign cards in order from softest to loudest or vice versa. Then ask students to play a five-finger scale, adding the gradation of sound indicated by the sequence of cards.

Game Show: B/I/A

- Modify television game shows, such as Jeopardy, to review or drill theory or music history concepts.

Written Exercises and Time Drills: B/I/A

- Written exercises and timed drills are excellent ways to assess student comprehension of theoretical concepts. To expedite the process of checking these assignments or exercises, request students to exchange papers, correcting any answers that may be incorrect.

Triad Building: B/I

- Students line up in groups of three. In rhythm, the teacher chants, "Build C major—ready, set, go." Students respond, in order, each offering a pitch: "C," "E," "G."

Chord and Inversion Building: B/I

- Three students select large note cards (e.g., hand-drawn on card stock or poster board) that display pitches used in a chord and arrange themselves in any order. The remainder of the class decides in what inversion the cards are arranged.
- Variation I: Students use the same procedure for seventh chords.
- Variation II: The teacher creates cards with the notes from two different chords. Each student draws a card and finds other students who have notes from their chord. They then must line up in front of the class in chord order. The first team to do so remains, while the opposing team must indicate what chord and inversion they see. They must also play it using correct fingering.

Form: B/I/A

- Following discussion of various forms, play recordings or perform works that display a recognizable form. Ask students to, in teams, identify the structure/form.
- Variation I: The class is divided into groups. Each group composes a part of a tune (ABACABA) based on given parameters. Students can assign a visual representation (e.g., animal, object) to represent each part of the form. Students can also chart what is happening in each section by drawing abstract symbols, dancing, and so on.

Learning Form and Structure through Movement: B/I/A

- Using any piece from the repertoire, the teacher teaches students simple dance movements that complement each part of the formal structure of the music. This exercise works particularly well at first for rondo-type forms in which material is clearly distinguishable and where the return of material is a defining attribute. Students may also wave scarves while dancing the piece to indicate phrase shape and contour.

Music History Activities

Composer of the Week or Month: B/I/A

- Students study a different composer each week or month, exploring works composed for the piano and other instruments. Listen to the works and discuss stylistic and compositional traits that characterize their works. Then assign repertoire by these composers to each student.

Talk Show Interview: B/I/A

- The teacher assigns students to learn a work by a given composer and then research the composer and piece. The student performs their piece on the "Talk Show" followed by an interview in which classmates ask the "composer" questions about his life and works.

Name That Tune: B/I/A

- Play music as students enter the classroom. Students must guess the composer and the name of the work as well as justify their comments. The student who identifies the composer and work correctly wins a prize.

Name That Composer: B/I/A

- The teacher writes the title of a famous composition on the board, and students must name the work's composer. Correctly matched responses receive a prize.

Composer Timeline: B/I/A

- Construct a composer time line, including important dates, compositions, and other important historical information (e.g., arts, politics, birth and death dates for world figures) during the period. This activity puts music history into perspective.

Sound Canvas: B/I/A

- Listen to music from any period, especially the Impressionist period, and ask students to draw or paint what they hear.
- *New York Times* Review: I/A
- Assign students to listen to a composer's "work of the week" and then write a review. Students read their reviews at the next class.

Musical Twenty Questions: I/A

- A student thinks of a composer or musical or historical event. Students are given twenty questions to determine which composer or event the student had in mind.

Technology

The definition of technology is dependent upon the device and the age in which it is discussed. For example, the fortepiano was cutting-edge technology around the year 1700, but it is now commonly seen as an important historical artifact. Indeed, technology is dynamic and constantly changing, with a barrage of new technologies hitting the market every year.

In many ways, technology has helped to shape music throughout history. From Cristofori's fortepiano to the advent of MIDI and now the ability to teach long-distance via videoconferencing applications, the powerful impact of technology has been clearly demonstrated over time. The implications of these advancements are far-reaching, as technology has permeated our culture, touching nearly every aspect of our daily lives. From the quality and capability of musical instruments to the powers of communication devices that break down the geographic barriers of learning, the acquisition and sharing of information are becoming more and more accessible for the piano teacher. As such, educators are forced into dialogue to discuss, assess, and determine the role technology will play in their instructional and professional pursuits. As technology becomes more and more embedded in our culture, at least to a certain extent our teaching studios and instructional approaches must reflect such advancements.

Keyboard technology can be a viable educational resource for instructional enhancement. The benefits of such applications are manifested in the following ways:

- Enrichment of musical development and theoretical comprehension.
- Enhancement of the creative process through composition and improvisation
- Expansion of learning opportunities beyond the traditional lesson through computer-assisted instruction and drill/review applications
- Tracking student progress through software applications
- Visual and aural representation of printed notation
- Fostering effective practicing with advanced practice and tutorial features

Technology must always serve, support, and enhance the global curricular goals and should never be used as a substitute. It should be employed to enrich and strengthen music instruction by making it more effective, efficient, and enjoyable for the participating students and teachers alike. Indeed, technology is meaningful and useful only when there is demonstrated improvement in the student's level of playing and comprehension of musical concepts and principles. Teachers must never get lost in the luster of new technology simply for the novelty, but rather should look carefully at how technologies can be best applied to produce optimum learning. It is wise to remember that technology is a tool. It is the automobile, but the teacher is firmly positioned in the driver's seat.

Educators must consider how technology can be best used to meet the needs of any given student population. We must contemplate the world as lived by our students and begin to make the connection between what we teach and how it can be most effectively delivered to our student audience. As a result of the pervasive impact technology has had on human existence, there have been significant modifications in the ways in which information is received, processed, and shared by our students. In most circumstances, younger student populations already have an expert understanding of this technology, which negates the need for extensive training and tutorial processes that are often necessary for older students. Furthermore, because of the proliferation of personal communication devices such as cellular phones, text messaging, and online communities, and because of our fast-paced lifestyle, students often exhibit extended attention spans and an uncanny ability to multitask. It is not uncommon for these students to complete homework while simultaneously listening to music and text-messaging friends. To be sure, the patterns of learning relative to a given student population will determine how technology is applied in the delivery and reinforcement of keyboard knowledge and skills.

Integrating Technology in the Group Piano Classroom

Digital Pianos

Modern digital pianos are designed to provide the performer with the capability of producing the sound of an acoustic piano along with many additional and expanded features. Most digital pianos include features that have specific instructional implications, such as the following:

- Timbral/sound effects—Can be used to "orchestrate" ensemble literature or to provide students with an opportunity to perform with period instrument sounds. Instruments with sampled sounds are usually far superior to their synthesized counterparts.
- Rhythm/drum machines—Provide users with a variety of stylistic rhythmic patterns such as salsa, rumba, waltz, march, and so on. The tempo and meter of each pattern can be manipulated. Sophisticated instruments allow the user to create and program their own rhythmic patterns. These devices can be used as focus music for eurhythmic exercises or for tapping rhythmic patterns with percussive sounds.
- Sequencer—Provides user with record and playback features. Sophisticated instruments provide multiple track capabilities (see expanded explanation later in chapter).
- Tuning features—Allow students to experience historical tuning systems such as Pythagorean, mean tone, and equal temperament. Provide an important historical perspective on early piano literature.
- MIDI interface—Permits the digital piano to interface with external hardware and software devices.
- Chord/harmony features—This feature can be used to allow the beginning-level performer to play a single-line melody while the device provides a complementary harmonic or rhythmic accompaniment.
- Onboard tutoring or instructional systems—Such as MusicTutor by Roland

MIDI

MIDI, or musical instrument digital interface, is a binary computer language and a fundamental component of modern keyboard technology, including intelligent software applications. The quality of MIDI playback is limited to the quality of the playback device. A high-quality digital piano with sampled sound usually produces a much higher quality of sound than that which is produced by most synthesized sources.

Standard MIDI Files/MIDI Discs

Most piano methods now include auxiliary MIDI discs. These discs include standard MIDI files, commonly known as SMFs, which can be excellent instructional aids. SMF discs are ultimately more flexible than compact discs due to the operator's ability to adjust the tempo. MIDI accompaniment tracks also provide students with practice loops, enabling them to repeat difficult sections that may require extra attention. Orchestrated accompaniment tracks encourage students to play with continuity by challenging them to read ahead despite missed notes or rhythms.

MIDI discs often include multiple-track recordings (e.g., track 1: right-hand material; track 2: left-hand material; track 3: rhythm; track 4: background accompaniment), which provide the teacher with a variety of instructional possibilities. For instance, if students are reading only the right hand of a given work, that track can be muted while the left-hand track plays along. Accompaniment tracks add interest and serve to engage students by filling out the texture with an orchestrated backdrop.

Because MIDI players permit the user to play one track or a combination of tracks, the applications of such technology are endless. The following are sample instructional and performance applications using MIDI accompaniments:

- Sight-read a new piece using the disc to play one hand while the class plays the other hand.
- Ask the class to play along with all tracks to provide a steady pulse, promote continuity, and encourage them to read ahead.
- Omit right- hand and left-hand tracks and play with accompaniment tracks to supplement and embellish a student performances.
- Improvise upon a given accompaniment track.
- Use for at-home practice of ensemble music. The discs allow students to play along with the other ensemble parts.

Sequencing Devices

The use of sequencing technology in the group piano learning environment can be a very powerful instructional means. Sam Holland writes in his book *Teaching toward Tomorrow,* "If you can identify a musical problem, a sequencer can become a tool to help solve it. If you can identify a musical skill, a sequencer can become a tool to help teach it." Although a bold statement, it certainly carries a great amount of truth.

Sequencing technology is any device that can be utilized to record, play back, and manipulate MIDI data. This technology permits one to rethink or redistribute a musical score into a form that is usable and can be practically used. Sequencers can be either onboard features of a digital piano or keyboard, a separate hardware device, or run as software application. In its most basic form, the sequencer may be used as a means to record and play back a performance, providing the user with immediate feedback. From this point, its functions extend exponentially. Recorded MIDI data can be critically analyzed both aurally and visually, as well as edited. The operator can virtually control every element or event of the recorded performance. A few popular sequencing software titles include the following:

- Cakewalk
- Band-in-a-Box
- Master Tracks Pro
- Digital Performer
- Logic Pro

The following are a few ways in which a sequencer or sequencing software can be applied to group piano teaching:

- Students record scales and visually and aurally analyze resulting data. The feedback provided underscores issues such as a particularly heavy finger, uneven tone, timing, rhythmic imprecision, and velocity.
- Students play scales with prerecorded accompaniment tracks. They may also create and record their own scale accompaniments.
- For those methods for which MIDI discs are unavailable, teachers can prerecord written teacher accompaniments included in most methods. If a student has a digital piano at home, he too, depending on his level and the complexity of the accompaniment, can prerecord the accompaniment and use it as a duet.
- While sight-reading, students may record their performance. On playback, they can visually evaluate their performance for accuracy and precision.
- For any given sight-reading example, students record each hand on separate tracks. The track that is played by the student is muted. Ultimately, students should be challenged to play with both tracks. This procedure promotes continuity. Gradually the tempo can be increased.
- Record the Alberti bass accompaniment of a sonatina on one track. To develop proper balance of melody and accompaniment, students may play the melody with the prerecorded accompaniment track, working to achieve proper melodic projection. They may also shadow play the Alberti bass accompaniment while playing the melody.

- When learning fugal textures, students may be asked to record the voices of a fugue on separate tracks, with each voice assigned a unique, distinguishable timbre. This procedure allows students to focus on the characteristics of each voice and how they interact with one another. Gradually students combine the voices. Similarly, the procedure can be used to learn open scores, such as choral works or string quartets.
- Loop features are invaluable tools for practice repetition. Gradually the tempo can be increased as the student becomes more confident in playing the passage.
- View a composition in graphic notation. This procedure encourages students to understand the fundamental patterns of a work, including the basic melodic contour and shape. It may also assist students in the memorization process, providing them with a logical diagram of the essence of the compositional structure.
- Throughout the various stages of learning solo literature and especially prior to performances or examinations, teachers may require students to record their repertoire using the sequencer and to conduct a personal evaluation of their playing using the playback feature. Students can be asked to write and submit a written assessment of their performance, as well as a detailed list of strategies for improvement.
- For harmonization activities, students may be asked to record the melody on one track. Using the playback feature, they can then concentrate on the accompaniment by experimenting with the various chord choices that complement the melody. To expand the activity, students may be asked to listen to a partner's harmonization and then dictate, by ear, the chords that were used. By using the transposition feature that is standard on many sequencers, students can be asked to play the harmonic progression along with the recorded melodic track in a new key.[6]

Computer-Assisted Instruction

Computer-assisted instruction (CAI) is rapidly becoming established as a highly regarded instructional supplement and extension of traditional educational programs. CAI software provides both teacher and students with many benefits, serving to teach, drill, and reinforce key concepts and skills discussed in the group lesson, ranging from theoretical principles like constructing major triads or harmonic minor scales, to basic sight-singing and sight-reading exercises. Many titles also integrate composition and other creative activities as a part of their offerings. These applications address all student learning styles simultaneously and are becoming a familiar learning tool to our students. Aside from being an efficient method for concept drill and review, most software systematically tracks student progress, which not only is valuable information for the teacher but also is appreciated by parents and helpful to students.

Many teachers require their students to complete weekly computer-based assignments on computer workstations, either prior to or immediately after the group lesson. If multiple workstations are not available, teachers may conduct team-based or partner computer work. Some teachers facilitate computer software tournaments in which students seek to achieve the highest score or complete drill exercises in the shortest time. For younger students, there are many available software applications that frame instructional and drill-based activities in a gamelike environment, which, for many students, serves to motivate. Parents often acknowledge the benefits of these programs and purchase software for their child to use at home. A comprehensive listing of many excellent software titles can be found in "Group Piano Resources" on the companion Web site.

Notation Software

Notation software is quickly becoming a standard tool in the music teaching studio. These applications make it possible to create and publish technical exercises, as well as other instructional materials such as theory worksheets or quizzes. The software provides the teacher with enormous flexibility by enabling the user to generate professional-quality materials to meet students' specific needs. Additionally, the software can be used by students to publish their own original compositions and other class-related activities.

The two leading developers and publishers of consumer notation software are Finale, including Allegro, PrintMusic, and NotePad (www.makemusic.com); and Sibelius (www.sibelius.com).

Intelligent Software

Home Concert Xtreme, by Time Warp Technologies, is an intelligent, interactive, score-following software application that can be used for purposes of instruction, practice, and performance. Home Concert Xtreme, compatible with both Mac and Windows, can be interfaced with any MIDI keyboard. Standard MIDI files are loaded, and the user selects either one or two tracks to be displayed in notational form. Most publishers of piano methods now offer auxiliary SMFs. These, along with free downloadable files as well as self-created files, are compatible with the Home Concert Xtreme software.

Depending on the selected settings, the software follows the performer in tempo and dynamic expression, matching the accompaniment tracks with the performer's playing. The software also intuitively displays the score, coordinating the performer's location in the score with that which is projected on the screen.

Audio

Audio devices that record and play back have been staples in piano studios since they were made available to the mass market many years ago. Technology such as compact disc players and, more recently, digital audio devices such as iPods and MP3 players serve music educators in numerous ways, such as the following:

- Provides students with an aural image of works that are being studied, drawing attention to issues of musicality and expressive playing.
- Provides opportunities for students to record their group lesson or performances. These performances can be recorded using programs like Garage Band, transferred to a digital music player such as the iPod, or burned to a compact disc. The recordings can be used as a reference resource during at-home practice to remind students of particular practice techniques discussed during the lesson. They may also serve to compare former with current performances of repertoire. This can be especially motivating when a student hears how far a work has progressed throughout the various stages of learning.
- Many teachers make weekly listening assignments and provide students with audio files either on a compact disc or via website downloads. Web resources like iTunes allow the user to purchase and download high-quality professional recordings to digital music players. Students can readily listen to and analyze contrasting performances by concert artists. This activity will serve to inform their performance of the repertoire and perhaps even inspire new expressive and artistic ideas.
- Convert SMFs that accompany group piano texts to MP3 file format and transfer these to students' iPods or other MP3 devices for use during practice.

Video

Similarly, video technology can also be an invaluable instructional tool, allowing the student to record lessons and performances for reference. Beyond this, teachers may elect to record recitals and other studio events. Excerpts from these performances can be used to deliver performances in video and audio format to audiences worldwide via podcasts or video sharing host sites like YouTube. These excerpts may also be used for purposes of marketing by uploading material to a studio website. It is true that students are challenged to produce their best quality of work when they are aware that their performances will be showcased on a global platform.

Additionally, student performances can be recorded, then viewed and their strengths and weaknesses discussed by the class during a postperformance review session. Here, students function as the teacher, identifying problematic issues, either musical or technical, and ways these could be improved.

Video equipment can also be used to record and play back one's teaching for purposes of instructional analysis and review. The feedback provided is objective, providing the instructor with an accurate view of his teaching. It can be used to give the teacher the opportunity to intensively observe classroom activity in a more relaxed environment outside of the fast pace of the group lesson. Teachers are able to assess student comprehension of concepts and skills or evaluate underlying causes of confusion or student disruption.

Many university group piano teachers elect to videotape student exams. Students are asked to bring a videotape that is compatible with the instructor's recording equipment to each exam. After the exam, students are asked to review the recording and write a detailed assessment or analysis of their work. This provides both teacher and student with an objective record of the quality of work rendered at the exam.

Essential equipment needed to record and produce student performances includes the following:

- Digital piano
- Tripod
- USB connector cable or firewire
- Computer with Internet connection
- Video editing software such as iMovie or Movie Maker

Keyboard/Staff Displays

Visualizer

The Key/Note Visualizer has had a profoundly positive effect on group piano teaching and has become a fixture in most university group piano labs throughout this country. The device, which is manufactured by SCI Music Products, is a digital music instructional presentation tool that enables the instructor to display what is played on a MIDI keyboard on the Visualizer screen. The operator can choose to display pitches or chords on the keyboard and/or staff.

Classroom Maestro

The Classroom Maestro is a new electronic blackboard display system produced by Time Warp Technologies. When interfaced with a MIDI keyboard and projector, the software enables the instructor to display pitches, intervals, chords, scales, and keyboard hand positions. The device allows the user to project pitches on the grand staff, on singular staffs in treble or bass clef, or on any of the five C clefs. The software also displays an analysis of the pitches or chords that appear on the keyboard or staff, including note names, intervals, chord names in either jazz or Roman numeral form, and even scale names.

Projection Equipment and SMARTBoard Technology

Projection equipment like document cameras enhances learning by enabling the instructor to display scores or other materials for class discussion and instruction. Additionally, these devices allow instructors to project multimedia presentations such as PowerPoint or DVDs.

SMARTBoard technology is an interactive, touch-sensitive whiteboard visual learning environment. The device and accompanying software, which are interfaced with a computer and projector, allows the instructor to display and manipulate material as it is projected. The user can write on the board using the accompanying writing device or even by using a finger, with the resulting marks illuminated in a choice of colors. Instructors can prepare demonstration slides prior to each class using presentation software such as PowerPoint and/or notation software such as Finale or Sibelius. Musical scores, saved as PDF files, may also be scanned and projected on the screen. Further, by using the playback feature in Finale, the instructor can display a notated score and also provide the class with an aural representation of the visible score.

Other Instructional Multimedia Tools

The instructional media market is permeated with exceptional multimedia instructional tools such as DVDs and CD-ROMs. These materials, which combine sound with images, can be used to teach or supplement instruction related to music history, literature, or theory. Films bring to life historical musical figures through presentations that illustrate their life and works. Many interactive CD-ROM packages engage students in imaginative interactive activities. Live recordings of master performers and performances provide students with priceless musical experiences that may otherwise be geographically inaccessible or prohibitively expensive to attend.

Web-Based Support

Martha Hilley, coauthor of *Piano for the Developing Musician*, has extended her instruction beyond the classroom by creating a pioneering Web-based instructional support site (http://pdm6e.music.utexas.edu). The site features tutorials in which lesson content is rearticulated and reviewed. Here, students are able to access supplemental exercises that can be used to drill and reinforce concepts and skills that were discussed during the lesson.

Enterprising teachers are encouraged to develop their own online instructional resources in order to tailor-make materials expressly for their students and their specific needs. This may include PowerPoint teaching tutorials and lesson demonstrations. Hilley suggests the following software programs for the creation of such a Web resource:

- DreamWeaver
- Flash
- Shockwave
- Peak
- Director
- PowerPoint

Course Management Software

Course management software such as Blackboard, WebCT, and Moodle provides virtual learning and communication environments that enable instructors to facilitate student interaction outside the classroom through discussion forums. Additionally, it provides instructors with a platform on which to post class announcements, assignments, relevant audio and video files, and other course information such as syllabi, study guides, supplemental reading materials, instructional reviews, and tutorials. Students can access their grades via an online grade book, which is maintained by the instructor. All information is accessed through a secure, password-protected log in prompt. Students may also submit class assignments electronically through a digital drop-box feature.

Blackboard and its subsidiary WebCT are used primarily in college and university learning environments, due in part to the exorbitant cost to purchase and maintain. Alternatives to the more expensive Blackboard system do exist. Moodle is a free and open source software application that offers similar Web-based learning opportunities as those offered by Blackboard.

Videoconferencing Technology

Videoconferencing programs such as iChat or Skype empower teachers with the tools to provide instruction and support regardless of geographic location. The technology enables the teacher to supervise or assist students' at-home practice. All that is necessary to launch long-distance instruction is a Web camera and microphone, a program such as iChat or Skype, and a high-speed Internet connection.

Chapter 7

Group Piano and the Precollege Student

Group Piano Lessons for Children

Children are eager and capable learners who possess an insatiable curiosity about the world around them. According to Jean Piaget, their cognitive equilibrium is constantly challenged by new situations and experiences, resulting in the learning of new cognitive constructs and the assimilation of new ideas and skills. They love to explore, discover new things, and learn how these things operate. Indeed, children are intuitive learners and possess competent learning instincts. Jerome Bruner supports this assertion by stating that "the foundations of any subject can be taught to anybody at any age in some form."[1]

Children are also unabashedly and instinctively musical, and their intrinsic love for music manifests itself in many ways. Through their boundless energy they exhibit an innate love of music by way of natural expressions such as dancing, marching, or drumming to music or by singing along with a tune on the radio. For most children, to perform is to live. They are free of inhibitions and leap at every opportunity to showcase their knowledge and musical skills.

Some researchers suggest that a child's musical aptitude is malleable and even expandable through the age of nine, at which point the window of opportunity begins to close.[2] Thus, early childhood is the prime time in which to engage children in music study. These formative years provide a perfect opportunity to nurture a love for music, as well as a time to lay a solid musical foundation, which can be of immeasurable value to future musical and artistic pursuits. These studies can transcend the realm of music, potentially having a positive impact on other areas of cognitive and social development.

The piano is an excellent instrument on which to commence a child's journey of musical discovery. For the young student, the piano provides immediate musical experiences and rewards, enabling the child to make music at the very first lesson.

Unlike other instruments for which quality sound production can take months and even years to develop, a well-maintained piano will produce a beautiful sound from the first note played. Although expert pianism requires a refined technique and mature sense of musical expression, a child is capable of producing music at the piano from day one. Beyond this, the keyboard is arranged in a logical manner in regard to the relationship of sound, with keyboard geography, key location, and pitch remaining fixed and constant. Further, the piano is an all-encompassing instrument involving both melody and harmony, with a full spectrum of colorful sonorities, making the performance of the instrument of great interest and potential for the young musician.

General Considerations

Before one begins teaching a group of children, several basic considerations must be addressed to ensure a positive learning experience for both students and teacher.

Readiness

- Age: Most people classify the young learner as one who is from three to six years of age. Each child is different, so the acceptable age at which a child begins musical instruction should be determined on a case-by-case basis.
- Attention: The young learner usually possesses a limited attention span, with boys typically displaying more restricted levels of concentration than girls. Indeed, attention is often closely associated with age and gender. A few months can make a world of difference in this regard. As a result, lessons must be designed with this issue in mind. The student must have the ability to concentrate for the given length of a lesson, as well as be able to focus for brief, distributed periods of practice time.
- Physical coordination: Young learners are engaged in a time of great physical growth, with coordination developing at varying rates. One should bear in mind that the younger the child, the more limited his fine motor skills, as well as his ability to coordinate the mind, ears, and hands. Additionally, he may have a difficult time discerning between the left and right hands. The young student must be able to demonstrate a minimum level of finger dexterity, such as an ability to use the fingers independently.
- Social issues: To ensure a positive learning environment for all involved, the young student must also demonstrate an ability to work with others cooperatively and to some degree independently from the parent. Although it advisable for parents to observe children's classes from a distance, the student should be able to participate in lesson activities without the immediate assistance of the parent.

Other Characteristics of the Young Learner

- Curiosity: Children are supremely curious and abound with a desire to learn new things. This is evidenced in the endless number of unsolicited questions they pose, such as, "Why does the piano have black and white *buttons?*" or "How does the piano work without being *plugged in?*" This is an enormous advantage to learning, and the successful group piano teacher will make the most of such inquisitiveness. This age is ripe with opportunities for discovery learning–based activities. It is wise to remember that children view the world through a different lens and with a completely unique perspective. It is especially important for teachers of children to take a step back in time and consider how the students might best relate to and ultimately grasp a given concept at their present age.
- Memory: Although children often demonstrate an ability to quickly memorize what they hear, the information that is truly learned is often shallow and thus temporal. Therefore, significant repetition and reinforcement is of particular importance for younger students. Young students should be introduced to only a limited number of concepts at each lesson, all of which should be thoroughly reviewed and repeated over the following weeks.
- Imitation: Children are much like parrots, often repeating everything they hear. This, too, can be a major benefit for the group piano teacher. One should frequently employ musical modeling as an instructional strategy, calling upon students to imitate the sounds and expressive qualities of that which is heard (e.g., soft and loud, staccato and legato)
- Praise: Children love to be praised for their accomplishments, and they endeavor to please their superiors. Teachers should wisely use praise to edify and reward young learners for their achievements.

Class Size and Length

- Class size: Most teachers agree that the smaller the class size, the better. Therefore, a maximum number of four to six students per class is usually recommended, unless an assistant is present, in which case additional students can be enrolled and properly taught.
- Class length: Again, the age of the participating students will figure significantly when determining the class length. Taking into account student attention and concentration, a forty-five-minute lesson is usually a desirable maximum duration for a class consisting of young children, whereas older students tend to be able to sustain concentration for lessons of an hour or longer. Younger students are often very energetic, and the environment can be quite exhilarating. Thus, the lesson must be quickly paced, with carefully timed transitions. One must be carefully attuned to student attention levels at all time during the class, always prepared to move to a new activity when one senses that students are losing interest in a particular exercise.

Learning Environment

- Space: Teaching young students requires much physical space in which to conduct various eurhythmic and other activities.
- Delivery: To maintain student engagement, each lesson should be rich in activities and games involving singing, listening, rhythm, and playing experiences. Directions should be concise and delivered using language that is understandable for the young learner.

Several early childhood musicianship programs seek to provide the very young learner with a solid musical foundation through curricula specially designed for this student population. Some of these programs offer a combination of general musicianship training with piano instruction. Although the piano is the primary instrumental medium for such instruction, these courses appear to be geared toward laying a sound musical framework to enable the child to later focus on any instrument with confidence. The following is a selected list of such programs. Programs that provide a combination of general musicianship training along with piano instruction are preceded by an asterisk (*).

- *Harmony Road (www.harmonyroadmusic.com)
- Kindermusik International (www.kindermusik.com)
- *Musikgarten (www.musikgarten.org)
- Music Together (www.musictogether.com)
- *Music for Young Children (www.myc.com)
- Dalcroze Method (www.dalcrozeusa.org)
- Kodaly Method (www.oake.org)
- Orff Method (www.aosa.org)
- *Suzuki Method (www.suzukiassociation.org)
- *Yamaha Music Education System (www.yamaha.com)

Placement Examination and Interview for Children

The placement interview for the beginning class for children is especially important. Here, the teacher evaluates the child's ability to discriminate between two pitches by playing one low and one high, and asking the child to decide which of the two notes is lower and higher. The teacher should next sing two pitches and ask the student to echo the same pitches. The teacher may also sing a familiar folk tune once, and then ask the student to sing along with him the second time. Additionally, students may be asked to play back simple melodies by ear. These exercises test students' ability to match pitch, as well as their pitch memory.

To assess rhythmic perception, the teacher can conduct clap-back exercises. This involves clapping or tapping a rhythm and then asking the student to respond by clapping the same rhythm. Muscular control and general physical coordination can be evaluated by teaching the C-major five-finger pattern by rote. Students should play both hands separately and then together. Tabletop or fallboard exercises such as slow trill patterns can also reveal important fine motor skill readiness. For the transfer student, sight-reading should be included on the audition.

The teacher should attempt to get to know the student by encouraging conversation about favorite activities, music, school subjects, animals, or other topics of interest. One might also ask the student to read instructions from a method book or a passage in a children's book to assess his reading level. This conversation should also determine the student's interest in piano study and his willingness to devote himself to the required practice time. The interview also yields an important perspective on the maturity of the student. Figure 7.1 provides a sample group piano placementt form to be used when assessing and placing children in groups.

The Parent Interview

The initial interview should be designed as a time not only to assess the student's aptitude but also to communicate valuable information to the potential student's parents. A studio policy should be distributed and discussed in detail during the interview. This policy should include all salient features of the studio, as well as critical logistical information such as the instructional schedule and calendar (including all studio events, festivals, competitions, etc.), scheduling procedures, tuition and fees, payment options, attendance and makeup policy, student practice expectations, and expectations for parental involvement. This document should clearly articulate the benefits of group instruction, as well as the teacher's philosophy of education, instructional approach, and methodologies. Both student and parents should sign a copy of the policy, with a copy of the document kept on file by the teacher for future reference. Policies that are clear and firm are much less likely to be abused.

The interview must also include a serious discussion of the expectations of the parents, including their role in facilitating and supervising quality practice at home, as well as methods that can motivate children to high levels of productivity. Parents should know their specific role in this regard and should be held accountable, at least in part, for their child's practice, which should be a joint

Student Name: Date:

Parent(s)/Guardian Name:

E-mail Address:

Phone Number:

Previous Music Study Experience:

Score students on the following elements using the numbers 1 through 5 (5 represents the most proficient playing). During the examination, note the student's attention span and interest level, attitude, and overall musical sensitivity.

1. Pitch Discrimination
   A. Play any two-note combination. Instruct students to indicate which of the two notes, first or second, is higher. 1 2 3 4 5
   B. Sing a folk tune such as "Twinkle, Twinkle Little Star." Request the student to sing along the second time. Note the student's intonation and ability to match pitch. 1 2 3 4 5
2. Rhythmic Perception
   Clap rhythmic patterns two times. Instruct the student to echo. 1 2 3 4 5
3. Muscular Control/Fine Motor Skills
   A. Teach the C-major five-finger pattern by rote.
      - Hands separately 1 2 3 4 5
      - Hands together 1 2 3 4 5
   B. Away-from-keyboard exercise
      - Alternating 1–2 1 2 3 4 5
      - Alternating 2–3 1 2 3 4 5
      - Alternating 3–4 1 2 3 4 5
      - Alternating 4–5 1 2 3 4 5
4. Sight-reading (for transfer students with previous experience only) 1 2 3 4 5

Total _____/50

Comments and Recommendations:

Examiner's Signature: ______________________________

FIGURE 7.1 Group Piano Placement Examination Form for Children

responsibility, at least for a time. They should be made aware of exactly how much practice the teacher expects. Additionally, parents should be informed of other critical issues such as prompt delivery and pickup of their child from the lesson, as well as on-time payment of tuition and fees. This is also an opportunity to provide parents with various resources, including a suggested reading list of materials that contain information regarding ways to enrich their child's piano study.

The meeting is also a good occasion to find out more about the child from the parent's perspective, including what motivated the child to study piano in the first place, as well as specific information that may be of assistance to the instructor regarding how the child best learns. This is also a time to discover if either of the parents or siblings play an instrument, particularly the piano. The teacher should also communicate the importance of having a quality instrument, either acoustic or a digital piano with weighted keys, and adjustable bench at home that is positioned in a distraction-free location, which is conducive to practice. If the instrument is acoustic, it is wise to articulate the value of regular tuning and maintenance. Parents can be referred to Larry Fine's *A Piano Book* for further information on this topic. For the very young child, a pedal extender might also be a good investment. An inexpensive alternative can be a stack of carpet samples or a simple wooden box on which the child can rest his feet.

The Role of Parents

The parent is a vital element of successful group piano study for children. The success of the child hinges, at least in part and many times significantly so, upon parental involvement and support. Parents hold a critical position in the pyramid of success, which involves three parties: the student, the teacher, and the parents. They will serve to encourage, guide, supervise, and facilitate at home practice. Because of their significant role in the educational enterprise, parents need to be made aware of and accept their responsibility from the outset. Parents must understand and fully agree to the expectations set forth by the teacher regarding the required participation in their child's piano studies.

The task of parents, especially those of young students, is to take the lesson home and repeat it daily with the child until the next lesson. Parents become the teachers and practice facilitators away from the teaching studio. They are an extension of the teacher, the eyes and ears during the student's daily practice.

Their level of involvement can often determine the success or failure of the child's musical experience.

It is my policy to require at least one parent to attend each class, sitting so as not to interfere with the student's focus. Throughout the lesson the parent is charged with taking notes and learning the concepts and techniques taught so he can model or, at least monitor, the student's practice at home. I also encourage parents to videotape the lesson in order to have an audiovisual reference should questions arise during the week of practice. The student and parent use this resource to replicate the lesson at home.

When the parent is unable to attend the entire lesson, it is a minimal requirement that he or a representative attend the summary portion of the lesson as the assignment is given. This will give the parent critical information regarding the requirements for the forthcoming week of practice. When parents are present during the announcement of the assignment, students will feel more compelled to fulfill the assignment. With this policy, both parent and student are aware of expectations and are thus accountable to fulfill them. Further, parents should freely and regularly discuss issues related to music study with their child. The drive home is a wonderful opportunity for the parent to engage the child on what was studied at the lesson and what specifically was learned. Such conversations should happen regularly throughout the week.

Parents should be committed to assisting their child in scheduling a daily practice time that is free of distractions, at a time when the child can be focused. This may require distributed practice—several short practice periods—especially for the young student. For the young student, it is necessary for the parent to practice with their child, duplicating the lesson material on a daily basis. For all others, the parent must help the child structure and focus each practice session. It is wise for the parent to conduct random practice checks in which the child is asked what he is specifically attempting to achieve in his practice at a given moment, and what strategies he is using to accomplish this goal. Practice must be a priority, and the parent is partly responsible for making it happen. After each practice session, the parent and child should plan the next one, discussing what was accomplished during the present practice and detailing what will be addressed at the next rehearsal. The parent should help the student foster good practice habits, as well as monitor and address any unproductive concerns. Eventually, as the student advances in his studies, parents can encourage independent practice, which can be facilitated by gradually relinquishing control of the practice to the student.

It is the job of the parent to provide the teacher with regular feedback regarding the student's practice at home. This should include information related to the amount and quality of practice, as well as insight into other relevant issues (e.g., educational, personal, emotional, social) that may be affecting the child's study. Parents should be encouraged to communicate openly with the teacher, knowing that the information they provide can have a significant impact not only on the success of their child but also on that of all students who participate in the class.

Some teachers may even encourage parents to take lessons so they can better assist their child. Whether or not this is the case, the teacher can regularly provide parents with suggested reading that can enhance their understanding of what the child is learning, as well as ways to aid the child during his practice at home. There are many fine resources available to the parent, including the following:

The Parent's Guide to Effective Practicing by Nancy O'Neill Breth (Hal Leonard)
The Practice Revolution: Getting Great Results from the Six Days between Lessons by Philip Johnston (Practicespot Press)

The parent can enhance a child's piano study in a multitude of additional ways aside from direct practice at the keyboard. First, and perhaps foremost, the parent should seek to instill a love of music in his child by regularly listening to classical and other styles of music with the child either at home via quality recordings or through live performances. The latter can be particularly inspiring for young students as they witness a "live" artist communicating the joy and wonder of their art. Whether the music be live or recorded, the student should be engaged in discussions regarding these performances to elicit his personal thoughts and stimulate critical thinking and listening. Indeed, parents are a vital component in a child's study of music, and play a critical role in ensuring that practicing is both fun and productive.

Communication with Parents

The teacher should provide parents with written evaluations of student progress on a regular basis. These term reports should detail the individual student's development, including both strengths and areas of deficiency. The assessment should address issues such as:

- Technical development and physical coordination
- Reading, rhythm, and ear training
- Musicianship and artistry
- Level of motivation and attitude toward the instrument
- Ability to concentrate and attend to task
- Overall work ethic
- Quality of preparation for the weekly lesson
- Ability to self-evaluate
- Social skills and participation in group activities

The teacher can take note of student strengths and weaknesses by writing brief comments for each student in a journal following each class. Some teachers may employ a grading system to evaluate student progress. Although inherently subjective, such a system may help to measure and communicate the quality of each student's work in quantifiable terms.

Many teachers produce a monthly newsletter and use the medium to communicate important studio informational updates (e.g., enrollment deadlines, competition regulations, recital details) and to provide parents with news articles or other relevant readings related to their child's piano education. The newsletter provides a means for the teacher to highlight student successes and to feature the specific accomplishments of selected groups.

Scheduling

Scheduling group piano lessons can be challenging, especially given the extremely full schedules of many present-day students. It can be difficult to find common times in which evenly aged and leveled students are available to meet. Despite these difficulties, it is true that anything worth doing is certainly worth the extra effort. Students who make piano a priority will be willing to adjust other activities to facilitate their piano studies.

It is wise to distribute a scheduling worksheet along with the studio registration form several weeks before the teaching year commences. The worksheet should list, by level, the possible lesson times. The parent is required to rank the choices in order of preference, while marking off those times that are unavailable. The parent should communicate a reason for the time marked as unavailable. Oftentimes students of a similar age will have the same conflicts, so this information can be of particular assistance.

Methods, Materials, and Equipment

Although a limited number of available methods are written expressly for teaching groups of average-age students, most standard methods can be readily adapted and modified for use in group teaching. Many teachers draw upon group piano textbooks created for use in university group piano programs and find these to be excellent supplemental resources. Teachers who use a combination of private and group instruction often employ supplemental materials and games for the monthly or quarterly group lesson and utilize repertoire that was assigned and studied in the private lesson. Again, it is important to remember that a method must not dictate that which is taught. One must be committed to delivering a comprehensive curriculum, which requires the teacher to draw upon a variety of resources.

A listing of the few methods that have been created expressly for teaching piano to children in a group environment can be found on the companion website.

Group Piano and the Adolescent Student

Like all student populations, adolescent students present the group piano teacher with unique challenges. Indeed, teaching these students can be both demanding and frustrating for the teacher. In an attempt to penetrate their complex facade, educators must seek to understand the adolescent student in order to successfully negotiate the idiosyncrasies involved in teaching them. Armed with this knowledge, the teacher stands to maximize his instructional impact, the result of which can be a rewarding and satisfying educational experience for students and teacher alike.

Adolescence is a volatile period in human development, characterized by dramatic physical, emotional, intellectual, and social change. Driven largely by increased hormonal activity, adolescence is a developmental stage that bridges childhood with adulthood. Students aged twelve through eighteen are typically regarded as adolescent, although the lines of distinction are becoming increasingly blurred. In this intermediary period of life, students can at times feel confused, as though they are lost in a vast chasm in which their identity is connected to that of neither a child nor an adult. During this transitional phase, adolescents possess a powerful desire to be treated as adults while attempting to shed the lingering vestiges of their childhood. Concurrently, adolescents seek independence from their parents, as validation from peers becomes increasingly important. Adolescents are intensely motivated by the acceptance they receive from their peers. In fact, adolescent self-esteem is often directly linked to the attention they receive from peers. In many cases, the popularity derived from one's peer interest group fuels and drives the adolescent student.

In the throes of rapid physiological development, the adolescent student can become very self-conscious and at times embarrassed by the dramatic bodily and emotional changes they face. In large part due to such dramatic physiological changes, many students are launched on what seems to be an emotional roller-coaster ride, which is exemplified by unpredictable and temperamental moods and emotions. At times adolescents may even struggle to separate emotional from rational responses. Here, an accurate perception of reality is distorted due to fluctuating emotions. Such personal and social issues frequently impact the adolescent student's ability to stay on task, which can directly affect the resulting quality and level of their productivity.

These years are often marked by contradictions in mood and behavior. The multifaceted personalities of the teenage student can exhibit moments of intellectual and social brilliance followed by periods of great immaturity and foolishness. The delineation between youthfulness and maturity is blurred. Conversation can be at once witty and charming, and then rapidly become indignant and recalcitrant. Attitudes can swiftly change from captivated interest to total ambivalence. On one day, the teacher might find his class to be collegial and productive, while at the next meeting it is defined by a negative attitude and unwillingness to work. To be sure, the adolescent student population can be one of great contradiction.

On a more positive side, the cognitive, intellectual functioning of the adolescent student becomes more advanced. Here, the student is capable of more sophisticated abstract reasoning, which enables them to deal with many variables simultaneously. Thus, they are able to engage in more complex problem-solving situations by generating multiple, appropriate solutions to any given problem. Advancements in verbal skills enable adolescent students to articulate their thought processes more clearly. Such language abilities permit students to express their inner turmoil and emotions, oftentimes in rather melodramatic fashion.

With this information in mind, the group piano teacher should adapt or adjust his instructional approach to meet the needs of the adolescent student. Communication with teenage students should be guided by careful, sensitive listening, taking note of what students say not only verbally but also nonverbally. Students speak volumes through body language, requiring the teacher to be perceptive to what is being said without a word being spoken.

With the best of intentions, some teachers may initially try to compensate for feelings of student disconnect by employing excessive humor and enthusiasm that may be perceived by the student as fabricated. Therefore, the language and delivery style used must resonate with our students without sounding artificial.

These students desire to be treated as adults and will respect the teacher who regards them as such. Teachers must be sincerely determined to connect with these students and attempt to relate and empathize with genuine interest in their present situations. The ability to do so will often determine whether they are open to our instruction. One way to accomplish this is by taking a personal interest in the success of each student, validating his achievements with honest praise in front of his classmates. In every case, the teacher should avoid embarrassing students in a way that may cause them to feel incompetent in front of their peers. Correction must therefore be given in a tactful, sensitive manner so as not to endanger students' delicate self-concept.

Flexibility and patience are hallmarks of an effective instructional approach when teaching adolescents. One must be willing to modify the content and method of delivery in a way that can successfully connect with the students' attitudes toward learning on any given day. A significant sum of fortitude and persistence is necessary, as well as the capacity to quickly adapt to and deal with student emotions with care.

Deeply impacted by socialization, students at this age long to fit into a community of like-minded people. They begin to develop a sense of identity that is built around those intellectual, artistic, and athletic pursuits to which they devote themselves. Consequently, adolescent students often wish to associate only with others who share the same passions, and thus develop communities of identity that are uniquely their own. The group learning environment, in which students are surrounded by peers who possess the same artistic drive, serves as a medium in which introspective students may gradually open up and engage in productive dialogue with their more extroverted peers. To be sure, the sociocultural nature of the group learning environment can exert powerful influence on adolescent student motivation. Students are deeply concerned about how they present themselves to their peers, vis-à-vis their preparation for the lesson and for public performances.

The early adolescent years often demonstrate an increased dropout rate for students who participate in private piano lessons only. It is usually during this period that students who have studied since childhood begin to face the challenges of the intermediate and early advanced literature. When compounded with the physical and emotional struggles inherent in this time in their lives, many students throw their hands in the air and yell "retreat." The group setting can serve to motivate and sustain interest. Students at this age like challenges as long as they are framed in a way that appeals to their curiosity. Therefore, the materials used with adolescent students must be relevant and engaging. Teachers must be willing to teach to the students' diverse interests in musical styles. Well-selected literature can be infinitely more motivating than nearly any other instructional tactic. As pianists we are blessed with a diverse and exciting repertoire. This vast collection provides students and teachers with a wide assortment of pedagogically sound literature from which to choose, based both on our students' stylistic interests and on the teacher's instructional objectives.

Adolescent students also appreciate the freedom to express themselves through their art. Thus, it makes pedagogical sense to attempt to channel their interest in the piano through such creative activities as composition and improvisation, in addition to performance repertoire of all styles.

When scheduling adolescent students, one must negotiate the many extracurricular activities in which they often are engaged. To complicate matters, adolescent students often hold after-school jobs. Therefore, it is important to identify a list of common times at which students are available. Depending on the size of one's studio, multiple groups of a given age-group may be formed to accommodate busy schedules. Sometimes scheduling conflicts become impossible to avoid. In these cases, the student may be called upon to prioritize his activities to determine which will take precedence. Some teachers may be willing to refer students to another teacher who has a group offering that is compatible with the student's schedule. Whatever the case, we must be guided by the principle that what is best for the student is best for us.

In light of their busy schedules, adolescent students often struggle to sensibly manage their time. To assist them in this regard, it is critical that we help students set reasonable, attainable goals that take into consideration the individual student's needs and current skill level. Beyond this, and very important, the group should collectively establish its own goals, which will guide and challenge students to increased levels of productivity.

Chapter 8

Group Piano and the Adult Hobby Student

Recent years have seen a considerable surge in adult piano class offerings in this country. Indeed, a steady and marked increase in adult participation in music study over the past thirty years can be evidenced in the findings of several longitudinal research studies and by the exponential growth of program offerings designed expressly for this population.[1] Some reports suggest that the segment of the population aged fifty and older is the fastest-growing group of new music students.[2]

Increased interest in adult education in general, and in music study specifically, may be attributed to several factors. Social perception of adulthood has been altered in recent decades, with the general attitude toward how one will choose to spend one's retirement years significantly modified from that of previous generations. Perhaps in part due to increased human longevity and an overall better quality of life for a large portion of the U.S. adult population, there has been augmented interest in and commitment to lifelong learning. Beyond this, current research suggests that such continuing education endeavors may have positive health benefits.

Statistics show that adults are living longer lives and are retiring at younger ages. Some indicators suggest that over the next sixteen years the population of people over fifty will grow by about 75 percent while the number of those under fifty will grow by only 1 percent. Other research suggests that over the next decade the percentage of the world's population over sixty-five will more than double, while the world's youth population will increase by only 6 percent.[3] Furthermore, some reports suggest that baby boomers, those born between 1946 and 1964, make up an estimated 28 percent of the U.S. population (about 78 million). Ten thousand boomers turn fifty years old every day; 8,000 turn sixty daily.[4] Such demographic information signals potentially significant social, psychosocial, and economic implications for our society.

As part of this transformation of our social complexion, adults have begun to reevaluate the now-antiquated linear life plan, which maintains that education occurs during one's youth, with the middle years being devoted to work and professional activity, leaving leisure activity reserved exclusively for the elderly during retirement. With the revised outlook, commonly referred to as a "blended life plan," retirement is now viewed as an opportunity to merge leisure activity with continuing education.[5] Many retirees now exhibit a desire to spend their retirement learning new skills and taking on new challenges. Perhaps influencing this development is the fact that we as a society are more educated than ever before in history. Trends show that the more education one has received, the more one desires to participate in the broad range of available educational endeavors. We are a society of learners who seek to stay abreast of rapidly changing advancements in technology and other new discoveries.

Motivating Factors and Goals of Adult Piano Study

What, then, motivates adults to study piano? To be sure, there are a variety of reasons. Many adults seek out new learning experiences as a way to fill increased time for leisure activity often generated by life-altering events such as retirement, the "empty nest" syndrome, or relocation to a new city or retirement community. Some adults desire to be involved in activities that boost their sense of pleasure or heighten their sense of self-concept. Piano study becomes a medium for personal enrichment and a way to enhance one's quality of life. Some working adults approach the piano as a deviation or distraction from demanding careers and the hectic pace of life. Their involvement in piano study serves a therapeutic role, providing a source of relaxation from the pressures of professional life. For others, piano study in adulthood is an opportunity to realize a lifelong ambition, to fulfill a dream of learning the instrument. Many adult students studied piano as a child but terminated their studies for various reasons. Others wish to build upon their existing knowledge of music and to develop preexisting pianistic skills, while others who did not have the luxury of piano study as a child desire to first experience these joys as an adult. Additional motivators for adult study may be a desire to serve a local church as an accompanist or rehearsal pianist. Still others may wish to accompany a dance class or accompany sing-along events at their community center.

A relatively recent trend shows that there are many adults who have children that study the piano and therefore decide to take up the instrument themselves in an effort to assist their child. One study indicated that children of adults who were involved in some form of music making were more likely to become involved in music themselves, maintaining this interest and participation throughout their adult years.[6] Many excellent materials are available that readily facilitate ensemble or collaborative music making between a parent and child.

A need for socialization may also play a motivational role in adult piano study. A study conducted in 1996 reported that a majority of adult respondents preferred to participate in leisure activities that were conducted in group-based, social environments.[7] Because of the potential for positive dynamics involved in adult group piano study, including peer encouragement and support, teachers usually observe a heightened sense of motivation among class members, as well as an overall decrease in student attrition when compared with private study. Despite the diversity of age, gender, education, and professional activity among adult group piano student populations, they all possess a unifying link: an intense love of music. This common denominator helps generate a pleasant, nonthreatening and supportive learning environment.

For many adults, issues of health become a motivating factor. As a result, many adults seek programs that help them enhance or maintain their quality of life. They are searching for ways to feel better—mentally, emotionally, and physically—and ultimately for ways to sustain quality health. They acknowledge the intrinsic value of music study as well as the positive health benefits that come along with such involvement, including relaxation and stress relief. They understand that mental and physical prowess is a "use it or lose it" proposition, and that music study is a means for exercising these "muscles." Many adults are aware of recent media attention highlighting research that suggests that stimulation of the mind can help to slow and even prevent loss of cognitive functioning commonly linked to aging. Further, there is evidence that such activity can preserve or at least retard the decline of fine motor movement ability.

Perhaps above all, the study of music and the piano is a vehicle for self-expression and an opportunity to express oneself artistically using piano as the medium. These students seek to learn for the subject's inherent value. Adult students who decide to study piano are wholly enchanted by music and acknowledge the joy found in the process of making music. Thus, piano study gives them an opportunity to be personally involved in this wondrous art.

The Adult Learner

Recent advances in adult educational research have elevated awareness of the potential and special attributes of the adult learner. Often referred to as *androgogy*, the academic discipline has gained significant attention, particularly since the

1960s. The term *andragogy*, derived from the roots *andr*, meaning "man," and *gogy*, meaning "teacher of," can be defined as the science of adult education and learning. Malcolm Knowles distinguishes pedagogy from andragogy to reflect the differences in teaching and learning for children and adults.[8] Jost Reischmann goes further to suggest that androgogic research explores both intentional and passive learning carried out by adults. He contends that this research attempts to understand and support, both in theory and in practice, lifelong and life-wide education.[9]

Research in the field of androgogy has helped to illuminate the capacity for learning as well as other characteristics of adult learners, serving to debunk the myth that humans reach a point at which they become too old or unable to learn. Although the rate of learning may slow gradually as one ages, intelligence does not necessarily decrease with age. Indeed, adults are usually capable learners who possess the ability to develop musical skills despite the process of aging.[10]

Characteristics of the Adult Learner

Adults bring a unique attitude to learning.[11] Unlike children, who are more naturally inclined to accept specific and controlled teacher direction, adults usually prefer a more flexible approach to learning in which they have a significant say in how classes are conducted. Consequently, the adult learning environment must be designed with mutual respect and partnership based on the support of the instructor. Communication must then be guided by a sense of collegiality, sensitivity, and an overall atmosphere of collaboration. Here, the teacher is a facilitator of learning. As such, the teacher should never speak condescendingly toward his adult student group, and an authoritarian approach should be avoided at all costs. Rather, the teacher assumes the role of peer and colleague. In this way, learning becomes a joint venture between students and teacher, guided by the principles of shared responsibility and cooperative decision making.

In many ways, adults are self-directed in their approach to learning, often displaying significant autonomy and independence. Adulthood and maturity typically bring about an increased awareness of the necessity to take charge of one's life. This understanding plays out in the educational realm, in which adult students seek to exercise some form of control over the learning process. In an effort to direct their educational pursuits, adults frequently approach piano study with a preset ideology that includes well-developed ideas for what they desire to accomplish, as well as how lessons should progress to help them realize these predetermined goals. For some, the goal may be simply to play their favorite "golden oldies," whereas others aim their sights on more lofty aspirations such as their version of Carnegie Hall. The wise teacher will strike a balance between permitting some self-direction and offering carefully guided structure as needed. With this said, it is important to note that too much freedom can generate an increased sense of anxiety for adult students.

Because "learning to play the piano" means different things to different people, it is important to have an honest conversation at the outset of adults' piano study to determine the specific goals of both students and teacher. Bach and the Beatles need not clash. There has to be give-and-take. Students will appreciate the opportunity to be actively involved in defining learning objectives. For that reason, goals should be established as a result of mutual agreement between student and teacher. Teachers should attempt to honor students' individual goals while seeking to provide a balanced piano education. Indeed, it is crucial that both students and teachers be on the same page prior to the commencement of lessons.

Many adult students come to piano study with high and often unrealistic expectations, having spent years listening to exceptional performances by the world's finest artists. They desire to creatively express themselves, and they desire to achieve advanced levels of artistry with immediate results. In turn, they may become impatient with the process involved in acquiring the highly sophisticated skills of a pianist. Therefore, teachers should employ pieces that are taught by ear early on in the learning process. These pieces provide students with the feeling of success through the creation of appealing music right from the start.

Perhaps the most helpful guidance that can be provided by the instructor, both during the initial conversation and throughout the entire learning process, is that of helping students establish and maintain practical expectations. Honesty is key. Students should be informed that musical mastery takes considerable time and patience. It is the responsibility of the teacher to promptly work to dissolve any unfair and lofty expectations. One should avoid offering the average student false hope of someday having a concert career. Although it cannot be ruled out, such chances are certainly very slim. Instead, goals such as performing one's favorite show tunes or accompanying the congregational singing of a hymn at church may be more appropriate and attainable. Careful goal-setting may mean the difference between progressive levels of improvement versus losing students early on due to frustrations caused by such impracticable goals.

With this said, the teacher must also communicate the specific expectations he holds for his students and clearly articulate the work and commitment involved to successfully learn to play the piano. Specific strategies for achieving agreed-upon goals should be notated, and copies should be kept on file. Assessment of student progress begins first with establishing achievable benchmarks. For the adult student, assessment and evaluation are based on mutual consideration of self-collected evidence. Especially in the case of adult students, there is significantly more shared responsibility involved in the process of assessment. Periodic reassessment conversations should be scheduled after classes have begun to ensure that both parties are assuming full responsibility for realizing their stated goals.

Adults are intrinsically and voluntarily motivated, often by a strong sense of curiosity. Usually they have made a personal decision to study piano, having decided to invest the time and money necessary to achieve their musical aspirations. Having developed a sense of self-discipline and a defined work ethic over the course of their adult and professional lives, many adult students are highly motivated learners bringing to their piano study a tremendous amount of enthusiasm and optimism.

Adults tend to be motivated to learn skills and information that is relevant and immediately applicable to their lives. Therefore, carefully crafted immediate and short-term goals are essential for sustaining adult student motivation and interest. To achieve this, the learning content and experience must be both meaningful and useful. Adults desire to directly employ learned skills via practical applications. Consequently, adult learning is often best facilitated using experiential and inquiry-based techniques.

Because of the accumulation of advanced-level verbal and analytical skills over the course of their lifetime, adults usually prefer a more verbally oriented approach to learning that is rich in analogy.[12] They are appreciative when we as teachers make connections or note similarities of a concept to an activity in which adults participate on a daily basis. Thus, a verbal or conceptual approach to learning is typically a preferred mode of learning. With this said, adult students should still experience a concept or skill before the symbol and name are given. This discovery-based step can be reduced somewhat in length, in comparison to learning sequences involving children, with more time spent on verbal explanation and discussion.

Although some will enjoy learning the intricacies of music theory and history, the majority of adults wish to skip directly to the repertoire. They desire to be able to play familiar music and demand instant gratification in this regard. Here, the trick for the teacher is to present and pace materials in a way that supplies the adult student with a well-rounded curriculum while satisfying their immediate desire to play familiar music.

It is critical to keep in mind that adult students maintain multiple roles, often juggling the demands and pressures of family, professional, and social responsibilities. Because of this factor, group piano teachers must be highly sensitive to their students' more primary obligations. This demands both flexibility and accommodation. For example, teachers should set event deadlines well in advance to provide students with enough time for preparation, while being able to adjust or adapt when incidents arise that cause these deadlines to be impossible to meet.

Similarly, teachers should seek to understand student limits by tailoring the curriculum to fit the needs of the student clientele and making any other necessary accommodations. Working adult students are often presented with a limited amount of available, uninterrupted practice time. For these and most adult students, piano study is purely a hobby. Therefore, teachers should be careful to avoid implementing rigorous practice requirements. Conversely, if students are encouraged to practice in small segments using distributed practice, many will actually spend longer periods at the instrument outside of class. Teachers can also assist students by teaching them how to practice using efficient, results-oriented strategies. Also, longer class periods can facilitate in-class practice, giving students ample time to rehearse to ensure that concepts are understood before they leave the classroom. Due to the expanded attention span of most adults, a longer lesson length divided by a brief break is not only possible but also most often appreciated.

Other accommodations include scheduling lessons at a time when students can easily attend. This may translate to evening or weekend hours, or perhaps even lunch hour programs. Some teachers offer biweekly classes for adult professionals who travel frequently. Depending on the number of adult students enrolled in one's program, it can be helpful to offer multiple sections at varying levels of advancement. Such offerings enable adults to attend a different class of similar level should they have an occasional conflict with their regularly scheduled class. For senior adults, accessible parking is greatly appreciated, as well as coordinated travel arrangements for lessons during the winter months or when other inclement weather conditions may make travel difficult.

One must also consider the vast accumulation of knowledge and previous learning that most adult hobby students bring to their piano study. This experience and knowledge base can be an invaluable asset, a sort of treasure trove, from which the instructor can draw. This clientele may include physicians, engineers, lawyers, scientists, professors, and other highly educated individuals. The teacher must consider this background and how the students' previous education and experience might impact their study of the instrument. Most adult students appreciate any attempts by the instructor to make associations between musical concepts and concepts related to their professional activity and life experiences.

The penetrating questions asked by adult piano students are typically quite different from the questions of the child beginner. Some adults approach the instrument through the scientist's or physicist's lens, often asking mathematically complex questions. Many attempt to overquestion or rationalize concepts. They are often decidedly analytical in their approach to learning, having developed significant higher-level reasoning. Such analytical thinking can prove to be both a benefit and a hindrance. Challenges often arise due to the adult student's disconnect between intellectual comprehension and refined motor skill control. As a result, these students can become easily frustrated when the cognitive and physical aspects fail to rapidly merge and immediate progress is not immediately experienced.

Potential Problems and Other Considerations

Although adults are typically highly motivated at the outset of their study, there exists a high potential for attrition. Some factors that may contribute to dropout include the following:

- Frustration due to an inability to realize high expectations in a short period of time
- An incomplete understanding of the time and patience required to learn a new instrument
- Discouragement related to an inability to rapidly develop the refined cognitive-technical mastery involved in piano playing
- An inability to devote oneself to the necessary practice
- The perception that one is not good at the piano, and that all efforts to learn are futile
- A lack of interesting and stimulating music and materials
- Stress resulting from required performances or recitals[13]

Teachers who are aware of these potential pitfalls may be able to successfully retain adult students who may otherwise fall through the cracks through the use of simple modifications along the way. First, and as previously mentioned, students must be made aware of the enormous amount of time involved in mastering the piano. The commitment to realistic and achievable goals is critical. Next, good intentions to practice are simply that—good intentions. Students have to be dedicated to scheduling and following through with consistent practice. The job of the teacher is to arm his students with efficient, systematic practice techniques that get results. Further, the selection and study of exciting, interesting repertoire is key to sustaining students' devotion to the instrument. In fact, this is what usually draws students to study the piano in the first place. Overly difficult and unappealing literature can just as easily turn our students off to music. Finally, teachers must keep performance situations low-stress and pleasurable. Stress derived from performance can kill an adult student's drive to continue his study.

Psychological Considerations

Adults often bring a significant amount of emotional and physical baggage to learning, usually the direct result of unpleasant or traumatic childhood educational experiences or failures. In many ways, these negative emotions can be more of a hindrance to the adult's efforts to learn to play the piano than any issues associated with aging. These feelings not only can have damaging effects to self-esteem but also can significantly limit the chances of success of any educational endeavor.

Many adults make unjust comparisons to the success of young musicians, declaring, "If they can do it, then why can't I?" Others unfairly compare themselves to successful concert artists. Such comparisons spawn negative self-judgments and cause them to inaccurately or unfairly assess their own capabilities. Some adult students approach learning with a sense of trepidation, fearful of not succeeding or of embarrassing themselves in front of their peers or teacher. Anxiety and abject fear of failure may translate to an overly cautious approach to their studies. Many simply lack confidence and are unwilling to take risks. Still others equate mistakes or errors with personal failure.

Indeed, adult students approach group piano study with much vulnerability. Because of their excessive self-conscious behavior, support from the teacher as well as from peers becomes even more imperative to help students rise above their insecurities. Every attempt should be made to set students at ease by creating fresh, comfortable learning experiences that are rich in encouragement and positive feedback. Students need to sense from their teacher a sincere admiration for the courage required to step out of their comfort zone to pursue music study. Through it all, teachers must stress the process rather than the product, emphasizing the remarkable journey students have chosen to travel. We can engender a feeling of personal and shared success from the outset by praising even the most minor accomplishments.

In the same way, we must encourage and reward risk-taking. Many adults will balk at the idea of improvising on a twelve-bar blues pattern because of the ambiguity of the task. For that reason, activities that involve a certain amount of risk should be facilitated early on in the learning experience, in order to foster an adventuresome and experimental spirit as a natural part of the learning process. It should be the goal of the teacher to penetrate these walls of resistance by showing students that some of the best learning occurs simply by doing through experimentation. All the while, we must be careful not to establish an atmosphere of strict perfectionism but instead foster an attitude that recognizes the benefits of learning from one's mistakes.

Physiological Considerations

It is true that adults, and especially older adults, may encounter some unique physiological challenges along the way. Indeed, adults at times possess vastly different physiological mechanisms than those of child learners as can be evidenced in minor deficiencies in fine motor skills and overall finger dexterity and coordination. While the challenges can appear to be insurmountable, students can be assured that many of these issues can be overcome. Some adults actually report that keyboard playing has provided them with increased digital dexterity, lessening the effects of arthritis and serving as excellent physical therapy. To address specific weaknesses, teachers must identify and assign technical exercises that serve both the individual and corporate needs of the students involved.

Additional considerations include vision-related issues, most often including a decline in visual acuity for the older adult student. Any information displayed, whether written or in musical notation form, should be large enough for students to clearly view from the back of the room. Teachers should seek out materials that are available in large-print editions or else produce materials that are enlarged to facilitate ease of reading. Also, appropriate lighting can play a significant role in generating a comfortable visual learning environment. This may involve dimming lights when displaying projected information. Furthermore, some auditory deficiencies may be found in older adult learners. In these situations, headsets can be of great assistance by permitting the teacher to adjust the volume of his voice. When off headset, verbal instructions should be clearly projected and articulated.

Recreational Music Making

In recent years there has been a popular trend in adult music making experiences commonly referred to as Recreational Music Making (RMM), which Karl Bruhn defines as "enjoyable, accessible and fulfilling group music based activities that unite people of all ages regardless of their challenge, backgrounds, ethnicity, ability or prior experience."[14] RMM programs place a primary emphasis upon the person rather than the product. Here, nonmusical outcomes are as important as the musical outcomes. Emphasis is placed more on the process than on the product, and the journey becomes more important than the destination.

The RMM approach is an attitude toward learning that is shaped by a desire to make music purely for enjoyment and pleasure, as well as a means to socialize with peers who have a common interest. Rather than placing demands on students to achieve high levels of musical performance, mastery, and competition, which in fact may induce stress, RMM seeks to provide participants with opportunities for fun, relaxation, and overall enhancement of their quality of life while making music.

Recreational Music Making courses are designed expressly for adults who do not perceive themselves to be musical or who indicate a lack of previous musical training. In this way, RMM classes are created for students who simply desire to make music for pleasure in a nonthreatening environment. The purpose of RMM classes is therefore to inspire students to enjoy the process and experience of music making in a positive, social learning environment rather than being preoccupied with the stresses of attempting to attain an established level of proficiency.

Bruhn describes the RMM philosophy as follows:

- RMM is NOT about inspiring extraordinary music-making. It is about inspiring extraordinary living.
- RMM is NOT about exceptional performance. It is about exceptional support and personal experience.
- RMM is NOT about teaching to play. It is about giving people permission to play.
- RMM's best facilitator's are NOT just talented musicians. They are caring, compassionate, and intuitive guides.[15]

In order for a program to be considered in keeping with the RMM philosophy, it must meet the following criteria:

- Enjoyable, accessible, and fulfilling
- Offered as a group-based activity
- Capable of uniting people regardless of their challenges, backgrounds, ethnicity, ability, or prior experience

- Based on promoting or supporting some or all of the following: exercise, nurturing, social support, bonding and spirituality, intellectual stimulation, heightened understanding, and enhanced capacity to cope with life's challenges
- Offered in a manner that fosters creative expression[16]

RMM programs offerings include not only experiences for piano and organ but also drumming circles, band ensemble experiences, and even a conducting/ exercise class. Many of the major digital piano manufacturers have created their own RMM curricular offerings. These include:

- Yamaha Clavinova Connection (www.yamaha.com)
- Club Roland (www.rolandus.com)
- Kawai Keyboard Experience (www.kawaius.com)

While it is true that a majority of RMM programs are designed for the adult demographic, there also are successful RMM programs being offered for children and young adults.

There currently exist two methods written expressly for RMM programs:

Piano for Fun and Fulfillment, by Brenda Dillon. Address inquiries to Brenda Dillon, 4518 Dolwick Drive, Durham, North Carolina 27713 or visit www.brendadillon.com.

Musical Moments: A Recreational Music Making Program, by Debra Perez. To order, contact Debra Perez at MusicalMomentsRMM@gmail.com.

Health Benefits

According to the National Institute of Occupational Safety and Health, 40 percent of American workers consider their jobs very or extremely stressful, and an estimated 40 percent of job turnover is related to stress.[17] *Newsweek* reported in 2004 that "60–90% of doctor visits involve stress related complaints,"[18] and the *New York Times* reported in the same year that "workplace stress costs the nation more than $300 billion each year."[19] A 2000 Gallup poll found that 80 percent of Americans feel stress on the job.[20]

In response to these statistics, the RMM community promotes music making as an ingredient for healthy living, just as exercise and proper nutrition contribute to a healthy lifestyle. Dr. Barry Bittman suggests that the power of group-oriented music making experiences can be quite significant, as evidenced in the biological and psychological benefits they produce, which are clearly demonstrated in the results of several recently published studies. In one study, researchers identified DNA indicators that are associated with increased stress levels. Study participants, who were involved in Yamaha's RMM Clavinova Connection class, demonstrated a reversal of nineteen out of the forty-five markers associated with increased stress levels.[21]

Another study conducted by a team led by Dr. Frederick Tims examined the general physical and emotional health of 100 senior adults. The experimental group was enrolled in a keyboard class while the control group did not participate in such a class. The study found that the keyboard participants exhibited a 90 percent increase in the human growth hormone (hGH), whereas the control group demonstrated no change in hGH levels. High levels of the hGH hormone are thought to increase energy levels and sexual function, as well as reduce other effects of aging such as wrinkling, osteoporosis, and the decline of muscle mass. Additionally, depression, anxiety, and loneliness all decreased for those who studied music.[22] The implications of this study are certainly noteworthy and support the assertion that group music study for older adults can produce significant health benefits.

Supported by the evidence from his research, Tims has identified a list of potential health benefits for senior adults who study music in a nurturing and enjoyable social environment:

- Stimulates brain activity and engages the mind
- Maintains healthy, optimal brain functioning
- Generates a heightened sense of quality of life
- Promotes stress reduction, relaxation, and decreased anxiety
- Provides a social network and outlet, which may combat loneliness
- Facilitates opportunity for continued learning and participation in life
- Develops concentration
- Fosters a sense of confidence and pride from achievement[23]

Business Aspects

For most adult students, the study of piano is a noncompulsory, pleasure-driven activity. These students have made a commitment, in terms of both their time and their money, to pursue the art. Many adults have disposable income that permits them to engage in music study. In fact, baby boomers control as much as 70 percent of the nation's wealth.[24] As these students involve themselves in fulfilling musical study, they are more likely to contribute to the artistic community both financially and through physical support as dedicated patrons of the arts.

Group piano courses for adults address a significant market need and translate to important artistic and educational opportunities for this rapidly growing segment of our population. For the teacher, this means greater opportunities to broaden curricular offerings, expand studio hours, and ultimately increase income.

Because of the relatively flexible schedules of many retired persons, group piano courses for this population can be offered during the normal workday. The morning and afternoon hours are particularly popular among adults for piano study. This schedule permits teachers to engage in teaching during the day while leaving open the prime after-school hours for school-age students. For working professionals, lunchtime "brown bag" classes or evening offerings often fit more easily into their busy schedules.

Marketing

To market a newly launched adult group piano program or to stimulate renewed interest in an existing program, teachers may choose to target the working professional by speaking at business, church, civic, or philanthropic organizations. Perhaps an even more effective approach is to offer demonstration classes at retirement and assisted living centers, or even shopping malls. Demo classes allow teachers to field questions from observers, explain the benefits of adult music study, and, most important, exhibit the pure enjoyment possible from participating in these classes.

Successful adult group piano programs are thriving throughout the county in community music schools, university continuing education programs, and private/independent studios. In an effort to encourage interest and commitment to the music programs of public and private schools systems, and with the permission of the administration, some teachers are utilizing these facilities and their digital piano labs to hold group piano courses. Such an action is just one way to increase awareness of the arts while also generating interest in adult music study.

Methods and Materials

When selecting materials, one should consider the length of the term of study for each class. Will the course run over the span of a fifteen-week semester, or will it be an eight-week introductory course? Is the class designed as a three-year sequence, or will it continue indefinitely?

Teachers must take great care to select methods and materials that will be of interest to adult students. Fortunately, many textbooks have been written expressly with this population in mind. Beyond this, average-age beginner methods can usually be adapted for adults as long as the material does not appear childish or juvenile. Special consideration should be given to the size of the print, especially for older adult groups. Because large-print editions are not readily available, enterprising teachers may, with the permission of the publisher, enlarge and photocopy materials in a suitable font size.

Adults like to be given additional reading on related topics. Teachers should be prepared to provide students with supplementary reading on any given class topic. Therefore, class handouts or resource lists are often much appreciated. For the busy adult student, concise readings from quality Web resources are perhaps more valuable.

A complete listing of available adult piano methods that can be adapted for use with hobby and recreational groups can be found on the companion website.

Equipment and Technology

The belief that all adults scoff at a technology-rich learning environment is simply not true. In fact, many adults are interested in and enjoy the use of such technology in learning to play the piano, and most learn how to operate it very quickly. The savvy group piano teacher will employ technology as a means for fostering creativity and musical sensitivity, demonstrating the benefits throughout all stages of the learning process. For instance, online resources such as YouTube, can be a source for class discussion of both celebrated concert artists and accomplished amateurs.

Adult piano students appreciate the use of audio resources such as compact discs and standard MIDI files, which accompany many of today's piano textbooks, and use these to enhance their at-home practice. From the teacher's perspective, accompaniment tracks can generate a feeling of excitement in the class, as students experience a fully orchestrated version of the music they are playing.

Group piano teachers have found the use of recording technology to be particularly beneficial with their adult students. This equipment enables teachers to record and produce high-quality compact disc recordings of student repertoire. Students feel compelled to meticulously prepare their repertoire when they are working toward the goal of making a CD. Further, these recordings can be used to document student achievement, which can be of enormous benefit, especially to students who feel as though they are not making suitable progress. They are also an excellent way for students to share their successes with family and friends.

Piano laboratories that feature individual digital instruments and headsets are helpful for older students who suffer from hearing impairment. This technology with coordinated controller systems permits students to hear teacher instructions more clearly and facilitates communication with classmates. Additionally, instructional technologies such as the Visualizer, Classroom Maestro, and SmartBoards serve those who are visually impaired by increasing the display size of projected information in contrast to simply writing this information on the board.

Performance Opportunities

Creating exciting and stress-free performance opportunities that are tailored to the needs and wishes of our adult students is one of the great joys of teaching this population. Teachers do well to provide both formal and informal performance outlets because most students will prefer either one or the other. Environments that present low-pressure situations are excellent venues for adult students to make their big debut. For those who are not comfortable being in the spotlight, the student may be given the opportunity to provide background music before or after a formal program.

Some teachers organize periodic informal gatherings such as musicales or piano parties in which students gather in the home of either the instructor or a fellow classmate. These casual, relaxed meetings provide students with opportunities to perform and socialize and are designed to foster a contagious love and enthusiasm for sharing one's music. Here, students should be invited, not required, to perform, and memorization is always optional. When the teacher creates an environment that is nonthreatening and nurturing, students stand to be encouraged and motivated to achieve their individual and shared musical goals.

Another way to bridge the public performance gap is to encourage students to prepare and perform duets and other ensemble literature. Besides the fact that ensemble repertoire is normally performed with the score, thus eliminating the pressure of memorization, the performers also share the spotlight in a collaborative effort. Students who determinedly avoid performing solo literature in public are more likely to attempt a performance if they do not have to go at it alone.

Some group piano teachers of adults encourage their students to form performance groups or societies based on a preferred style of music or other special interest. These subgroups encourage dialogue and exchange of insight and provide students with an additional performance venue.

In an attempt to prepare students for a debut performance, adult groups may attend professional solo or chamber music recitals together and write reviews of these performances. Following the recital and at the subsequent class, the group may discuss features or qualities of the performance they would like to translate to their own performance. Other topics may include characteristics of expert performance and common issues faced by all performers.

Confident performers who enjoy sharing their music with others often enjoy opportunities to present community outreach performances. These recitals may occur in nursing homes or hospitals and can bring great satisfaction to performer and audience alike.

Planning for and Teaching the Lesson

Teachers have found the application of a "whole-part-whole" approach to be particularly beneficial for the instruction of adults. The idea is to introduce and present materials in a way that first provides the student with an overview of that which is to be learned. This might be accomplished by giving a complete performance of a piece to be studied. From here, with the help of the instructor, the class disassembles the piece to its most basic form, identifying the individual issues posed by the composition and discussing creative ways to solve them. It is during this phase that students can learn new concepts and skills or apply and integrate those that have been previously studied and mastered, and that are particularly relevant to the work at hand. Once this has been achieved, students reassemble the aggregate pieces by learning and performing the entire work. Adults especially appreciate this step-by-step approach on how to achieve mastery of a new skill or piece.

Lessons should be problem-centered and mastery-based rather than focused too extensively on content. Furthermore, class exercises should be broken into small, manageable tasks. The study of repertoire fits this bill nicely. A musical score wraps specific technical and musical problems into one composition, presenting the learner with a composite goal to be mastered.

One must not assume that his adult students understand a concept at first hearing or experience. It is also a mistake to assume that students already know what one might consider a basic concept. Every element must be covered. Along these lines, adult students appreciate the opportunity to extensively review old concepts as well as significant time to mindfully integrate new concepts. Reinforcement, review, and drill are all critically necessary even for adults. Older students desire to feel a sense of mastery before they proceed to the next skill or concept. With this said, repetition must serve a clearly defined purpose. Likewise, drill and review must be meaningful and serve an explicit goal. As previously mentioned, adult learning hinges greatly upon the acquisition and application of relevant information and skills. Therefore, learning, and similarly drill and review, must be framed in a substantive, practical manner.

Unlike most children, adults are typically more analytical in their approach to learning. Therefore, open-ended questions that require a problem-solving-based approach are most appropriate. We do well to encourage active, participatory learning that is rich in dialogue and discussion. A common practice must be that of students identifying shared problems and engaging in class discussions on how these problems can be resolved. In the same way, we must create an environment that encourages creativity and a spirit of experimentation, exploration, and risk-taking. This can be facilitated by engaging students in activities such as improvising on a twelve-bar blues progression or composing a work for solo piano using extended piano techniques.

It is important to provide adult students with frequent, genuine feedback. Adult students have a need to feel validated and to be assured that they are on the right track and making steady progress. When offering feedback, it is wise to emphasize the positive attributes of student playing while carefully presenting ideas that will enhance their work.

Periodic breaks in the lesson may be necessary, especially for extended lesson lengths of more than one hour. Such pauses provide students with opportunities to reengage both the mind and the body, thus refocusing attention.

As is the case in all learning situations, pacing is an especially critical component of successful adult learning. Classes that move too quickly can generate feelings of anxiety and overwhelming stress. Similarly, too much freedom can also create stress, which is often the by-product of a lack of structure. Most adult students prefer to establish a pace that is suitable for their individual needs. Therefore, the application of some measure of self-pacing is desirable.

Teachers do well to challenge their adult students just slightly beyond their present level of ability. It is our responsibility to identify that threshold at which our students perceive that success is possible but not wholly guaranteed. Teachers must exercise great discernment on this issue while always seeking to monitor and assess student attitudes in relation to their current level of proficiency. Indeed, students are encouraged when we highlight the concepts or skills that have already been mastered and show them how these can be directly applied to address problems at hand. Supported and driven by the confident notion of "We can do this," students will perceive forward momentum toward achieving a common goal.

It is important that we regularly invite student feedback regarding the pace of learning, encouraging either corporate or individual discussion of this issue. Teachers must be attuned to student questions, monitoring student attitudes and observing student performance so that an accurate assessment of comprehension and mastery can be made. This information will guide the instructor as to when his students are ready to move on to a new concept or piece. Discouragement and boredom often ensue when students feel that progress is too slow, and an attitude of retreat occurs when the pace is too swift. Finding the perfect balance requires perceptive judgment and sensitivity to students.

Flexibility and an ability to adapt our instructional approach to meet the specific needs of our students are hallmarks of exemplary adult education. Successful teachers of adults are able to anticipate and assess age-related issues that may impact learning and provide strategies to negotiate these problems so as to avoid frustration. These teachers emphasize that a key to learning to play the piano is a willingness to experiment with a variety of procedures to determine those that work best for each individual student.

Repertoire

As was alluded to previously, learning to play a favorite tune is often what drives adult students to enroll in a piano class. Therefore, a successful curriculum for adult piano study should be designed around high-quality, exciting repertoire that is supplemented with just the right amount of technique and theory. Because repertoire is at the heart of adult piano study, it is an issue that demands thoughtful attention from the teacher.

To be sure, there is a vast quantity of literature available to pianists. The teacher is charged with the task of assisting his students in selecting appropriate literature that is aurally appealing and supports musical and technical development. This is very much a joint venture when working with adult students. Musical taste and stylistic preference are indeed highly individualized. Some students may wish to play only folk and pop tunes, "oldies," jazz, and classic rock; others prefer to focus strictly on sacred music, hymns, and the classical literature. The task of the teacher is to provide recommendations of literature that would appeal to students based on their stylistic preferences and present playing level.

Teachers and their students may reference Jane Magrath's *The Pianist's Guide to Standard Teaching and Performance Literature,* published by Alfred Publishing Company. The student should be able to master and eventually perform this music with relative ease. Ultimately, the adult student should be given the opportunity to select from several choices of literature to be studied.

Fortunately, many excellent, accessible editions of music are available for the adult amateur population. With this said, there also exist many poorly arranged or transcribed materials that are rife with awkward, unmusical passages that could potentially create much frustration for even the most precocious student. Therefore, teachers must guide students in finding literature that is of the highest quality. Our job is to instruct students in how to discern the difference between high-quality music versus that which is lacking in such integrity. To accomplish this, the teacher should read through as much literature as possible to identify those materials that would best serve the needs of his students while enhancing the student's musical growth.

Both teachers and students can use the following checklist when selecting repertoire:

- Is the music aurally appealing?
- Can the student relate to the music?
- Would the piece fulfill a need in the student's collective repertoire?
- What are the challenges found in the music?
- How easy will this piece be to learn?
- Is the piece a reasonable length?
- Is the piece melodically and rhythmically straightforward?
- What is the tempo? Does the piece require great speed and facility?
- How long should this piece take to learn?

A few available methods provide students with many options, in terms of both repertoire and approach to learning. *Play by Choice* by Fred Kern is one such method. For example, Kern lays out several approaches to reading in the early units and permits the student to choose what works best. Additionally, the method provides a step-by-step approach for learning repertoire, including warm-up and technical exercises that prepare the student for the challenges found in the music.

Adult students often appreciate exploring background information related to the music they are learning, including the sociocultural context of a composer and his work. For some, this information can be what initially motivates a student to study a work. For others, it may be the impetus for additional exploration into similar works by the same composer. This information should always be a part of one's introduction to new works. Teachers should also supply students with print, audio, video, and Internet resources should they desire to further explore a topic.

Consequently, teachers should seek out editions of repertoire that include performance notes and supplementary information. Several such publications of the standard repertoire are available, many of which contain clearly defined, step-by-step strategies for learning the piece. One example is Ingrid Jacobson Clarfield's Artistic Preparation and Performance Series, published by Alfred Publishing Company.

Some teachers choose to maintain a supplementary music library to provide students with opportunities to explore new literature either in class or through a library-type checkout system. Such a program encourages students to read through volumes of literature, which in turn helps develop reading skills and enhances knowledge of the literature, including the various styles and genres available to the pianist.

To further facilitate a self-directed approach to learning, which is preferred by most adult students, teachers may elect to give students opportunities to engage in self-study pieces. These are pieces that students select and prepare over the course of a several weeks or a full term entirely unassisted and without guidance from the teacher. This procedure allows the instructor to assess whether or not his students are internalizing and applying the musical concepts and principles that have been discussed in class. The literature should be selected in consultation with the teacher so that an appropriate level is identified. Teachers can best serve adult students by offering enough flexibility and freedom to promote self-directed learning, all within the parameters of a well-structured curriculum supported with guidance by the instructor.

Every class should include the learning of a simple piece that can be mastered easily and quickly. These pieces should be relatively brief and undemanding, yet introduce important concepts and skills that can be applied in more challenging literature. By doing so, students are armed with a sense of accomplishment and will in turn be invigorated during their practice at home.

Technique

Unlike their younger counterparts, most adults have developed quite an extensive repertoire of fine motor gestures and movements throughout the course of their years. Despite these years of fine motor experiences, many adults bring to piano study motor movements that are quite different from those required of effortless, efficient piano technique. Compounded with this issue is the fact that many adults feel embarrassed of and at times seemingly disconnected from their bodies. Therefore, teachers must work to guide students on how to reintegrate this vital element of the physicality of learning the piano rather than relying purely on a cognitive approach.

Adults often have certain age-specific physical obstacles that will need attention. As a general rule, older adults usually possess joints that are not as flexible as those of children, with some affected by arthritis or muscular degeneration. Some may have impaired vision or other specific fine motor control deficiencies, which directly affect hand-eye coordination. Other technical issues that are often found in the adult student's technique include excessively high or low wrists, awkward hand positions, strange fingering choices, and lack of finger independence. Some students may also use excessive or extraneous movements or unproductive and unnecessary gestures.

Many adults also demonstrate muscular rigidity and stiffness, which are often linked to an overzealous attempt at perfection, in addition to psychological and emotional tension. In regard to the latter, one must take into consideration the lives of working adult students. Many come to class following a long, stressful day at work. Along with their books and materials, adults also bring a day's worth of tension to the lesson. The adult hobby student should be given a succinct series of warm-ups to be applied both in the lesson and before each practice. This is essential to properly warm up the body and rid oneself of tension. These should begin with large, gross motor movements and progress toward fine motor movements. The exercises should be applied periodically throughout the class or practice session to disperse any unnecessary tension that may have developed.

Adult students should be encouraged to take inventory of tension whenever they are at the instrument. They are particularly susceptible to this, due in part to their intense desire to achieve immediate results and succeed in their pianistic endeavors. Therefore, the instructor must carefully teach students how to assess the accrual of unwanted tension and ways to combat it. To achieve this, students must be aware of their complete playing mechanism, while being constantly open and perceptive to bodily feedback.

The teacher can employ a variety of strategies to achieve these goals. The use of imagery can be very beneficial when attempting to produce relaxation in students' playing. Demonstration is also critical to illustrate a proper, comfortable approach to the instrument that yields beautiful sound production. One might consider the instruction of weight technique at the outset of the learning sequence, using large gestures to promote a relaxed, warm tone. Phrases like, "Imagine that your arms weigh one hundred pounds each" can help to generate a comfortable approach to sound production. Teachers may also elect to employ eurhythmic activities in which students walk or respond physically to music. These activities help to inspire freedom in one's technique. In the end, one may choose to videotape and play back students playing. There is no better way to assess and critique one's approach than by watching it directly. The video camera never lies.

Adults should be encouraged throughout this process to help them understand that development of such freedom of piano technique requires thoughtful attention and patient repetition. The adult's repertoire of unproductive movements and gestures acquired over a lifetime will need to be carefully modified and shaped to generate an overall healthy and efficient technical approach to the instrument. Most adults will welcome the use of a specific technical regimen to develop these motor skills.

Chapter 9

Group Piano and the University Music Major

The University Group Piano Teacher

The university group piano teacher is faced with a host of demanding responsibilities, not the least of which is the enormous task of meeting students where they are, usually having little or no previous piano experience, and taking them to a level of proficiency, all within the span of a few short academic terms. For the university group piano teacher, the primary objective is to enable his students to become competent in the application of piano skills in their work as professional musicians. This is certainly no small task.

Diagnostic Examinations for the University Music Majors

The diagnostic/placement audition for the university music major is imperative to properly measure each student's present level of ability and to ensure that students are placed in a section that is commensurate with their specific skill level. The ultimate aim is to produce relative homogeneity within each class.

An audition should be administered according to the individual student's experience level and may take place prior to the first week of class or during a freshman/transfer student audition or orientation program. Prior to playing, students should complete a questionnaire regarding their previous piano study, as well as their perceived strengths and weaknesses.

The exam will assess a cross section of functional keyboard skills, not repertoire alone. Examinations that include solely repertoire can provide a distorted perspective of the student's skill level. Indeed, many students can play a well-polished piece, but this can certainly be misleading because it provides an incomplete view of the student's overall functional keyboard abilities.

The placement examination should evaluate skill competencies that will be mastered upon completion of each level of study. Students who prove proficient at each level examined are exempt from that level of coursework.

Following are suggested placement examinations by level:

- No previous piano study
- One through three years of piano study
- Four or more years of piano study

See figure 9.1 for a sample assessment tool to be used for university group piano placement.

No Previous Study

For the student who has had no prior piano experience, an audition may include teacher modeling and student playback of major five-finger patterns, as well as one-octave major scales, both hands separately and hands together. This exercise reveals student fine motor control abilities. These students should also be asked to sight-read single-staff melodies from both the treble and bass clefs. Because some students may read one clef more easily than another due to the study of their primary instrument (e.g., a flute player will read the treble clef well but may struggle with the bass clef), this drill will expose any specific weaknesses in clef-reading ability.

One to Three Years of Study

Students who have completed roughly one to three years of previous piano study should be asked to play an examination that includes major scales, harmonization, transposition, and sight-reading. During the scale-playing portion, the examiner must carefully observe the student's hand position and choice of fingering, noting any technical deficiencies. The student should also be asked to harmonize a simple melody using single notes from the primary chords. The exercise will reveal the student's understanding of basic harmonic principles. Using this same melody, the student should then transpose the example to a closely related key. Regarding sight-reading, examples may focus primarily on linear textures with some chords included.

Four or More Years of Study

For students who have had four or more years of piano experience, major scales should be rendered hands together without assistance from the examiner. The

Student Name: Date:

E-mail Address:

Phone Number:

Major:

Previous Piano Experience:

Check One:

- ○ No Previous Piano Study
  1. Five-Finger Patterns
     Hands Separately 1 2 3 4 5
     Hands Together 1 2 3 4 5
  2. Major Scale (Playbacks)
     Hands Separately 1 2 3 4 5
  3. Sight-Reading (Single Staff Melody) 1 2 3 4 5

  Total _____/20

- ○ One through Three Years of Piano Study
  1. Major Scale
     Hands Separately 1 2 3 4 5
  2. Harmonization
     Simple Melody Using Single Notes 1 2 3 4 5
  3. Transposition
     Single-Line Melody to Closely Related Key 1 2 3 4 5
  4. Sight-Reading
     Linear Textures with Some Simple Chords 1 2 3 4 5

  Total _____/20

- ○ Four or More Years of Piano Study
  1. Major Scale
     Hands Together (Two Octaves) 1 2 3 4 5
  2. Harmonization
     Simple Melody Using Primary Chords 1 2 3 4 5
  3. Transposition
     Grand Staff 1 2 3 4 5
  4. Sight-Reading
     Linear Texture 1 2 3 4 5
     Chordal Texture 1 2 3 4 5

  Total _____/25

Comments and Recommendations:

Examiner's Signature: ______________________________

FIGURE 9.1 University Group Placement Examination Form

harmonization example should include primary chords, and the transposition exercise should include a grand staff example rather than a single-line melody as per the previous category. Sight-reading should include both linear textures and four-part chordal textures.

The Student Population

University group piano courses for the nonkeyboard music major serve a diverse constituency, enrolling students who are majoring in music education, performance, therapy, theory, composition, and musicology, and other areas. Each area of emphasis demands certain keyboard skills from the student. Indeed, the purpose and objectives of group piano study for the nonkeyboard music major are certainly not the same as those of the piano major. As such, the curriculum and subsequent student training must be meticulously crafted and carried out to accommodate the specific needs of each music major.

Furthermore, the typical group piano class consists of a complex conglomeration of student ages, personalities, and attitudes toward the subject matter. In most cases, the traditional undergraduate college student is between seventeen and twenty-two years of age, spanning the gap from late adolescence to early adulthood. There are of course exceptions to this rule, as trends indicate a rise in the number of nontraditional students returning to university studies. The teacher must be prepared on all fronts to address this complex web of diversity.

Many group piano students approach piano study with mixed feelings. For some, what may begin as excitement at the prospect of learning a new instrument can easily disintegrate into an environment fraught with feelings of disinterest, frustration, and even resistance to learning altogether. Group piano courses can become yet another hoop through which students must pass on the way to fulfilling degree requirements and thus are often relegated to the bottom of the student's list of priorities.

As a teacher, one cannot assume that one's students fully understand the importance of acquiring functional keyboard skills. Students must come to know and believe not only that the development of keyboard proficiency is an integral part of a comprehensive music education mandated by the National Association of Schools of Music but also that these skills are essential for the success of any professional musician. How does one convey the significance and enormous value of these skills?

First, teachers have to be willing and prepared to address students who challenge the system with questions like "Why do *I* have to learn piano? I am a violinist! How could I possibly need these skills?" Indeed, a certain amount of coaxing, persuasion, and at times cajoling is necessary.

Nonkeyboard music major group piano students are indeed accomplished musicians in their own right, having achieved a certain degree of success on their respective primary instruments. These students may feel overwhelmed when faced with the task of mastering a new instrument in such a short time. Group piano teachers must acknowledge the high level of artistry these students have achieved on their principal instruments. At the outset of group piano study, students can be asked to give an introductory performance in which they play an excerpt on their primary instruments and demonstrate to their classmates that "this is really who I am and what I do." When students realize that they are all novices at the piano, it builds a sense of common ground and generates a feeling of confidence that they are all "in this together."

Students must know that we as their instructor are dedicated to equipping them with the requisite keyboard skills necessary to be effective, confident musicians who are prepared to meet the demands of the profession. They must know that we are not preparing students only to survive in the profession but to be successful and thrive. Students must be assured that we are their resource and that we take pride in our role in helping them achieve these goals and expectations.

We must also assure our students that the curriculum has been carefully designed to prepare them for the various ways in which keyboard skills will be used in their daily work as musicians. This involves highlighting throughout our teaching how the skills presented are both practical and relevant to their professional preparation. We must engage our students in conversations regarding the topic, asking them to identify specific skill competencies they wish to address more frequently or in greater depth. Additionally, one may distribute questionnaires to students at the beginning of the term to identify strengths and weaknesses so that the curriculum can be modified to meet their particular needs (figure 9.2).

One may also reference several research studies that clearly illustrate the necessity of functional keyboard skills for the music professional.[1] A study by Tollefson found that 96 percent of music educator survey respondents who completed piano proficiency exams indicated that the piano was employed in their classroom instruction.[2] Additionally, a survey of choral conductors directed by Jamila McWhirter found that choral educators employ keyboard skills very frequently, if not daily, and that they consider these skills to be important and critical to their success.[3]

Student Name: ______________________ Date: ________________

Attitude Inventory	Disagree				Strongly Agree
A. I look forward to studying piano.	1	2	3	4	5
B. I believe I will use piano skills in the future.	1	2	3	4	5
C. I believe learning to play piano will be challenging.	1	2	3	4	5
D. I am taking this course only to satisfy a requirement.	1	2	3	4	5
E. I enjoy working with others cooperatively.	1	2	3	4	5
F. I expect to achieve an A grade for this course.	1	2	3	4	5
G. I feel very nervous about playing the piano.	1	2	3	4	5
H. I prefer to learn individually, not in groups.	1	2	3	4	5

Skill Assessment Inventory
In which of the following skill areas do you feel the weakest and the most confident?
Weak skill area = X
Strong skill area = O

_____ Sight-Reading	_____ Reading Treble Clef	_____ Reading Bass Clef
_____ Hands Together	_____ Rhythm	_____ Chord Progressions
_____ Scales	_____ Arpeggios	_____ Improvisation
_____ Harmonization	_____ Transposition	_____ Score Reading
_____ Theoretical Knowledge		

Anticipated Practice Inventory
Approximately how many hours per day do you anticipate practicing alone? (circle one)

A. Less than thirty minutes
B. Thirty minutes
C. One hour
D. More than one hour

Approximately how many hours per day do you anticipate practicing with someone else? (circle one)

A. Less than thirty minutes
B. Thirty minutes
C. One hour
D. More than one hour

FIGURE 9.2 Self-Assessment Questionnaire

For some, the most convincing argument comes not from the group piano teacher but from professional mentors. Teachers may invite recent graduates who are presently working in various facets of the music profession to share with group piano students ways in which keyboard skills are employed in their daily professional activity. Personal testimonials will pack a powerful punch, communicating the necessity of developing these essential keyboard skills. These meetings will also provide students with opportunities to discuss with young professionals particular keyboard skills that are employed daily in the classroom or other professional setting, as well as suggestions for how one might make the most efficient use of practice time and other valuable tips.

Some teachers may assign first-year group piano students to complete a "Piano and My Profession" project. For this assignment, students are placed in groups according to their major emphasis. The groups are charged with researching, experiencing, and demonstrating ways in which piano is utilized in their respective career paths. Each group must interview a professional in their area (e.g., choral or band ensemble director, elementary or general music teacher, music therapist, private voice or instrument instructor) from a list provided by the instructor. They are encouraged to discuss specific strategies that will be of benefit in achieving the established level of proficiency. After the interview, students collectively meet to discuss their findings and then present an oral report to the class. During the class presentation, students are asked to demonstrate a variety of ways piano will be employed in their professional work.

Curriculum

To be sure, many factors must be considered when creating a group piano curriculum for music majors. The skills taught must be relevant to the needs of the students' professional goals. Real-life application is key. All in-class activities and out-of-class assignments must be applicable to students' future careers. When it comes to curricular design, Fred Kern has been quoted as saying, "Students must be able to know it, read it, play it, and fake it."[4] Traditionally, the following skill competencies are commonly held as core curricular components of the university group piano program for music majors:

- Technique, including scales and arpeggios
- Chord progressions
- Sight-reading
- Harmonization

- Transposition
- Improvisation
- Playing by ear
- Open score reading
- Multiclef reading
- Reading from a lead sheet
- Realization of figured bass
- Repertoire, including solo, ensemble, and accompanying

In recent years there has been a trend that indicates a diminished emphasis on advanced-level technique and the study and memorization of repertoire, with more emphasis being placed on those skills that will be used in day-to-day activity of the music professional. For example, the choral music education student should gain experience doing the following:

- Learning to play and lead choral warm-ups from the piano
- Preparing and rehearsing open scores
- Singing one part while playing one or more additional parts
- Sight-reading and performing choral accompaniments
- Preparing, rehearsing, and performing accompaniments with soloist or ensemble

Regardless of the major, the foundational curricular building blocks of any group piano curriculum include the following:

- The development of a basic technique to enable students to function at the instrument with confidence and ease
- A knowledge of chords, inversions, and chord qualities—how they feel, and how chord progressions are applied in the repertoire and in other functional keyboard activities
- Sight-reading, which is perhaps the most central, vital element of any group piano curriculum

Importantly, the university group piano curriculum must be created in alignment with the specific skill competencies mandated by the National Association of Schools of Music (NASM). These standards can be referenced in the NASM handbook.

Furthermore, it is advisable that the group piano curriculum for music majors be developed in consultation with the school's academic areas, especially theory and aural skills curricula. Congruency between these programs creates valuable laboratory opportunities for students in which theoretical and aural skills can be transferred, applied, and reinforced at the piano, resulting in a unified program of study that promotes practical, efficient, and powerful learning.

Group piano program coordinators must work closely with colleagues from all academic, professional, and performance areas to encourage the integration and application of piano skills across the music curriculum. Honest conversations among faculty are necessary to identify the knowledge and skill sets that are central to the success of all music graduates. In turn, stimulating curricula can be developed to meet the professional training demands of our students. Group piano teachers should solicit information from their colleagues regarding resources, textbooks, and other materials that students will use in the classroom or professional setting. These materials can then be used as supplementary resources from which exercises and activities can be drawn.

In an effort to encourage students to continue to practice and utilize their piano skills even after the piano requirements have been fulfilled, group piano coordinators may encourage their colleagues in the academic, professional, and performance areas to create opportunities for students to employ these skills on a regular basis, especially in upper-division course work and practicum experiences.

Methods

A complete listing of available group piano methods that are designed for the university nonkeyboard music major can be found in the companion website.

The Syllabus

A comprehensive syllabus is an essential document for any university course. For the group piano instructor, the syllabus is the culmination of detailed curricular planning and a means for delivering critical course-related information to students. For students, the syllabus is an indispensable tool that serves both as a guidebook and in some ways as a contract that delineates students' responsibility regarding what they must do to achieve maximum benefit from the course. The syllabus is a map or blueprint, which gives students an overview of the course and provides a complete picture of the intended destination. It serves to communicate curricular objectives and goals, including the knowledge and skills to be developed and mastered throughout the course. The syllabus also reflects an instructor's teaching philosophy and methodologies that will be used to facilitate student learning. Syllabus content may include the following:

Course Information

- Course title
- Course number
- Credit hours
- Prerequisites
- Academic term
- Meeting days/time
- Location
- Academic campus (if applicable)

Instructor Information

- Instructor name and title
- Office location
- Office phone number
- E-mail address
- Office hours

Course Description

- Course catalog description
- Course content
- Course objectives and goals
- Course requirements, assignments, projects
- Instructional methodologies and teaching techniques

Textbook and Materials Information

- Required textbooks
- Supplemental textbooks
- Additional materials and resources

Course Calendar and Schedule

- Course calendar and time line
- Assignments and project due dates
- Quiz and examination dates and materials

Assessment and Evaluation

- Procedures and standards for evaluation and grading
- List of competencies to be evaluated on all quizzes and examinations
- Grading scale

Attendance and Tardy Policy

- Attendance requirements
- Penalties
- Excused absences (e.g., family emergency, university holiday, religious observance)
- Makeup policy

Other Policies

- Academic honesty and integrity
- Disability statement and accommodations
- Other university-mandated policies

Practice Strategies and Other Tips for Success

- Clear definition of student responsibilities for success in the course
- Additional learning and practice strategies and resources
- Suggested supplementary materials
- Tutoring opportunities

Graduate Teaching Assistants

Graduate teaching assistants can be enormous assets to any group piano program. Likewise, the opportunity for these students to instruct university-level courses is an invaluable educational experience that can prepare them well for their own professional pursuits.

Most group piano program coordinators acknowledge that graduate teaching assistants may require a certain amount of training, as most are hired based largely on the student's performance audition rather than previous group piano teaching experience. To this end, program coordinators may host orientation and training seminars at the outset of each academic year. These meetings provide graduate assistants with a crash course in program logistics, including piano lab equipment and operation, grading policies, examination materials and protocol, and standardization of assessment techniques and procedures. Furthermore, these sessions can be used to discuss lesson planning and instructional strategies. An instructional handbook that includes program policies, syllabi, exams, and templates for various forms can be distributed to teaching assistants at this time, both as hard copies and in digital format.

Group piano program coordinators may find it beneficial to convene weekly or biweekly meetings with their graduate teaching assistants to give teaching assistants an opportunity to ask questions of their supervisor and solicit ideas from their colleagues. Such meetings are also a platform for the discussion of fresh instructional strategies, teaching tips, the use of technology, and new materials. Prior to the meetings, graduate assistants may be given an assignment to create a novel approach to the instruction of a given skill competency to be demonstrated and discussed at the meeting.

Providing graduate teaching assistants with regular opportunities for observation and subsequent feedback regarding their teaching is one of the primary responsibilities of the group piano program coordinator. Both scheduled and unannounced observation by the program coordinator keeps teaching assistants accountable for quality preparation and presentation of class lessons.

Graduate teaching assistants should be asked to regularly videotape their teaching. This should be followed by a self-analysis of their work through critical review of the video. It is advisable that teaching assistants complete a written assessment of their work to be submitted with the video to the program coordinator for review. This assessment challenges students to critically evaluate their work, noting positive attributes and areas the need to be improved. Students should be asked to articulate possible strategies that may be used to enhance their teaching.

The supervisor will then examine the video and provide written feedback (figure 9.3). A private meeting with the teaching assistant will follow, in which the supervisor will discuss his written remarks. The supervisor may choose to play back clips from the student's video to illustrate points made and to engage the teaching assistant in discussion of how the lesson segment could be improved.

Teaching assistants should be strongly encouraged to observe group piano faculty and other graduate teaching assistants regularly to broaden their perspective and knowledge of teaching piano in group environments. Teaching assistants may be asked to exchange teaching videos with other teaching assistants and construct a list of inventive ideas gleaned from this exercise. These strategies can be discussed at the weekly graduate teaching assistant meeting. (See chapter 5 for more information on procedures for evaluating teaching effectiveness.)

Technology

Keeping abreast of current trends in group piano laboratory and instructional technologies is of critical importance for the university group piano program coordinator. In addition to the many educational benefits afforded the students

SAMPLE UNIVERSITY GROUP PIANO PROGRAM
GRADUATE TEACHING ASSISTANT TEACHING EVALUATION FORM

NAME: DATE:

CLASS OBSERVED:

TEACHING EVALUATION

	Excellent	Satisfactory	Needs Improvement
Appropriate content			
Organization of material			
Presentation			
Pacing			
Well-defined objectives			
Speaking voice			
Ease of presentation			
Rapport with students			
Enthusiasm			

ADDITIONAL COMMENTS

Graduate Assistant ______________________ Date ______________

Faculty Observer ______________________ Date ______________

FIGURE 9.3

who use these facilities, high-quality, modern piano laboratories enhance program visibility, which has positive implications for successful recruitment of graduate students and teaching assistants.

In what seems to be a pervasive problem plaguing music programs across the country, grim fiscal climates and the resulting restrictive budgets make purchasing and maintaining state-of-the-art group piano equipment and instructional technology a seemingly impossible task. Consequently, group piano program coordinators must be industrious in addressing this issue by seeking out alternative solutions.

First, it is advisable to develop a relationship with retailers and industry manufacturers. Special pricing, which may include drastically discounted instruments and technology, may be made available as a result of these partnerships. In return for an institution's loyalty to and endorsement of a given product, the institution and its testimonial may be included in product marketing campaigns.

Further, there may exist opportunities to participate in institutional leasing and placement programs, which provide instruments and equipment for a fraction of the cost of purchasing these items outright. Retailers or manufacturers may require the use of university facilities to host an institutional sale at the close of the year at which time the instruments will be made available to the community for purchase.

Assessment and Evaluation

Unbiased, objective assessment of student progress and achievement must be a top priority for the university group piano teacher. Therefore, one must give careful thought to how assessment will be conducted. Although group-based assessments can be an effective means for evaluating student comprehension and skill mastery, and certainly play an integral role in assessment, individual student examinations can be of particular benefit to both student and teacher. This arrangement gives the instructor an opportunity to offer students individual attention and suggestions for addressing specific problems they may be encountering.

Class size will have some bearing on the amount of time granted to each student to perform his exam. The use of multiple class periods may be necessary for large-scale examinations such as midterms or finals to accommodate the many skill competencies to be evaluated. Thus, it is quite necessary to conduct examinations in an efficient yet thorough manner. Students should arrive a minimum of five minutes prior to their scheduled examination appointment, warmed up and ready to render their exam. Students can facilitate efficiency by having materials appropriately marked to ensure quick transitions from skill to skill.

The instructor should do his part to set the class at ease by warmly greeting students as they enter and by permitting the student to select the first skill to be heard. For technique or skill drill exercises, the instructor may allow the student to select the first key from a set of scales to be prepared, followed by a selection from the instructor. This empowers the student, granting a sense of confidence to start him off on the right foot.

Some teachers may elect to give special consideration to classes that consist of students of varying skills levels by allowing students to select from an approved list of repertoire or a list of melodies to be harmonized, each of a slightly varying degree of difficulty

Preparing Students for Examinations

Students must have a clear understanding of the grading policy and procedures from the very outset of their group piano experience. The grading policy, which must promote equity and should uphold the integrity of the course, should be made readily available to students and be posted in the piano lab or classroom, included in the course syllabus, and may also be published online on a program website or by using Blackboard or other classroom management software. To this end and prior to the first assessment experience, the teacher should demonstrate to students what constitutes an A, B, C, D, or F grade. The teacher may play sample performances of exam material, some with deliberate mistakes. He can then reveal the grade that would be assigned for such a performance. Such information delineates clear benchmarks, leaving no room for ambiguity or assumption, and guides students in their preparation.

Further, exams should be announced well in advance, preferably at the beginning of the term as detailed in the course syllabus or on a course management site. A scoring rubric may be distributed to students at this time. This document, which includes the exam content to be evaluated and the criteria by which a grade will be assigned, provides students with a clear picture of the exam expectations and may assist them in their preparations. If exams are rendered on an acoustic instrument, students should be encouraged to practice on as many acoustic instruments as possible.

Promoting Assessment Consistency

When operating a group piano program in which multiple faculty, including graduate teaching assistants, are involved in the instruction and assessment of students, consistency in grading is critical. Grading criteria should be clearly laid out at the beginning of each academic year, and all faculty should be familiar with the established grading standards. To accomplish this, sample video clips or mock exams performed by teachers can be analyzed and discussed among faculty to help convey how each performance should be scored.

In an effort to monitor the progress of students enrolled in a university group piano program, the program coordinator may choose to hear all final exams or may periodically sit in on quizzes or exams throughout the term.

Grade Documentation, Storage, and Dissemination

A scoring rubric or grade report form can be divided by skill area/competency and should include point value and points received (quantitative data) and written comments and remarks (qualitative data) to justify the point distribution (figure 9.4). The form should be given to students only after grades have been recorded and stored by the instructor. Some teachers may wish to provide students with access to their grades via course management software so that progress can be tracked across the term. Although potentially time-consuming, discussion via student conferences either immediately after an exam or at a later time can dispel any confusion surrounding the assessment experience.

SAMPLE GROUP PIANO EXAMINATION REPORT FORM

Name: ______________________________

Date: ____________

Course/Section Number: ________________

TECHNIQUE (20 points)

Content: All white key harmonic minor scales and arpeggios, two octaves, hands together

Hand Position	_____ /5 points	
Fingering	_____ /5 points	
Precision/Accuracy	_____ /5 points	
Continuity	_____ /5 points	Skill Area Total _____

Comments:

FIGURE 9.4

SIGHT-READING (20 points)

Content: Example to be read at sight. You will be permitted five minutes to preview prior to scheduled appointment

Pitch Accuracy ______ /5 points

Rhythm Accuracy ______ /5 points

Dynamics/Articulation ______ /5 points

Continuity ______ /5 points Skill Area Total ______

Comments:

HARMONIZATION (20 points)

Content: When Love Is Kind, p. 60 (Waltz-style accompaniment)

Melodic Accuracy (Pitch and Rhythm)______ /5 points

Chord Selection and Placement ______ /5 points

Accompaniment ______ /5 points

Continuity ______ /5 points Skill Area Total ______

Comments:

INSTRUMENTAL TRANSPOSITION (20 Points)

Content: Page 110–111 (B-flat clarinet and trombone)

Pitch Accuracy ______ /5 points

Harmonic Accuracy ______ /5 points

Rhythmic Accuracy ______ /5 points

Continuity ______ /5 points Skill Area Total ______

Comments:

REPERTOIRE (20 Points)

Content: Preapproved Student Repertoire

Pitch Accuracy ______ /5 points

Rhythmic Accuracy ______ /5 points

Expression and Musicality ______ /5 points

Continuity ______ /5 points Skill Area Total ______

Comments:

Summative Comments:

Total Points ______ /100

Popular tools for the electronic storage of data such as student grades and attendance include Blackboard, Gradebook, Microsoft Excel, and FileMaker Pro. It is advisable for teachers to back up grade information in multiple locations and on a regular basis.

Strategies for Assessment and Evaluation

The Checklist Approach

Although evaluating musical performance will always involve a subjective element, one must strive to make the process as objective as possible. To this end, some teachers employ a checklist system in which the evaluator circles "yes" or "no" in response to questions regarding an assessed skill or competency, such as "Did the student use the correct fingering?" or "Did the student maintain a steady tempo?"

Videotaped Exams

The act of videotaping student exams can curtail any student disputes over grades. Such documentation allows the teacher to play back and discuss areas of weakness that may have impacted a student's grade.

ePortfolio

The ePortfolio is a compilation of a student's work in the form of video clips, recordings, learning plans, and records.[5] The procedure allows students to document their own progress by establishing and tracking achievement of short- and long-term goals. It also encourages students to reflect upon their learning and accomplishments in the form of self-assessment, bringing a heightened sense of awareness to the educational process. Such an approach helps motivate students as they chart progress and observe how learned skills are applied in their work as professional musicians. Teachers may use the ePortfolio as a capstone project for students' group piano experience.

Daily Preparation Assessments or Quizzes

A numeric daily grade, either as an informal assessment or as the result of a more formal quiz, allows the teacher to measure and track student progress on the micro level while keeping students accountable for daily preparation. Teachers may choose to hear only excerpts from the day's assignment or may listen to complete assignments. This process can be as brief or as extensive as the teacher deems necessary and may vary from class to class. Although the process is potentially time-consuming, the fostered benefit of student accountability to solid daily preparation certainly far outweighs the alternative. If instituted at the outset of study, such quizzes can become a natural part of the assessment process, in turn potentially diminishing student anxiety associated with test taking.

Pretest or Mock Quizzes

Pretest performance quizzes are of great benefits to students. Here, students can select one or two skills to perform for the class that will be evaluated on a forthcoming exam. Each student performs an excerpt or sample of a skill or competency. Following the performance, classmates offer feedback and suggestions for improvement. The instructor follows this with the grade that would be awarded based on the given performance and then provides a justification for his mark. This procedure allows students to become comfortable with the instructor's grading procedures and expectations, while alerting them to areas that need to be addressed prior to the graded exam.

Written Quizzes

All too often, written quizzes are neglected as assessment tools for group piano teachers. Such quizzes allow the instructor to evaluate cognitive mastery of theoretical concepts. They can range from naming notes to constructing/spelling secondary dominant chords or writing scale or chord fingerings.

Scheduled or Random Student Self-Evaluation

Self-evaluation is a critical component of any educational endeavor. In the group piano learning environment, this can take the form of a videotaped performance analysis. Students may be asked to record exam content and on playback complete a self-analysis. Instructors can provide a checklist or assessment protocol by which students evaluate their performance. Students should state positive attributes of their playing, identify weaknesses, and articulate methods for improvement.

Because students are given the option to record multiple takes in order to document their best possible work, they gain valuable practice via drill and repetition. By doing so, they are challenged to listen critically to their work to discern their most exemplary performance. The recorded performances can be discussed in class among classmates or can be e-mailed to the instructor for feedback. This strategy may be most effectively used as a preparatory exercise or pretest simulation prior to a formal examination. It is also central to the aforementioned ePortfolio approach to assessment.

Group- or Team-Based Practice Exams

Team-based practice exams are excellent strategies to prepare students for exams by way of healthy competition. For example, the class can be divided into two teams. One member from team A performs an exam component. Afterward, members from the other team discuss the performance, write comments, and assign a point value from 1 to 10, with 10 being the highest possible score. The roles are then reversed. The team that receives the most collective points wins.

Mock Interview

As a culminating assessment project or in preparation for the proficiency examination, group piano program coordinators may elect to conduct mock interviews in which students demonstrate keyboard skills before a panel of faculty or guest professionals who represent the various major areas. After each performance, the panel offers feedback and comments on whether or not they would consider the student to be a viable candidate for a professional position.

Proficiency Examinations

College and university group piano program coordinators must decide, in consultation with school administrators and curricular committees, whether or not a piano proficiency examination will be required of every music major. Some programs have decided to forgo the requirement of a proficiency exam and have instead chosen to deem successful completion of group piano coursework with a passing grade as demonstration of proficiency, thus fulfilling the keyboard requirement. While the practice of proficiency exams varies from institution to institution, many programs have retained a required piano proficiency exam separate from group piano coursework. Although this practice is potentially more time-consuming and creates more work for group piano program coordinators, most maintain that the proficiency exam remains the best method for evaluating students' cumulative keyboard competency.

The proficiency exam can be administered in a variety of ways. The following are a few questions that require consideration:

- Must the proficiency exam be attempted after the group piano coursework has been completed, or can it be attempted at any point during the student's group piano study?
- Will students be given multiple attempts, or is it a "one chance only" exam?
- Must students attempt all portions of the exam at one setting, or can they elect to play only a portion of the exam over a period of several examinations?
- In the instance where multiple opportunities are given, must a certain period of time pass before a student is permitted to retake the exam?
- Will a proficiency exam or barrier exam be used at the close of each term or year of a group piano course sequence?
- When will the proficiency exam be offered? Multiple times per term or year? Only once at the close of each term or at the close of each year?

It is common for students who matriculate with advanced keyboard skills to be granted an opportunity to test out of the group piano sequence altogether. These music majors for whom piano is a secondary instrument are typically required to take a piano proficiency examination to fulfill their keyboard requirements. Upon successful completion of the exam, the students are typically given the opportunity to study piano privately or in an advanced group piano course with the intent of continued enrichment and development of their keyboard skills.

When considering the competencies to be evaluated as part of the proficiency examination, one must survey the composite group piano curriculum, highlighting those particular skills that are especially relevant to the needs of each area of emphasis among music majors. As a result, exam requirements will vary by area, thus reflecting those competencies necessary for success in a given sector of the music profession (figure 9.5).

Practice

Just because the university group piano class involves the instruction of music majors who have achieved advanced levels of expertise on their respective instruments does not in any way translate to innate knowledge of how to practice the piano. Therefore, significant instruction and coaching in this regard are often necessary.

Group piano instructors acknowledge the burden of the packed schedules kept by music majors and the resulting limited available time to practice the piano. To address this issue, we must seek to educate our students on how to be most effective and efficient in their practice. Teachers must stress that a

INSTRUMENTAL MUSIC EDUCATION OR INSTRUMENTAL PERFORMANCE

1. Harmonize and transpose melodies using blocked chords, proper voice leading, and inversions for ease of movement. Appropriate accompaniment styles must be used. Examples are placed on reserve in the music library. Additional melodies to be harmonized and transposed at sight will be provided during the examination.
2. Transpose at sight various single instrumental lines to concert pitch. Melodies will be provided during the examination.
   - B-flat instruments
   - E-flat instruments
   - F instruments
3. Perform instrumental accompaniment with soloist.
4. Sight-read selected fragments of a band or orchestral condensed score.

CHORAL MUSIC EDUCATION

1. Harmonize and transpose melodies using blocked chords, proper voice leading, and inversions for ease of movement. Appropriate accompaniment styles must be used. Examples are placed on reserve in the music library. Additional melodies to be harmonized and transposed at sight will be provided during the examination.
2. Perform a vocal accompaniment with soloist.
3. Prepare and perform a four-staff choral work from an open score. The composition will be made available one week prior to the examination.
4. Perform choice of two popular/community songs. These may be selected by the student and approved by the instructor. High level of performance is expected (e.g., appropriate tempo, musicality, fluency).

KEYBOARD OR VOCAL PERFORMANCE

1. Harmonize and transpose melodies using blocked chords, proper voice leading, and inversions for ease of movement. Appropriate accompaniment styles must be used. Examples are placed on reserve in the music library. Additional melodies to be harmonized and transposed at sight will be provided during the examination.
2. Prepare a vocal or instrumental accompaniment with soloist. Students will also sight-read a simple vocal or instrumental accompaniment during the exam.
3. Prepare and perform a four-staff choral work from an open score. The composition will be made available one week prior to the examination.
4. Perform choice of two popular/community songs. These may be selected by the student and approved by the instructor. High level of performance is expected (e.g., appropriate tempo, musicality, fluency).

MUSIC THEORY, HISTORY, OR COMPOSITION

1. Harmonize and transpose melodies using blocked chords, proper voice leading, and inversions for ease of movement. Appropriate accompaniment styles must be used. Examples are placed on reserve in the music library. Additional melodies to be harmonized and transposed at sight will be provided during the examination.

FIGURE 9.5 Sample Proficiency Examination Requirements by Major

2. Prepare and perform a vocal or instrumental accompaniment with soloist. Students will also sight-read a simple vocal or accompaniment during the exam.
3. Prepare and perform a choral-type texture from a standard hymnal or the Bach *Choralbuch.*
4. Prepare and perform short excerpts from both a string quartet and choral score. Examples will be made available one week prior to the examination.

MUSIC THERAPY

1. Harmonize and transpose melodies using blocked chords, proper voice leading, and inversions for ease of movement. Appropriate accompaniment styles must be used. Examples are placed on reserve in the music library. Additional melodies to be harmonized and transposed at sight will be provided during the examination.
2. Sight-read a hymn from a standard hymnal.
3. Perform a prepared vocal or instrumental accompaniment with soloist.
4. Perform choice of two popular/community songs. These may be selected by the student and approved by the instructor. High level of performance is expected (e.g., appropriate tempo, musicality, fluency).

commitment to consistent, thoughtful practice will in the end usually reduce the overall amount of time necessary at the instrument.

Students appreciate having a variety of step-by-step procedures at their disposal that serve them in working toward the goal of efficiency. Accordingly, teachers should make an effort to incorporate the discussion of at least one new practice strategy into every class. After all, teaching students how to become independent and skillful at practicing is at the heart of what we do.

Students should also be encouraged to maintain a practice journal in which they collect a list of questions that may emerge during their practice. They should be asked to record any new discoveries or valuable practice tips. Class time should be devoted each period for questions related to practice, as well as opportunities for students to share and demonstrate their new discoveries.

Instructors who use classroom management software may find it useful to maintain an online chat room where students can dialogue about practice issues, ask questions, or make suggestions. By doing so, students are likely to get more immediate responses rather than having to wait until the next class period to solicit help.

The Piano Student's Guide to Effective Practicing, by Nancy O'Neill Breth, is an excellent resource for the study and practice of the piano repertoire. Specific practice strategies are organized and indexed according to musical and technical problems. Students are able to reference the chart and apply the strategy according to their specific needs.

In an effort to better understand how our students approach their practice, teachers may assign students to generate a learning plan for their repertoire or other class assignments. As part of the plan, students must lay out in writing how they will approach learning their repertoire within a given time frame. The learning plan, which is a daily plan of attack and guide to practice, should articulate specific practice strategies that will be used. Students may be asked to cite a minimum number of strategies from *The Piano Student's Guide to Effective Practicing* and describe why these are of particular relevance and how they will be specifically applied to their chosen piece. A copy of the plan is submitted to the instructor, who reviews it and provides written feedback. Upon return of the plan to the student, the instructor may take a few moments to explain his written remarks and answer any questions the student may have. This should be conducted as a group activity so all may glean helpful instruction and strategies.

The use of Practice Partnerships can be of immeasurable benefit to students both in the realm of practice and for providing mutual support and accountability to practice throughout the group piano sequence (see also chapter 4, "Cooperative Learning Theory and Group Piano Teaching").

Group Piano Tutoring Programs

Group piano tutoring programs can be an invaluable asset to students who require additional guidance and assistance in their practice. The weekly tutoring sessions may be conducted by graduate assistants or by piano pedagogy students as part of an internship or practicum requirement.

Group piano teachers may require students who are struggling with specific issues to attend these meetings. In preparation for the tutoring session, the teacher may complete a tutoring form (figure 9.6), which explains the skills to be practiced with the tutor. The student delivers the form to the tutor at the beginning of the session. The tutor uses the form to guide his work with the student, provides written feedback, signs the form, and returns it to the student's teacher. This procedure keeps students accountable for attending the session and also provides a means for tracking student progress.

Courses for Non-Music Majors

Group piano course offerings for non–music majors are extremely popular on campuses across the country. For many institutions, these courses fulfill arts education electives as part of general education requirements, thus attracting

To be completed by the instructor:

Student Name: ____________________ Date Assigned: ______________

This student needs help with the following:

(list book name, page number(s), exercise(s), etc.)

To be completed by the tutor:

Did the student attend the above session and receive help on the listed materials?

Yes ☐ No ☐

Please comment on what was/was not covered:

Recommendations:

____________________ ______________

Tutor Signature Date

FIGURE 9.6 Sample Group Piano Tutoring Form

students from throughout the university. Group piano program coordinators who choose to offer these courses must determine, in consultation with their administration, whether the school will offer a course sequence or only a single introductory-level course. A fee may be assessed to maintain and upgrade equipment.

Notes

Chapter 1

1. The history of group piano teaching is treated in the following doctoral dissertations: William H. Richards, "Trends of Piano Class Instruction, 1815–1962" (D.M.A. diss., University of Missouri–Kansas City, 1962); Sally Monsour, "The Establishment and Early Development of Beginning Piano Classes in the Public Schools, 1915–1930" (Ed.D. diss., University of Michigan, 1960); Diana Skroch, "A Descriptive and Interpretive Study of Class Piano Instruction in Four-Year Colleges and Universities Accredited by the National Association of Schools of Music with a Profile of the Class Piano Instructor" (Ph.D. diss., University of Oklahoma, 1991); and Shin Young Kim, "Development of Materials and Teaching Strategies for Comprehensive Musicianship in Group Piano for College-Level Piano Majors" (Ed.D. diss., Columbia University Teachers College, 2000).

2. Richards, "Trends of Piano Class Instruction."

3. Skroch, "Descriptive and Interpretive Study of Class Piano Instruction in Four-Year Colleges and Universities."

4. Monsour, "Establishment and Early Development of Beginning Piano Classes in the Public Schools."

5. Richards, "Trends of Piano Class Instruction."

6. Skroch, "Descriptive and Interpretive Study of Class Piano Instruction in Four-Year Colleges and Universities."

7. Edith E. Wagner, "Raymond Burrows and His Contributions to Music Education" (D.M.A. diss., University of Southern California, 1968).

8. Richards, "Trends of Piano Class Instruction."

9. Ibid.

10. James Bastien, *How to Teach Piano Successfully*, 3rd ed. (San Diego: Neil A. Kjos, Jr. Publishers, 1995).

11. Sarah Steigerwald, "Artist/Educator Archive Interview—Dr. James Lyke," http://pianoeducation.org/pnojlyke.html.

12. Richard Chronister, "Why Do You Advocate 'Three or More' Teaching?" in *Proceedings from Pedagogy Saturday III*, ed. M. Lorince (Cincinnati, OH: Music Teachers National Association, 1999), 15.

13. Guy Duckworth, "Why Do You Advocate 'Three or More' Teaching?" in *Proceedings from Pedagogy Saturday III*, ed. M. Lorince (Cincinnati, OH: Music Teachers National Association, 1999), 16–18.

14. Richard Anderson, "From Paper Keyboard to MIDI: A Brief Look at Group Piano Through the 20th Century," *Piano Pedagogy Forum* 9, no. 2 (July 2006).

15. Duckworth, "Why Do You Advocate 'Three or More' Teaching?"

Chapter 2

1. Adapted from Doris Harry, "Personal Profit Sheet," in *Group Piano Studio Operations Manual* (Johnny Appleseed Project: KTV Publications, 1988).

Chapter 3

1. Mel Levine, *A Mind at a Time* (New York: Simon & Schuster, 2003).

2. Jerome Bruner, "The Act of Discovery," *Harvard Educational Review* 31, no. 1 (1961), 26.

3. Jerome Bruner, *On Knowing* (Cambridge, MA: Belknap Press, 1962). 87.

4. John Holt, *How Children Learn* (New York: Da Capo Press, 1995), 116.

5. Ibid.

6. Based on my studies with Dr. Sylvia Coats.

Chapter 4

1. Dorwin Cartwright and Alvin Zander, "Origins of Group Dynamics," in *Group Dynamics: Research and Theory*, 2nd ed., ed. Dorwin Cartwright and Alvin Zander (New York: Harper and Row, 1960).

2. Herbert Thelen, *The Classroom Society* (London: Croom Helm, 1981).

3. Morton Deutsch, "Field Theory," in *International Encyclopedia of the Social Sciences*, ed. D. L. Sills (Englewood Cliffs, NJ: Educational Technology Publications, 1968), 412.

4. Joan Reist, "It's a Group Thing: Getting Started in Group Teaching," *American Music Teacher* 51 (April–May 2002), 35–36, 94.

5. Guy Duckworth, "Group Dynamics," in *Proceedings from Pedagogy Saturday III*, ed. Margaret Lorince (Cincinnati, OH: Music Teachers National Association, 1999), 78–79.

6. David Johnson and Roger Johnson, *Learning Together and Alone: Cooperative, Competitive, and Individualistic Learning* (Boston: Allyn and Bacon, 1994), 39.

7. Ibid., 40.

8. Quoted in Shin Young Kim, "Development of Materials and Teaching Strategies for Comprehensive Musicianship in Group Piano for College-Level Piano Majors" (Ed.D. diss., Columbia University Teachers College, 2000)), 33.

9. Steven Roberson, "Motivating Groups," *American Music Teacher* 41 (June/July, 1992), 22–25.

10. Johnson and Johnson, *Learning Together and Alone.*

11. Elizabeth Cohen, *Designing Groupwork: Strategies for the Homogeneous Classroom*, 2nd ed. (New York: Teachers College Press, Columbia University, 1994).

12. Johnson and Johnson, *Learning Together and Alone.*

13. Joseph Goliger, "Implementation of a Program of Cooperative Learning in an Urban Secondary Piano Laboratory" (Ed.D diss., Columbia University Teachers College, 1995).

14. Ibid., 370–372.

Chapter 5

1. Sylvia Coats, *Thinking as You Play: Teaching Piano in Individual and Group Lessons* (Bloomington: Indiana University Press, 2006).

2. Stephen Covey, *Seven Habits of Highly Effective People* (NY: Free Press, 1990): 235.

3. Quoted in Anna Muoio, "All the Right Moves," *Fast Company* 24 (1999), 192.

4. Robert Duke, *Intelligent Music Teaching: Essays on the Core Principles of Effective Instruction* (Austin, TX: Learning and Behavior Resources, 2005).

Chapter 6

1. Émile Jaques-Dalcroze, *Rhythm, Music and Education*, trans. Harold Rubinstein (New York: Knickerbocker Press, 1925).

2. Ibid.

3. Edwin Gordon, *Learning Sequences in Music: Skill, Content, and Patterns* (Chicago: GIA Publications, 1993). See also Marilyn Lowe and Edwin Gordon, *Music Moves* (Chicago: GIA Publications, 2007).

4. Richard Chronister, "Independence Day: Music Reading," *Keyboard Companion* 3 (Spring 1992): 14.

5. Christopher Hepp, "Does Group Teaching Help You Teach Reading?" *Keyboard Companion* 7 (Winter 1996): 13.

6. I learned this activity and its variations from a presentation given by Dr. Lisa Zdechlik at the National Group Piano and Piano Pedagogy Forum.

Chapter 7

1. Jerome Bruner, *The Process of Education* (Boston: Harvard University Press, 1960), 12.

2. See writings by Edwin Gordon.

Chapter 8

1. National Research Center of the Arts, *Americans and the Arts* (New York: Associated Council for the Arts, 1975 &1981); Thelma Cooper, "Adults' Perceptions of Piano Study: Achievement, Experiences, and Interest" (Ph.D. diss., University of Texas–Austin, 1996) (this study reported that 20 million adult amateur pianists were studying piano in the United States); Chelcy Lynn Bowles, "An Assessment of Self-Expressed Music Education Interest and Music Experiences by Adult Music Audiences: Implications for Music Education" (Ph.D. diss., University of Texas–Austin, 1988) (this study reported the keyboard to be the most frequently selected instrument among adult students); Peter J. Jutras, "The Benefits of Adult Piano Study as Self-Reported by Selected Adult Piano Students" (Ph.D. diss., University of North Texas, 2003). The website www.pianonet.com reports that adults aged twenty-five to fifty-five are the fastest-growing population of piano students.

2. Karl Bruhn, "Take Two Music Lessons and Call Me in the Morning: Interview with Karl Bruhn," *Keyboard Companion* 18 (Summer, 2007).

3. Ibid.

4. As reported by Brenda Dillon in the introduction to her book *Piano for Fun and Fulfillment.*

5. Patricia K. Cross, *Adults as Learners: Increasing Participation and Facilitating Learning* (San Francisco: Jossey-Bass, 1981).

6. C. Bowles, "Self-Expressed Adult Music Education Interests and Music Experiences," *Journal of Research in Music Education* 39 (1991): 205.

7. Cooper, "Adults' Perceptions of Piano Study."

8. Malcolm Knowles, *The Adult Learner: A Neglected Species* (Houston, TX: Gulf, 1986).

9. Jost Reischmann is professor of androgogy, Bamberg University, Bamberg, Germany. See www.androgogy.net for more information.

10. A.C. Gibbons, "Musical Aptitude Scores in the Elderly and Their Relationships to Morale and Selected Other Variables." (Ph.D diss., University of North Texas, 1979).

11. This section is based largely on the writings of Malcolm Knowles.

12. Barbara English Maris, *Making Music at the Piano: Learning Strategies for Adult Students* (New York: Oxford University Press, 2000).

13. On reasons for dropout, see also studies by AMC 1988 and Dyal 1991 as cited in Thelma Cooper's dissertation, "Adults' Perception of Piano Study."

14. Bruhn, "Take Two Music Lessons."

15. Ibid.

16. Barry Bittman, M.D., and Karl T. Bruhn, *Creating the Right Fit: Understanding Key Recreational Music Making Criteria.* http://rmm.namm.org/industry/white-papers/white-paper-pdfs/7%20Creating%20the%20Right%20Fit.pdf.

17. Steven Sauter, Lawrence Murphy, Michael Colligan, Naomi Swanson, Joseph Hurrell Jr., Frederick Scharf Jr., Raymond Sinclair Paula Grubb, Linda Goldenhar, Toni Alterman, Janet Johnston, Anne Hamilton, Julie Tisdale, "Stress…at Work." 9, *National Institute of Occupational Safety and Health,* http://www.bychan.de/procrastination/stress_at_work.html.

18. Herbert Benson and Julie Corliss, "Relaxation: Ways to Calm Your Mind," *Newsweek*, September 27, 2004.

19. John Schwartz, "Always on the Job, Employees Pay with Health," *New York Times*, September 5, 2004.

20. "Attitudes in the American Workplace VI," annual Gallup poll, 2000, sponsored by the Marlin Company.

21. Barry Bittman, Lee Berk, Mark Shannon, Muhammad Sharaf, Jim Westengard, Karl Guegler, and David Ruff, "Recreational Music-Making Modulates the Human Stress Response: A Preliminary Individualized Gene Expression Strategy," *Medical Science Monitor* 11, no. 2 (2005), BR31–40.

22. F. Tims, *Scientific Study Indicates the Music Making Makes the Elderly Healthier* (unpublished manuscript, Michigan State University, 1999).

23. M. Koga and F. Tims, "The Music Making and Wellness Project." *American Music Teacher* 51, n0.2 (October/November, 2001), 18–22.; F. Tims, *Scientific Study Indicates the Music Making Makes the Elderly Healthier* (unpublished manuscript, Michigan State University, 1999).

24. "Who Are the Baby Boomers?" *BabyBoomerMagazine.com*, March 16, 2009.

Chapter 9

1. Linda Christiansen, "A Survey of the Importance of Functional Piano Skills as Reported by Band, Choral, Orchestra, and General Music Teachers" (Ph.D. diss., University of Oklahoma, 2000).

2. Mary Tollefson, "Rethinking the College Piano Proficiency," *Piano Pedagogy Forum* 4, no. 2 (June 2001).

3. Jamila L. McWhirter, "A Survey of Secondary Choral Educators Regarding Piano Skills Utilized in the Classroom and Piano Skills Expectations of Student Teaching Interns" (Ph.D. diss., University of Missouri–Columbia, 2005).

4. Remarks by Fred Kern given at the National Group Piano/Piano Pedagogy Forum, 2006.

5. I was first introduced to this technique at the 2004 National Group Piano/ Piano Pedagogy Forum as part of lecture given by Dr. Cynthia Benson.

Index

CPSIA information can be obtained at www.ICGtesting.com
Printed in the USA
BVOW02s1458110216

436308BV00001B/3/P

9 780195 337044